Content Area Literacy

Interactive Teaching for Active Learning

Second Edition

ANTHONY V. MANZO

University of Missouri-Kansas City

ULA C. MANZO

Central Missouri State University

Merrill,
an imprint of Prentice Hall
Upper Saddle River, New Jersey   *Columbus, Ohio*

Library of Congress Cataloging-in-Publication Data

Manzo, Anthony V.

    Content area literacy: interactive teaching for active learning / Anthony V. Manzo, Ula C. Manzo.—2nd ed.

      p.   cm.

    Rev. ed. of: Content area reading. c1990.

    Includes bibliographical references and index.

    ISBN 0-13-532102-6

    1. Content area reading—United States.   I. Manzo, Ula Casale. II. Manzo, Anthony V.   Content area reading.   III. Title.

LB1050.455.M36   1997

428.4'07—dc20

                                                     96-29160

                                                           CIP

Cover art: ©Mark Ari/Superstock

Editor: Brad Potthoff

Production Editor: Julie Anderson Peters

Design Coordinator: Karrie Converse

Text Designer: STELLARViSIONS

Cover Designer: Russ Maselli

Production Manager: Patricia A. Tonneman

Director of Advertising: Kevin Flanagan

Advertising/Marketing Coordinator: Julie Shough

Photo Researcher: Angela Jenkins

Electronic Text Management: Marilyn Wilson Phelps, Matthew Williams, Karen L. Bretz, Tracey Ward

This book was set in ITC Century by Prentice Hall and was printed and bound by R.R. Donnelley & Sons Company. The cover was printed by Phoenix Color Corp.

© 1997 by Prentice-Hall, Inc.
Simon & Schuster/A Viacom Company
Upper Saddle River, New Jersey 07458

Earlier edition, entitled *Content Area Reading: A Heuristic Approach*, © 1990 by Macmillan Publishing Company.

Photo credits: Scott Cunningham/Merrill, pp. 2, 16, 56, 76, 102, 118, 138, 160, 182; Anne Vega/Merrill, 36, 200, 236; Tom Watson/Merrill, p. 256.

Printed in the United States of America

10 9 8 7 6 5 4 3 2 1

ISBN: 0-13-532102-6

Prentice-Hall International (UK) Limited, *London*
Prentice-Hall of Australia Pty. Limited, *Sydney*
Prentice-Hall of Canada, Inc., *Toronto*
Prentice-Hall Hispanoamericana, S. A., *Mexico*
Prentice-Hall of India Private Limited, *New Delhi*
Prentice-Hall of Japan, Inc., *Tokyo*
Simon & Schuster Asia Pte. Ltd., *Singapore*
Editora Prentice-Hall do Brasil, Ltda., *Rio de Janeiro*

To our boy, "Brynie,"
whose extra hours in daycare
contributed immeasurably to this effort.

Preface

This book is intended to introduce teachers-to-be to the *why* and *how* of promoting basic and higher-order literacy. It does so in the context of promoting reading and thinking as a collateral part of specific subject instruction and in an increasingly interconnected local and global environment.

The ideas and methods presented reflect nearly a century of progress and the continuing evolution of the field into this age of local and worldwide telecomputing. Understandably, there is somewhat more here than a professor necessarily will wish to fully cover or a teacher initially will use. About eight of the initial ten chapters constitute the core of most courses and the last section largely serves as optional, or reference, chapters.

Section I, including Chapters 1 through 3, focuses on what content teachers need to know about literacy and content reading and about their students' abilities to learn from reading and the language arts. The four chapters in Section II address the specifics of how to provide support to students in comprehension at every stage of that process: prereading, during reading, and postreading. Section III chapters focus on higher-order literacy: how to build language and concept development, strategies to advance analytical and constructive thinking, and study habits. Section IV, Reference Information in Content Area Literacy, is included because there is a good chance that some preservice and veteran teachers will need much of these contents quickly and that all readers will need them eventually, as experience and professional demands further unfold and personal readiness peaks.

To further advance self-examination and personal–professional development, each chapter concludes with a "Trade Secret." This feature includes evocative thoughts that might be overlooked during formal education but are part of the education that teachers tend to receive in the faculty lounge.

To take full advantage of the book's possibilities, students will need the advice and recommendations of the course instructor and, ideally, the interactive advantages offered through one of several local and Internet web sites devoted to the topics of text. With such experience and guidance, preservice and veteran teachers should be able to better select the ideas and methods that will suit them and their students in their initial efforts to teach subject matter and reading–learning strategies.

ACKNOWLEDGMENTS

We thank our editors at Prentice Hall, Brad Potthoff and Julie Peters. We would also like to thank Andy Lang and Darlene Beeman for their personal assistance with referencing, completing permissions, and manuscript preparation. Finally, we wish to thank the following reviewers for their helpful comments: W. Gale Breedlove, University of South Carolina; Marilyn G. Eanet, Rhode Island College; Cindy Gillespie, Bowling Green State University; Judy C. Lambert, University of Wisconsin—Oshkosh; Michael McKenna, Georgia Southern University; Gary A. Negin, California State University; Deborah Nieding, Gonzaga State University; Robert J. Rickelman, University of North Carolina at Charlotte; Albert Shannon, St. Joseph's College; and Edward A. Sullivan, Providence College.

Brief Contents

Contents

SECTION I

Interactive Teaching Begins with Knowing Students

The purpose of this section is to help you to find, fan, and even ignite the embers of your own experiences as a reader, so that these can serve as a basis for well-structured and accessible professional knowledge. The three chapters that compose Section I focus on what content teachers need to know about literacy and content reading and about their students' abilities to learn from reading and the language arts.

Chapter 1 begins with a discussion of why all teachers need to have an understanding of the process of reading to learn as well as the more rudimentary process of decoding words, or translating groups of letters into spoken sounds.

Chapter 2 provides a closer look at the reading process, or models of reading. It explains why reading has been called an invisible process. In the past fifty years, these newer models have challenged many of the assumptions on which traditional teaching approaches had been based. Chapter 2 concludes with an example of a simple instructional method for teaching students at any grade and in any subject area how to read to learn. This method is intended to symbolize a class of hands-on teaching approaches that tend to instruct teachers as well as students.

Chapter 3 is about assessment. It provides a number of practical techniques for evaluating students' reading levels and for estimating the readability or difficulty level of textual materials. With these techniques, teachers will be able to make more informed selections of materials for their students' abilities. The appraisal of students' reading needs and the selection of appropriate materials are the first two steps in ensuring successful learning experiences for all students.

CHAPTER 1

Why and What Teachers Should Know About Content Literacy

No one can reveal to you aught but that which already lies half asleep in the dawning of your knowledge.

—Kalil Gibran

✦ *Organizing Thoughts* ✦

The purpose of this chapter is to urge teachers to become content area literacy providers. It tells the story of the content area reading movement in terms of the questions that impelled its evolution to where it now is more properly known as content area literacy. The underlying theme of the chapter is that teaching students to learn on their own moves them toward becoming literate, more than simply *not being illiterate*. The chapter concludes with a brief explanation of the so-called constructivist elements of interactive instruction that characterize the teaching methods found in the remainder of the text.

TEACHING IS MORE THAN TRANSMITTING INFORMATION

New teachers often come away from their first classes feeling that they had wonderful lessons prepared, but the wrong students showed up. This mismatch in expectations happens largely because many teachers still feel that teaching is a process of transmitting information. This view is strengthened by the fact that some students can receive new information relatively effortlessly. They have sufficient background of information, appropriate independent learning strategies, and motivation to learn more about the subject. For many students in most subjects, however, merely presenting information is not enough. Most new learning is far from effortless. It requires some prior knowledge and, ideally, some concrete experience with the topic. Next, learners must somehow become engaged, or interested, in and attentive to the new information and ideas at hand. Further, learners must explore the information by questioning, comparing, and testing it against those elements of prior knowledge and experiences. Finally, learners must categorize and connect the new information with what they already knew—which often means adding to and even revising previously held ideas. For these reasons, learning has been called a *constructive* process. To initiate this process—to grab students' interest, and then maintain and focus it—teachers must start from where students are—socially, emotionally, and intellectually. This means that teachers need to have a good sense of what interests students, what background of information and experience they are likely to have, and what obstacles and misconceptions might prevent them from actively participating in the learning process. Students have been shown to sense when teachers show such caring and to respond positively to their strategies for reading and learning (Moje, 1996).

FROM CONTENT AREA READING TO CONTENT AREA LITERACY

Content area reading evolved from an idea sparked in the 1920s and into a movement that swept the nation by the 1960s. Before the 1920s, education tended to follow a "survival of the fittest" model. Those who fell behind simply were permitted to drop from the system. A growing awareness of the need for an educated citizenry led to mandatory schooling legislation. It eventually became clear, however, that equal access to education meant more than requiring all students to stay in school until a certain age. If all students were to profit from staying in school, then schools would need to find ways to help them learn while they were there. In this context, educators began to believe that instead of simply presenting information, we could and should find ways to help students to *learn how to learn*—and especially how to learn through reading. This was a dramatic role change for schools and for teachers. It raised a host of questions. Just who was supposed to be responsible for figuring out why some students learn to learn and others do not? Who was supposed to help those who fell behind? And how could this be done? Some educators still question whether it really *can* be done, or even really *should* be done, given spiraling costs and competing priorities.

Nevertheless, this new concept of public education was an idea whose time had come. The need to equalize opportunities for all citizens was growing into a national priority that was fueled by the civil rights movement and the increasing skill demands of the job market. Today, most schools and teachers understand that they are not merely responsible for teaching a subject but for teaching all students to be flexible and independent learners. It is this shift in perspective that has driven the rapid development of the content area reading movement.

Early proponents of this movement laid the foundations for extending the definition and practices of reading instruction from an elementary grade focus on merely learning how to read to a new and broader focus on learning from reading. To meet this expectation, schools and teachers needed answers to immediate and pressing questions about how students learn and about how to help students to become better learners. They welcomed the answers that the field of study known as content area reading was beginning to offer. In many cases, however, these answers conflicted with teachers' attitudes and expectations. Changing teachers' views of their roles and responsibilities, like most change, has not been easy. It has been an ongoing process that continues to unfold within one teacher at a time, among both practicing and beginning teachers.

Know the Questions, Know the Answers

Several key questions influenced the early organization and direction of the content area reading movement. These questions are stated next, along with brief answers summarizing the past forty years of research and experience.

1. Haven't students learned to read by the time they finish grade school?   The answer to this question must begin with a basic definition of *reading*. Many people think of learning to read as learning to *decode*, or translate the little squiggles we call letters into the sounds we call words. Reading, however, means much more than this simple translation process. It means constructively comprehending, or making meaning from, print. Reading comprehension generally is defined as follows:

+ *Understanding* the author's intended message (reading the lines)
+ *Interpreting* the message's meaning and implications (reading between the lines)
+ *Applying* the message in meaningful ways (reading beyond the lines)

Most children do master the decoding aspects of reading by about the fourth grade. At each higher grade level, however, the reading materials become more difficult. To express increasingly complex ideas and information, authors must use more technical vocabulary and more complex language forms. Thus, learning to read is a process that continues as long as one continues to learn.

Even children who master beginning reading in elementary school must continue to develop effective strategies for learning from more difficult materials and about increasingly specialized subjects. Some students acquire these strategies rather effortlessly, but many others do not. Even in elementary school, some children begin to fall behind their peers in comprehending what they read. As middle and high school teachers' expectations increase, these children begin to have more frequent unsuccessful experiences in attempting to learn from reading. And, of course, a few children fail to master even basic decoding.

For these reasons, content area teachers can expect to have several categories of students in their classes. A few students will still have basic decoding problems. Some will have fairly serious comprehension problems. Many will simply need assistance in acquiring the comprehension strategies appropriate to each higher grade and subject area. Finally, some students will continue to read and develop the needed comprehension strategies on their own. In the past, teachers could concern themselves primarily with presenting information and materials to the latter category of students. Learning to read content materials was treated as a "sink-or-swim" challenge: You figured out how to do it, or you failed to learn the subject.

Today, most teachers are willing to accept more responsibility for helping *all* children to learn to read and think. As they do so, they are accepting the challenge to teach in ways that don't simply *require* but that help students *acquire* the thinking strategies they need to actively construct meaning from print.

2. *If some students acquire reading–thinking strategies naturally, simply by reading increasingly difficult materials, why do others fail to do so?* The fundamental premise of this book, and a large sector of the content area literacy movement, is that *if all students did spend time reading and working at understanding in every subject through the grades, they all might continue to develop the reading–thinking strategies they need.* However, for a variety of reasons, this does not always happen.

One simple reason why some students do not spend sufficient time reading and working at understanding every subject is that at each higher grade level students' personal interests begin to influence how much reading they do in different subjects: They read more in subjects they prefer and often avoid reading in subjects they do not like. Thus, they may continue to acquire the specialized vocabulary, language, and thinking strategies needed in some subjects but not in others.

Another reason why some students do not do enough reading to make so-called natural progress is related to their personal experiences with being taught to read. Reading instruction, even in the elementary grades, often is structured and conducted in ways that cause some children to see themselves as poor readers. For example, when children are grouped for reading, children placed in the low group know that they are seen as poor readers by their teacher and their peers and learn to see themselves as poor readers. The strength of this learning is evidenced in the fact that they seldom advance to a higher group. Another familiar elementary school practice that undermines the self-confidence of young readers is round-robin reading. In this familiar activity, students take turns reading aloud, a paragraph or two at a time. Few students gain much that is profitable from this. Better readers are bored, most others are occupied with looking ahead to the section they will be reading, and struggling readers are dreading humiliation. When children begin to view themselves as poor readers, for whatever reason, they read less, and progress at a slower rate. By the time these struggling readers reach secondary school, they have had years of negative experiences with reading.

Thus, at each higher grade, in any given subject, there are students who have fallen behind in acquiring the necessary natural reading–thinking strategies: some simply because of stronger interest in other areas, and some because prior failures have caused them to stop trying. Secondary teachers, faced with increasing numbers of students who cannot or will not learn from reading, sometimes make the well-meaning but ironic attempt to present information in other ways that involve little or no reading. The irony in this approach is that it removes any possibility of students' acquiring greater ease and self-confidence in reading. Even those students who might have developed grade-level reading strategies through continued reading may fail to do so if no reading is required. The better alternative, and one of the most influential things a secondary teacher can do, is to use teaching methods that structure reading-based lessons in ways that enable more students to have more successful experiences with reading. It is only through repeated successful reading experiences that appropriate thinking strategies are acquired, and the effects of years of negative experiences can be counteracted.

3. Aren't there some students who just can't be taught to read better? Since reading comprehension is almost synonymous with thinking, many educators once believed that there was a simple, one-to-one relationship between general intelligence and reading comprehension. It was assumed that intelligent students would acquire the ability to read and comprehend well and that unintelligent ones would not and could not be taught to do so. Today, few educators hold this simplistic view. We now know, for example, that intelligence is much more multifaceted than is measured by most conventional tests of intelligence. Several aspects of critical and creative thinking, in fact, appear to be only minimally related to conventional IQ test scores. In fact, some educators have proposed that poor reading comprehension may be a causal factor in low IQ scores, rather than the reverse. In recent years, educational researchers have provided convincing evidence that thinking can be improved and that the methods for doing so are not terribly complex. Content area literacy is based on the premise that all students can be taught to read, learn, and think better, and that all teachers can share the challenges and rewards of helping them to do so.

4. Why can't reading be taught in a separate pull-out class? For those few students who have not acquired basic decoding strategies, reading *should* be taught in a separate class by a reading specialist. Reading disabilities this severe usually have multiple causes and may be accompanied by emotional and behavioral disorders.

Students who can decode adequately but simply do not seem to understand what they read are a different matter. At the beginning of the content area reading movement, and sometimes still today, separate reading classes were designed for these students. The problem with the separate-class approach is that, even though it seems to be the most logical solution, it simply doesn't work very well. Why it doesn't work seems to be related to at least three conditions. First, whenever students are grouped by ability, a multitude of negative factors tend to outweigh the logical advantage that might be gained by offering them instruction that is geared to their achievement level. Second, as discussed previously, most secondary students are stronger readers in some subjects than in others. Identifying which students are lagging in which subjects and trying to provide this level of individualized assistance is practically impossible. Finally, the pull-out approach assumes that students will be taught general reading–thinking strategies that they will then modify and apply when reading their various subject area assignments. This kind of transfer of training is a higher-order thinking process that is, almost by definition, what poor readers have difficulty doing.

Gradually, after years of trying various approaches, two things have become clear: (1) Pull-out programs are necessary for those students who have not mastered basic decoding. (2) However, all students, including those receiving separate remediation, need specific coaching in the particular grade-appropriate reading–thinking strategies of each subject. And, who is more experienced in reading, thinking, talking, and questioning in the respective subject fields than the content teachers themselves?

5. *How can content teachers be expected to find time to teach reading and thinking?* The fact that content teachers are being held responsible for the learning of *all* students is the strongest argument for all teachers to be prepared to coach students in the particular reading strategies relevant to their subject areas. Coaching reading and thinking need not be done *in addition to* teaching content. In fact, it is best done *while* teaching content. When such coaching accompanies the teaching of content, students (including mainstreamed students with learning disabilities) become more able to learn independently. Thus, in the big picture, teachers who help students to read on their own are able to teach more content rather than less.

Teaching methods that result in effective coaching of subject area reading and thinking have two important characteristics that make them appropriate for subject area teachers. These methods tend to be concurrent and interactive. *Concurrent* methods permit the teacher to teach toward several objectives at the same time. *Interactive* methods are designed to encourage what is called the *constructivist* side of education—that is, increasing student involvement in instructional exchanges and supporting the use of thinking strategies for making, or constructing, meaning. Many good teachers teach some reading without labeling, or even realizing, it as such. Teachers are teaching reading, for example, when they introduce a reading selection in a way that engages students' interest, or when they invite meaningful discussion following reading, or even when they just ask some questions to check comprehension following reading. Teachers who do these things naturally will want to know more; those who do not do so naturally need to know more.

6. Why should all subject areas be included in the schoolwide reading program? Some content areas, such as English, science, and social studies, have an obvious connection with reading. Others, such as physical education, art, music, and mathematics, traditionally involve far less reading. Yet most states require that all teacher certification programs include at least one course in the teaching of reading. This consensus is in part due to two concepts that are central to effective schools. First, schools are more effective when *all teachers accept responsibility for the overall goals of the school,* not simply for those of their own discipline and classes. Accordingly, every teacher is expected to contribute to the schoolwide literacy program. In some subject areas, this contribution may be as simple as including just a few reading-based lessons that are carefully designed to permit even poor readers to have more successful experiences as readers in that subject. Second, effective schools are organized not merely to teach a given body of information but also to develop interests and abilities that will allow students to continue to be reasonably well versed in their subjects in the future. In this information age, it is not enough to merely acquire information; students must know how to acquire it and, more importantly, to interpret and use it.

7. What level of reading achievement can content teachers expect students to have, and how can they evaluate their students' reading? Naturally, the higher the grade, the higher the overall average reading level of the class. However, this fact tends to mask another more important one: the higher the grade, the wider the *range* of students' reading abilities from lowest to highest. This is because children who encounter difficulty in beginning reading often make far less than a year's progress for each year in school. Others, however, make more than a year's progress in a school year. Thus, a typical seventh-grade class may be expected to have reading levels ranging from the third- to the tenth-grade level, while a tenth-grade class is likely to range from the fourth-grade to the college level.

Some basic information about students' reading levels usually can be gathered from standardized test scores that are on file. Students with particularly low scores can be noted and observed during the first weeks of school to verify this test-based information. As discussed previously, however, students' reading abilities are likely to vary from subject to subject according to their personal interests, experiences, and prior knowledge. Subject area teachers can use a variety of techniques to cross-verify standardized test score information. These include observation, informal assessment procedures, and systems for portfolio collection, all of which are detailed in Chapter 3.

8. How can students of varying reading achievement levels learn from a single textbook or supplementary material that is written more or less on grade level? Over the years, the field of content area reading has proposed and explored many solutions to this puzzling question. Most of the early solutions had a certain logical appeal but were not very practical. One frequent suggestion, for example, was to collect a variety of reading materials at different difficulty levels and to match these with student reading levels. Individual students, or groups of students, could then explore the topic of study through reading at their own levels. Another suggestion was to prepare reading guides at different difficulty levels and to assign these based on student reading level. For example, lower-achieving readers were guided through acquiring the basic information, and more advanced students were asked questions that required more complex analysis of the information. These early attempts, while reasonable and still viable in some situations, tend to require an extraordinary amount of preparation and continuous monitoring. They also raise troublesome questions about how to evaluate students' work on these differentiated assignments and about whether lower-achieving students would be penalized rather than assisted by a steady diet of literal-level questions and easy material.

Content area literacy has moved to simpler, more manageable, and more equitable solutions. The basic approach is based on *interactive methods* for teaching reading–thinking *concurrently* with subject area knowledge and applications. Regular use of such methods from grade to grade and across subject areas supports student development of independent reading–learning strategies and empowers even relatively poor readers to read and learn from materials that they otherwise would find difficult.

CONTENT AREA LITERACY

The research-supported answers and perspectives that have evolved in response to the preceding questions represent a fairly complete picture of the traditional field of content area reading. A substantial body of research now supports the propositions that teachers *can* teach reading–thinking strategies, that they *can* meet the needs of a fairly wide range of student reading levels in a single classroom, and that the most effective schoolwide reading programs are those that enlist the participation of *every* educator in the school. With that groundwork established, the field has begun to broaden its focus, viewing reading within the broader context of literacy. Whereas the term *reading* connotes acquisition of strategies needed to successfully complete schooling, the term *literacy* speaks more to the breadth of education needed to function in modern life, where ordinary citizens are given the executive power of the vote but also must live in a milieu of rapid technological change and job displacement.

In today's world, the acquisition of large amounts of information is less important than the acquisition of effective strategies for accessing and evaluating information, problem solving, and communicating and interacting with interested parties. We once assumed that learners must first acquire information before they could be challenged to critically analyze and apply it. Many frustrating hours have been spent in trying to teach/learn isolated history facts, math facts, grammar rules, and the like. These required so many hours that teachers often despaired of students ever acquiring sufficient information to enable them to operate at higher levels of evaluation and application. Research in the field of constructivism, also called critical literacy (Shannon, 1990), is refocusing our attention on what many effective teachers have long intuited: If students are initially engaged in an authentic, relevant problem, situation, or challenge, the relevant information is acquired almost effortlessly and in a fraction of the time.

Similarly, reading and subject area specialists are redirecting their attention toward creating educational environments in which students are challenged to analyze, reflect, communicate, and create. In such environments, effective strategies for reading, writing, speaking, listening, and thinking are more likely to develop more naturally and easily than when these are addressed as isolated elements. Thus, there is a growing trend to refer to this emerging field as *content area literacy*. This reorientation shifts the emphasis from reading as a somewhat isolated function toward its role in overall communication and higher-order thinking. Ironically, the need to write and to read highly technical information has been greatly intensified by telecomputing and related technologies that once were expected to reduce the demand for every citizen to be highly literate.

Interactive Teaching for Active Learning

The broad goals of content area literacy are best achieved through interactive teaching methods that involve students in instructional conversations (Tharp & Gallimore, 1989) and hands-on experiences that cause them to be active learners. Teaching toward content area literacy, as discussed previously, begins with the need to create authentic contexts for active thinking and effective communication. To do this, we still need to begin with the question, What *facts* do students need to know? But this needs to be attached to the question, *Why* these particular facts? Helping students to see the relevance or purpose for learning is the first step in involving them in meaningful interactions designed to show them how to read and think through textual material and give them adequate opportunities to try out appropriate reading–thinking strategies. This process of interacting with competent models of a given thinking strategy is the most effective way known to improve thinking and motivation to learn. Interactive methods for teaching reading–thinking strategies mirror the three basic stages of the reading process:

✦ *Prereading:* teaching students to recall and use prior experience and knowledge about a topic, to identify and define difficult vocabulary words, and to set clear purposes for reading

✦ *Guided silent reading:* teaching students to apply a variety of active thinking strategies during reading

✦ *Postreading:* teaching students to check basic comprehension after reading and to apply information in a variety of ways

Interactive teaching is an ongoing, cyclical process that is characterized by the following elements: *assessment, engagement, scaffolding, modeling, reciprocity,* and *fading,* followed by reassessment to continue the cycle. Each of these elements is briefly described in Figure 1.1 and is more fully elaborated on throughout the text.

On a Professional and Personal Career Level

So who, in conclusion, should have knowledge about content area literacy? In our judgment, everyone who teaches, and certainly anyone who will teach in a conventional school setting, should know about content area literacy. The interactive teaching methods of content area literacy permit students with a wide range of reading levels to learn from the same reading materials and in the same classroom. These methods offer practical ways to satisfy today's expectation that students of quite varied learning aptitudes and even those with special learning needs and from diverse cultural backgrounds should have the opportunity to learn in the traditional class setting. And, given the additions of new, electronic communication and computing systems, traditional class settings are now anything but traditional. Nonetheless, all teachers, including those who might think they have the least need for content literacy methodology, have the obligation to be informed about what constitutes enlightened instruction so that they can participate in the school's primary mission.

On a more personal career level, an understanding of content area literacy precepts and practices prepares all who work in a school setting to be ready to step in for their colleagues and to have sufficient flexibility and preparation in their education to be able to take on other related jobs, as often as is required over a typical lifelong career. It is not unusual today for those who originally prepared to teach in a conventional classroom to find themselves teaching in other settings: in adult basic and high school equivalency programs; in one of the burgeoning educational programs within business and industry; or extending their certification to work as school-based consultants or central office administrators. (See Appendix B for a sample portfolio system to help teachers better record and prepare for such varied career options.)

Figure 1.1
Elements of an interactive teaching cycle.

Assessment

Assessment of student needs is the starting point for effective classroom instructional interactions. Standardized test scores and prior grades in school provide information about students' general achievement levels. In addition, the teacher should begin to accumulate information about the nature and extent of students' prior knowledge and experiences, as well as their personal interests, talents, and possible areas of learning difficulty. This more specific assessment information can be collected from structured observations of students and from a variety of informal assessment techniques.

Engagement

Engagement is a concept derived from motivational and learning theories and simply means getting and holding students' attention during instruction. It is, logically, the single most essential element in teaching/learning: If the learner is not paying attention to the learning environment, none of the subsequent elements can be achieved. Whereas traditional instruction has tended to rely on external sources of motivation (such as grades) to encourage, or force, engagement, the interactive methods approach emphasizes building internal motivation as the key to developing interested and lifelong learners.

Scaffolding

Scaffolding refers to elements of instruction that support the learner during the early stages of learning. Learning anything new involves an initial trial-and-error period that, in the social context of a classroom, can threaten the learner's self-esteem. Classroom interactions can be structured in ways that reduce this threat and encourage the learner to experiment with new ways of thinking and communicating. One of the best ways to build self-esteem and internal motivation is to provide lessons with sufficient scaffolding to build students' sense of their own competence as learners.

Knowledge of content area literacy is basic to understanding the pedagogic side of teaching. Like the so-called foundations courses, such as history and philosophy of education, content area literacy prepares teachers to make sound curricular and instructional decisions. It could be argued that content area literacy contributes even more to a teacher's education than do the typical foundations courses, since it grapples more directly with many of the most practical aspects that such courses introduce. For example, how, precisely, can mainstreaming be accomplished, and how can students with different learning styles and from culturally diverse backgrounds be given fair representation and accommodation in the conventional heterogeneous content class?

Figure 1.1, *continued*

Modeling
Modeling is a means of teaching by showing. Although it has long been used to teach complex manual procedures, as in art and craft apprenticeships, only recently has it been applied to teaching *thinking* processes. This forward step in teaching came about with a simple realization. This realization was that just as toddlers first learn to speak by interacting with skillful language users, each of us continues to acquire more sophisticated language and thinking processes in the same way: by observing models of these behaviors, imitating those models, and self-evaluating our progress toward some personally desired level of competence.

Reciprocity
Reciprocity is a term used to characterize teaching situations that are structured so that students and teacher are encouraged to influence one another's thinking. This ingredient is necessary for effective modeling and interactive teaching. In reciprocal teaching situations, the teacher is still responsible for outlining and maintaining the general content and direction of instruction, but interactions are structured in ways that require the teacher to allow student response and encourage students to learn from one another. When teachers and students are connected reciprocally, they tend to create a communal learning spirit in which everyone, including the teacher, learns.

Fading
A final element of interactive teaching is fading of teacher support, in a gradual release of responsibility for learning from the teacher to the students. As each lesson nears its conclusion, the teacher returns to the beginning of the cycle by assessing students' developing competence, gradually removing the instructional scaffolding, and transferring control and responsibility for learning to the students. It is during this fading process that learners internalize new learning strategies by adjusting them into forms and formats for personal use.

As you read ahead in the text, you should feel your own confidence as a professional growing in proportion to your understanding of solutions to several school-based problems that others tend to only talk about. Of course, there is much more to learn. We will try to be candid, too, about what is not yet known or cannot adequately be done.

✦ *Looking Back and Looking Ahead* ✦

This chapter offered a rational basis for urging all teachers to become content area literacy providers. It briefly described how interactive teaching and certain related elements have helped to make this a dynamic and effective field of study. The next chapter focuses on your theoretical base for making effective instructional decisions.

✦ ✦ TRADE SECRET ✦ ✦

Every field has its tricks of the trade. In this section of each chapter, we share some insider secrets and tricks of the teaching trade or suggest some that you might adopt from other fields.

A Memo on Memoranda

TO: Our Newer Colleagues

FROM: Veteran Teachers

RE: Tips on Writing Memoranda

Sooner than you expect, you will be writing notes and memoranda to students, parents, colleagues, and your principal. Here are some simple guidelines to keep in mind:

1. Check your spelling.
2. Check your punctuation.
3. Watch your penmanship in handwritten notes.
4. Ask a colleague to read and react to notes that will leave the school building.
5. Hold a note for a day if you wrote it in anger.
6. Picture everything you write being reprinted in the evening newspaper.
7. Reread your note as though you were the recipient.
8. After rereading your note, rewrite it.

The value of these tips is easily tested. One day, ask colleagues in the teacher's lounge whether any of them has had a bad experience with a note they wrote hurriedly. You may hear the reply, "I haven't, but you should hear what happened to one teacher I used to work with. . . ."

CHAPTER 2

Foundations of Teaching and Learning

Let no one imagine that they are without influence. The person who thinks becomes a light and a power.

—Henry George

✦ *Organizing Thoughts* ✦

This chapter begins by summarizing what we know about the reading process. It opens with the concept of three distinct levels of reading that can be identified for each person who reads. It then discusses the benefits of sound theory as a rationale for describing three different theories, or models, of the reading process. Interactive teaching is discussed as a means of aligning instruction with theory, and the chapter concludes with an example of a simple teaching method that facilitates interactive teaching for active learning from print.

READING TO LEARN: A CLOSER LOOK

Reading can be defined, simply, as the unlocking and construction of meaning from a coded message. What is not so simple is why some things are easy to read and others are hard or why one student can accurately decode a page and comprehend 95% of the information while another student accurately decodes the same page but comprehends only 60%. To answer these questions, it is necessary to consider what happens when one reads. The reading process is quite complex, and much of it is performed subconsciously. Therefore, what we know about reading is in the form of various theories and findings from research designed to test the accuracy of these theories.

One thing we know for sure about reading is that, for each of us, some things are easy to read, other things are more difficult, and still others are next to impossible. The next section introduces the terminology and specific criteria for categorizing and examining these levels of reading. To know these is to have the conceptual basis and the language for understanding and discussing much of what needs to be done instructionally in a content class to ensure that students will be able to learn from textual material.

LEVELS OF READING

The level at which materials are easy to read is technically referred to as the *independent level*. Reading feels effortless at this level, because we often know something about the topic and are familiar with the language, style, and vocabulary used. All we need to do is fit the new information into existing categories. At this level, we are able to read and comprehend without assistance. The independent level typically is defined as the highest level at which we can accurately decode 99% of the words and comprehend with 90% accuracy. For most people, independent-level reading—whether it is nonfiction, news, or novels—is enjoyable, relaxing, and entertaining.

Most of us occasionally have had the experience of reading and suddenly realizing that we have not understood the last sentences, paragraphs, or even pages. What usually has happened is that we have been trying to read something that is somewhat difficult for us, using the same passive reading process that works for independent-level reading. When the topic, language, style, and/or the vocabulary are less familiar to us, we reach what is referred to as our *instructional-level reading*. To comprehend material at this level, we often need to create new categories or stop to decipher the meanings of unfamiliar words and/or language patterns. This is the level at which we probably would be able to read and comprehend with the type of assistance a teacher might provide in a classroom setting. This level is defined as the highest level at which we can accurately decode 95% of the words and comprehend with 75% accuracy. Instructional-level reading requires a more active stance and some external assistance, and it still can be painstakingly slow.

Beyond this point, some reading materials are so difficult for us that they are next to impossible to understand without an extraordinary level of effort and assistance. This *frustration level* is defined as the point at which decoding falls below 90% or at which we comprehend with less than 50% accuracy. It is next to impossible to learn from materials at frustration level, even with the assistance a teacher could provide within a regular classroom.

Considering the reading process in this way, essentially as three *different* processes, helps to explain why many teachers fail to see the need for providing guidance in reading strategies. One reason is the frequent misinterpretation of the *grade-level* designation of textbooks. We tend to assume that this designation means that students at that grade should be able to use the book for independent study. In fact, it means that the book is intended to match the *instructional* level of the student's grade. It should be manageable for them, but only with a reasonable degree of guidance from the teacher. A second reason why teachers sometimes fail to provide reading strategy instruction is that they simply are uninformed about these levels and about the dramatic difference between passive, independent-level reading and active, instructional-level reading. Textbooks that are written at students' instructional level require active strategies for constructing meaning. Since these same textbooks will be at the teacher's independent level, the teacher can read them quite easily and passively and may be puzzled as to why students are not understanding what seems perfectly clear.

The kind of guidance that teachers can provide depends largely on their understanding of the nature of the reading process. What do teachers think they do when reading? Recent research related to the reading process suggests that many of our assumptions about the reading process may be inaccurate. This research is changing not only the way beginning reading is taught but how it is guided through the upper grades and even through professional school levels.

THEORIES OF COMPREHENSION

The Value of Theories

Good theory is always practical. Often, good theory is simply the articulation of what occurs in practices that have been found to be effective.

The purpose and power of effective theory can be illustrated with an anecdote. A while ago, we became acquainted with a fellow junior high school teacher, Frank, who had a side business as an air conditioning and refrigerator repair person. Frank was respected by a large and wealthy clientele on Long Island's North Shore because he often could fix air conditioning problems that were not covered in the manufacturer's repair manual or that lay not in the machine itself but somewhere in its operating environment. Frank was a science teacher. He deeply understood the theoretical underpinnings of cooling in addition to the mechanics of coolers. In this same way, an understanding of the theoretical underpinnings of reading comprehension can enable teachers to help students fix comprehension problems in some very practical ways.

COMPREHENSION AS GUIDED PROBLEM SOLVING

The scientific basis for the study of the comprehension process began around the time of World War I with a study designed to demonstrate that acquiring understanding from reading was far more than the simple act of reading words. Edward L. Thorndike (1917), one of the most eminent educational psychologists of the twentieth century, made the following observation:

> Understanding a paragraph is like solving a problem in mathematics. It consists in selecting the right elements of the situation and putting them together in the right relations, and also with the right amount of weight or influence or force for each. The mind is assailed as it were by every word in the paragraph. It must select, repress, soften, emphasize, correlate and organize, all under the influence of the right mental set or purpose or demand. (pp. 327–328)

In this single paragraph, Thorndike makes it clear that reading comprehension is a process of actively engaging text. It requires that the reader be attentive, analytical, purposeful, flexible, self-aware, world-aware, and emotionally sound.

Contemporary theories of reading comprehension typically are presented in the form of models that describe or illustrate, in flowchart form, the sequence in which various elements of the process are activated and the ways in which they interrelate.

MODELS OF THE READING PROCESS

Models of the reading process tend to be categorized as primarily bottom-up, top-down, or interactive. *Bottom-up models* build from details and specifics toward a global concept. *Top-down models* start with a global concept and use reading to clarify details and specifics. *Interactive models* explain the reading process as partly top-down and partly bottom-up. Each of these three categories of models has distinct implications for how reading should be taught.

Bottom-Up Models

Bottom-up models define reading as a text-driven process that begins with perception and recognition first of letters, then of phonetic elements, then of words, then of word groups, and ultimately of sentence meaning and passage meaning. The reader's role is to process these units accurately and rapidly, building meaning from the smaller to the larger units—that is, from the bottom up. It is assumed that if children master each successive reading subskill, they eventually will attain overall reading competency (Gough & Cosky, 1977). Educators who hold bottom-up models of reading would assume that the most important thing a teacher can do is to organize and present the information and skills to be taught in a logical sequence. If this is done, and each child is permitted sufficient time to master each step, then all children will learn. This assumption has been challenged, however, by linguists and cognitive psychologists, who tend to advocate top-down models (Goodman, 1984; E. Smith, 1979).

Top-Down Models

Top-down models describe reading as a meaning-driven process. The learning process does not start with the information and skills, but with readers, who have a unique collection of prior knowledge and experience that they actively apply and compare to the material being read. Top-down models imply that reading instruction should deemphasize subskills and focus on prereading activities that develop students' background of information and on spending more time reading. Founders of the popular whole language movement (Goodman, Bird, & Goodman, 1991) state that if children are immersed in a literate environment, they do not even need to be taught to read but will acquire print literacy in the same way they acquire spoken language. Another top-down theorist believes that comprehension instruction is valueless and that the only thing that accounts for reading gains is *time* spent reading (Carver, 1985).

Interactive Models

Interactive models propose that readers apply both top-down and bottom-up processing, using information gleaned from one process to inform and advance the other (Rumelhart, 1977). For example, when reading material on a familiar topic, readers can use top-down processing: reading quickly to check the information against prior understandings and experiences. When the material moves into unfamiliar territory, readers may need to switch to more active bottom-up meaning-constructing strategies. Other factors that may cause difficulty for readers and require them to switch from top-down to bottom-up strategies can be viewed as external—outside the reader's mind—and internal—inside the reader's mind (Schell, 1988).

The interactive model views reading as an active, strategic process of questioning, predicting, confirming, and self-correcting. Good readers have a variety of such strategies at their disposal and can apply them as needed to accommodate any internal and external factors that may be contributing to the difficulty of a given reading selection. The implications of this model for effective teaching of reading are only recently being recognized. Schell (1988) summarizes these implications as follows:

> An interactive view of reading comprehension minimizes or ignores some aspects we have long focused on, such as levels of comprehension (literal, inferential, and critical) and comprehension skills (main idea, sequencing, drawing conclusions, etc.). Instead, it emphasizes aspects such as the reader's oral language, prior knowledge of the topic, and ability to reason. It focuses more on causes than on symptoms and de-emphasizes the role of reading tests in comprehension diagnosis and increases the importance of the teacher as gatherer of information. (p. 13)

In general, interactive models appear to hold the most promise as a basis for developing effective instructional strategies. Bottom-up models tend be too narrow: They describe only what children do when they are first learning to read. Top-down models also have a shortcoming: They tend to describe what skilled readers do when reading familiar material but fail to account for how readers handle unfamiliar text. Interactive models reflect a broader range of factors, describing what both beginning readers and skilled readers must do when constructing, as opposed to simply reconstructing, meaning from the printed page and somehow moving it into consciousness.

For further information on models of reading, see Geyer (1972), Harker (1972–1973), Lovett (1981), Mitchell (1982), R. B. Ruddell and Ruddell (1995), Samuels (1977), Singer (1976), Singer and Ruddell (1976), and Williams (1973).

HOW READERS ACTIVELY CONSTRUCT KNOWLEDGE FROM PRINT

Interactive models of reading describe what readers do in three basic stages of the process: as they begin to read, while they are reading, and after they have read. The thinking strategies readers use in each of these stages are more or less automatic in independent-level, or easy, reading. For instructional-level, or study-type, reading, however, the strategies must be used much more actively and consciously.

Prereading

Effective reading begins with readers quickly scanning some or all of the selection, consciously calling to mind what they know about the topic, and making some initial predictions about the content and the difficulty level of the selection. This process, in general, is called *schema activation.*

Schema is a term used in learning psychology to refer to an organization of information and experiences about a topic. Schemata (the plural form) are unique to each individual, both in content and in organization. Readers' schema for a topic can be thought of as a kind of net that screens incoming information and experience. The more information and experience that readers have related to a topic (the more finely woven the net), the better able they will be to learn, or catch, the new information (see Figure 2.1). This relatively passive process, which simply involves adding to and refining information and categories within the existing net, was described earlier in the chapter as independent-level reading. When readers have an undeveloped schema for a particular topic (very few strands in the net), it is more difficult to read and to learn. At this instructional level, reading requires active construction or reorganization of the net to recognize, evaluate, categorize, and retain new information.

Put simply, the more you know, the better able you are to learn more. However, there is another important aspect of the function of schemata

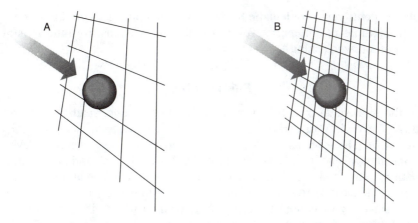

The incoming information is more likely to be caught (perceived and remembered) by the well-developed schema represented in *B* than in the less well-developed schema represented in *A*.

Figure 2.1
Schema theory.
Note. From *Teaching Children to Be Literate: A Reflective Approach* by A. V. Manzo and U. C. Manzo, 1995, Fort Worth, TX: Harcourt Brace College Publishers. Copyright 1995 by Harcourt Brace College Publishers. Reprinted by permission.

in learning. No matter how much one knows about a topic, it must be consciously called to mind in order to function effectively as a *learning net*. This process of consciously calling up related information and experience is called *schema activation*. It is the most essential element of the prereading stage.

Active Silent Reading

Once the reader has an appropriate mindset for reading a particular selection, the general characteristic of active silent reading is referred to as *metacognitive monitoring*. Metacognitive monitoring is the continuous awareness of when one is understanding and when one is beginning to lose the thread of meaning. It involves continuous and active questioning: Is the author saying that . . . ? Is this like when . . . ? Does this really mean that . . . ? Or simply, What does this mean?

Metacognitive monitoring helps readers avoid lapsing into a passive, unproductive independent reading mode. When comprehension begins to falter, active readers use a variety of *fix-up strategies* to actively construct meaning even from difficult text. Depending on the situation, these may include simply pausing to reflect and refocus, rereading, reading aloud, identifying problematic terms and using context to predict or confirm possible meanings, paraphrasing difficult sections, forming mental images, or even asking for help.

Postreading

In the final stage of active, instructional-level reading, readers may use any of a variety of strategies for *schema enhancement* or *schema building.* These terms correspond to the learning processes that developmental psychologist Jean Piaget called "assimilation" and "accommodation." The reader consciously compares the new information to existing schema categories and either adds it (assimilation) or constructs a new category or categorization system to incorporate it (accommodation). This process is best done through review and reflection and can best be taught through some form of writing in response to reading and/or questions and activities that require discussion and application of the new information.

Having considered some of the levels, theories, and stages of the reading process, we turn next to the more practical problems faced by teachers in translating this information into interactive classroom practice. This is followed by a simple interactive teaching method designed to help students acquire reading–thinking strategies by aligning instruction with what is known about the reading process. In doing so, it simultaneously causes teachers to discover many of the principles and guidelines for successful teaching.

ALIGNING INSTRUCTION WITH THEORY

Problems Facing Students

Schooling and education cannot always be the same, but educators must continue to try to make them such. The reason is simple. Students tend to have the greatest difficulty internalizing appropriate strategies for independent learning when classroom practices are markedly incompatible with natural processes for learning. Accordingly, the goal of effective instruction is to try to parallel our best understanding of natural learning processes, since such practices are more likely to put the wind at the students' backs as they try to learn and at the teachers' backs as they attempt to teach. Of course, even meeting this objective is no panacea for all possible problems, since there are students with unusual, though not unnatural, styles of learning.

Nonetheless, the interactive teaching approach advocated here intentionally tries to parallel the interactive, and presumably natural, model of the reading process described previously. In this way, both teacher practices and student learning processes move in the same direction. Ideally, too, each of these processes periodically should guide the other since the necessarily more contrived aspects of operating institutions called *schools* occasionally conflict with the more natural ways that humans learn.

Problems Facing Teachers

At every career stage, there are developmental problems to face and resolve in working toward ideal goals. For most new teachers, it is much easier to teach in the traditional manner they experienced as students than it is to acquire a more interactive teaching style. Most of us have had far fewer personal experiences with interactive teaching than with traditional methods. Furthermore, for new teachers who have been successful students, it can be difficult to realize the problems that many of their peers experienced in those more familiar instructional settings. These impediments are intensified by the fact that they must learn to use these new methods while standing before a class of youngsters who have their own preoccupations, unique histories, and concerns. In a typical classroom setting, teachers must continually evaluate progress toward instructional goals and make many complex "in-flight" decisions based on their perceptions (Padak, 1986). The high potential for stress and job frustration that exists when youngsters with growing pains are brought together with young professionals who are also feeling their own way suggests the need to support teachers so that they can effectively support students.

Interactive Teaching Methods
Benefit Students and Teachers

The interactive teaching methods of content area literacy parallel the needs of students and teachers during these difficult decision-making periods. They generally are fashioned around what research has revealed about what effective readers and teachers do. Interactive methods such as the Listen-Read-Discuss procedure, discussed next, are designed to produce a well-thought-out, but not confining, teaching–learning environment. This is accomplished in several ways:

✦ Because interactive methods are step-by-step guides, they help keep instruction and learning on course through most student disruptions as well as during teacher lapses resulting from inexperience. This structure helps to create a classroom environment that is conducive to the kind of cognitive and social risk taking that is essential to effective learning.

✦ Because interactive methods are general enough in nature to be easily applied across grade levels, subject areas, and types of reading materials, they can reduce lesson-planning time. They can be drawn on to create a lively interaction in virtually any teaching–learning situation, freeing teachers to add as much subject-specific creativity as time and physical and mental resources permit.

✦ Because interactive methods are designed to encourage greater student participation, teachers tend to be more responsive and empathetic. Teaching and learning become more interesting and engaging for both students and teachers.

Listen-Read-Discuss: A Self-Initializing Method

Effective learning, including learning how to be an effective teacher, needs something to get it started, something to keep it going, and something to keep it from becoming random or misguided (Bruner, 1971). The Listen-Read-Discuss (L-R-D) procedure (Manzo & Casale, 1985) tends to meet these requirements for both teachers and students. The L-R-D is a simple lesson design that can be tried almost immediately and that offers several variations that can be phased in as a personal program of professional development. The L-R-D is a heuristic, or hands-on, activity designed to induce self-discovery about effective teaching by teachers and about effective learning by students.

Steps in the L-R-D
Following are the recommended steps for use of the L-R-D as an initial interactive method for teachers and students:

1. Select a portion of a text to be read.
2. Present the information from that portion of the text orally in a brief, organized summary for about half the class period.
3. Have students read the textbook version of the same material. Students will then be empowered to read material with which they have some familiarity.
4. Discuss the material students have heard and read.

Facilitating the Postreading Discussion
Three questions are recommended for provoking an active discussion following reading:

1. What did you understand most from what you heard and read?
2. What did you understand least from what you heard and read?
3. What questions or thoughts did this lesson raise in your mind about the content and/or about effective reading and learning? (E. Smith, 1978)

Anyone who teaches is certain to like the example in Figure 2.2. It is realistic and professional. Notice how students in this lesson were (1) informed on a difficult topic; (2) reinforced in their reading; (3) assessed in their ability to extend and verify their understandings; (4) permitted to articulate those understandings or possible misconceptions; and (5) redirected to continue their search for verifiable knowledge in their textbooks, in other texts, and implicitly from other sources. Notice too, how

Figure 2.2
L-R-D postreading discussion.

Ms. Hailey:	What did you understand best about matter from what you heard and read?
Sam:	That matter means things that take up space.
Mike:	Anything that has mass and takes up space.
Ms. Hailey:	Okay, that's the definition given in your book. Can you, or someone else, give us some examples? *(Various ideas are shared by several students.)*
Ms. Hailey:	What did you understand least about matter?
Julie:	I don't get what isn't matter. Like, we can't see air, so it's not matter, right?
Several students (disagreeing with Julie):	But air takes up space.
Ms. Hailey:	Julie, do you agree with that?
Julie:	No. . . . at least not if. . . . No, I don't agree.
Jenny:	All things take up space. Take blowing up a balloon, for example. . . .
(Interrupted by the teacher)	
Ms. Hailey:	What happens to your balloon? What's inside?
Julie:	*(Thinking, still looking puzzled)* Then there's nothing on earth that isn't matter?
Ms. Hailey:	I can't think of anything, but maybe someone can. *(Teacher models a personal uncertainty.)*
Sam:	Nope. *(No one else volunteers a response.)*
Ms. Hailey:	Well, what other questions or thoughts did this lesson raise in your mind about matter?
Mike:	I'm still wondering about the matter of certain stuff—like the earth and air—what's it made up of?
Jenny:	Yeah, and how do scientists figure out what matter is made of?
Ms. Hailey:	Those are both good questions. Let's read further to see if the author of our textbook answers them. If not, we'll talk about where we might go to find the answers.

Note. From *Using Discussion to Promote Reading Comprehension* (pp. 36–37) by D. E. Alvermann, D. R. Dillon, and D. G. O'Brien, 1987, Newark, DE: International Reading Association. Copyright 1987 by the International Reading Association. Reprinted by permission.

the students began to interact with one another as well as with the teacher. When a class is structured so that students are engaged to the extent that this occurs, it is safe to say that real progress is being made toward content area knowledge and literacy.

Other Values and Benefits of Listen-Read-Discuss

Use of the L-R-D tends to benefit teachers, students, and the school program in ways that are not always immediately apparent. One such value emerges almost immediately in the lesson-planning stage. When teachers select textual material for use in an L-R-D lesson, they find themselves looking at the textbook more carefully and from more points of view than they might otherwise. They begin, quite naturally, to sense where students' comprehension is likely to falter and to better align the phrasing, facts, and organization of the lecture material they are preparing with the textbook material that students will read. With better alignment and organization, teachers automatically begin to heed a basic dictum of effective reading instruction: to stimulate active reading by preteaching key terms, pivotal questions, and new concepts before reading. Better organization and alignment also are likely to raise teachers' levels of tolerance for reasonable digressions in the form of comments about how the new information relates to real-life events and experiences. In so doing, teachers help students to better recall and develop relevant background information and appropriate anticipation, both of which have been shown to be natural to proficient readers and of great value in effective comprehension (Crafton, 1983; Harste, 1978; Stevens, 1982).

Careful preparation of L-R-D lessons actually raises students' ability to read a particular piece beyond their typical reading and thinking levels. This can be a positive and enabling experience for students and teachers. It tends to become a new benchmark for students to strive for in learning from text and for teachers to strive for in helping students to learn from text.

Following the lecture and empowered reading, the lesson design calls for discussion, providing a third repetition and elaboration of the material. This built-in redundancy factor is a most basic—and often overlooked—practice of effective teachers and principle of effective learning.

Finally, a teacher who follows the L-R-D guidelines will have begun to restructure class time and expectations from the typical 90% lecture format to one containing greatly increased proportions of purposeful reading and informed discussion. This achieves yet another important practice of effective teachers and precept of effective learning: increased time on task. Some have argued that the simple lack of attention to reading in typical content classes accounts for a great part of the current higher-literacy crisis in the schools. This conclusion seems justified by the fact that several observational studies of subject teaching at the postelementary levels reveal that virtually no purposeful reading goes on during class time (Feathers & Smith, 1987; Greenewald & Wolf, 1980; Mikulecky, 1982; Ratekin, Simpson, Alvermann, & Dishner, 1985).

Overall, the greatest value of the L-R-D seems to be its ability to provide a simple, hands-on way to introduce and initiate oneself to the principles and practices of content area literacy. The reapportioning of class time offers teachers with defensive teaching styles—who overuse either lecture or seatwork—an opportunity to experiment with reasonable alternatives (Manzo & Manzo, 1996). This tends to leave teachers with more energy and a greater willingness to try more sophisticated teaching methods and potentially benefit more fully from in-service workshops, consultations, and graduate coursework (Watkins, McKenna, Manzo, & Manzo, 1995).

A Self-Instructional Ladder

To help teachers' self-discovery, that is, to ease their way into the actual use of more sophisticated, interactive teaching methods, and to provide rich alternatives for different learning styles, we have developed a ladder of variations and elaborations on the basic L-R-D procedure (see Figures 2.3 and 2.4). You can use L-R-D variations and elaborations to develop your sophistication as an interactive teacher and to explore possible diverse student learning style needs. Try ascending this ladder as your own readiness and students' needs suggest. It's a good idea to keep notes of your thoughts and questions as you try different variations. Your notes and thoughts will be useful in discussions with your instructor and coursemates and in processing your own teaching experiences.

✦ *Looking Back and Looking Ahead* ✦

The combination of the concepts, principles, and the teaching method presented here should have you ready, set, and able to go as a content area literacy provider. Attention to the next chapter on assessment will provide you with the map you need to get there safely and efficiently.

Figure 2.3
Ladder of variations and elaborations on Listen-Read-Discuss.

1. Have students reread the information covered in the L-R-D format rapidly to increase their speed of reading and thought processing. Reading speed tends to rise as a result of increases in prior knowledge, although it can also be easily improved simply by systematic attention and practice.

2. Inform the class that you will lecture, intentionally omitting a few important details that they will need to read their texts to discover. This gives practice in recognizing what is not yet known and experience in careful reading and knowledge seeking.

3. Inform the class that your lecture will cover all the details of a lesson but that they will need to read to discover what questions these details answer. This is one way to teach students to actively seek an understanding of the concept base, or central question, around which an area of study is focused.

4. Inform the class that a quiz will follow the L-R-D sequence. Allow a short study period. This is recommended to activate a high level of focused attention, give practice in test taking, and set the stage for questions and discussion about how to study effectively.

5. Invert the core process occasionally by having the class R-L-D, or read (for about 15 minutes), then listen, and finally discuss. This variation tends to focus and improve listening attention and the ability to learn from an effective lecture. This effect can be further heightened when joined with the other listening training and note-taking techniques covered ahead.

6. Watch a videotape, educational film, or multimedia presentation on a text topic *before* reading about it in the text. Such visual representations are compatible with the habits of contemporary youngsters and can help build new bridges to print. (See Figure 2.4.)

7. Ask students which portions of the text struck them as inconsiderate, that is, poorly written, poorly organized, or presuming too much prior knowledge. This activity can help students learn when to ask for help with textual and class material. It also helps the teacher become more aware of student learning needs. Analysis of the writing in texts is also a good way to informally teach some of the basics of effective writing.

8. Provide the class with a definitive purpose for reading and discussing that will require critical and/or creative expression or application. State that purpose clearly on the chalkboard for easy reference, for example, "As you read this section on the steam engine, try to determine why it was bound to be replaced by the gasoline engine." This will serve as a reminder to read actively and with reference to real-life problem solving.

9. Hold postreading discussions on teaching and learning strategies. Make the discussion positive by asking students what they or you may have done that resulted in solid learning. Such discussion gives credit to student intuition, develops reciprocity, and furthers meta-cognitive processing, or thinking about thinking.

10. Create research teams, and provide time for students to delve into a topic in greater depth. One group could simply see what other textbooks say on the topic. Another could check with other authoritative references—persons, books, and the InterNet. Another could write a best estimate of which real-life problems the information learned might help solve or answer. Still another group, where appropriate, could try to identify and discuss theme-related stories, poetry, music, or art. Activities such as these provide links between text topics and nonprint resources and among school learning, artistic expression, multicultural perspectives, and the rest of the real world.

Figure 2.4

Example of L-R-D elaboration 6: Viewing a videotape or film before reading in a world geography class.

Purposes for Viewing

Teacher: Today we are going to continue our study of Kenya by focusing on the Maisi tribe of Southern Kenya. First, we will watch a 20-minute National Geographic tape on this most unusual tribe of people. Listen carefully as you watch for two things, which you will then read about: the diet of the Maisi and the names of three other tribes of the north whom few people know of but who figure in Kenyan life in a big way.

Brief Review Following Viewing

Teacher: OK, what were the two points we listened for?

Student: The Maisi basically live off their cattle, eating meat and drinking their blood and raw milk.

Teacher: And?

Student: Well, there were three other tribes mentioned, but I can't remember any of them.

Teacher: OK, read pages 66 to 71 in your text now to learn more about the Maisi diet, and let's get the names of those tribes. If you happen to finish reading early, there are a few copies of a recent magazine report on cholesterol here on my desk that might help answer the question "Why aren't the Maisi dying of clogged arteries and heart failure from their high-fat diet?"

Postreading Discussion

Teacher: What did you understand best from what you watched and read about?

Student: The names of the three other tribes.

Teacher: Say and spell them, and I'll write them on the board.

Student: Samburu, Turkana, and Hamitic.

Teacher: What did you understand least from what you watched and read about? [When students have understood what they have viewed and read, they will take this question to mean pretty much the same thing as the next one: What questions or thoughts did this lesson raise in your mind?]

Student: I pretty much understood what was said, but I don't understand why the Maisi don't raise things the way the other tribes do.

Teacher: The land they live on is not arable. There is poor topsoil and little water. But that really doesn't explain why they don't move to where there is arable land.

Student: I was wondering about their high-fat diet, so I read fast to get to the article you talked about. It seems that there are at least two reasons why they don't have high blood cholesterol. The raw milk has enzymes that break down fat in the blood. Also, they lead very active lives. They burn off the fat as fast as they put it on.

Teacher: If raw milk is so good for you, why do we homogenize and pasteurize ours, I wonder? Why don't you ask Mrs. Shell in science today if she can help us out with this.

✦ ✦   **TRADE SECRET**   ✦ ✦

Methods Prompters

Television personalities use TelePrompTers, or idiot cards, to help keep them on track during TV shows. Master musicians and conductors follow musical scripts. Commercial pilots rely on loose-leaf binders containing step-by-step instructions to get huge planes off the ground and navigators to guide them once they are aloft. Nonetheless, as teachers we tend to make many difficult "in-flight" decisions with no map or on-board navigator to guide us.

You will find it valuable to construct, and even laminate, a set of cards outlining the procedural steps of acknowledged and published lesson designs (as well as, eventually, those of your own creation). Use a large-size font, and prop these up on your desk to guide you as you teach. The security they provide will make it easier for you to digress from a lesson plan and attend to student needs and/or seize a moment to pursue a point that may be incidental to the lesson but nevertheless important and timely. You can collect these lesson prompters in a loose-leaf binder and/or a computer and share them with other teachers. Begin with a lesson prompter on the L-R-D method.

CHAPTER 3

Interactive Assessment for Active Self-Monitoring

The examiner pipes and the teacher must dance—and the examiner sticks to the old tune.

—H. G. Wells, 1892

✦ *Organizing Thoughts* ✦

Interactive teaching begins with interactive assessment. To achieve this, it is essential that assessment techniques are selected that invite a reasonably high level of student involvement. This chapter details several such techniques that are both timely and have withstood the test of time. These include an informal textbook inventory designed to assess and teach students about the parts of their books, a rationale for portfolio analysis of student progress, and a rubric system for easy evaluation of student writing. The chapter concludes with several simple ways to estimate the difficulty level, or *readability*, of textual material. Appropriate shortcuts and computer-based alternatives are noted along the way.

THE POWER OF THE EXAMINER

The power of the examiner is a long-standing and deeply rooted issue in education. In fact, the influence of testing may be greater now than at any time in our prior history. There are a variety of assessment movements with puzzling titles throughout the nation. In the past ten years, most states have first instituted and then dropped or redirected assessment procedures with names like *basic competencies, mastery learning, criterion-referenced* testing, and more recently, *holistic, authentic, outcomes-based,* and *performance-based* assessment.

HIGHER-ORDER AND PERFORMANCE-BASED ASSESSMENT

Of the current variety of assessment movements, the movement toward higher-order thinking and performance-based assessment, or the representation of real-life tasks in assessment, may be the most welcome (see Figure 3.1). The logic of mastery learning, which so strongly influenced teaching and testing in the past, now finally is being replaced with assessment more firmly grounded in interactive and integrated performance. Where mastery learning stressed the passive acquisition of facts and skills, newer interactive assessment models tend to emphasize the active role of readers and learners in using print to construct meaning and solve problems. Thus, there is a decreased emphasis on product outcomes of learning, such as information acquisition, and an increased

Figure 3.1
Performance-based, or authentic, assessment: the current trend.

The goal of traditional assessment is to evaluate *acquisition* of information. The goal of performance-based assessment is to evaluate the *processes for acquiring and using* information. To do this, performance-based assessment is expected to have several of the following characteristics:

- Is problem-centered
- Requires use of facts rather than recall of facts
- Requires higher-order thinking along inferential and evaluative lines
- Is more constructive in format than reconstructive
- Does not necessarily have a single correct answer
- Involves more hands-on doing than conventional knowledge testing
- Is more authentic, or real-life
- Reflects more fairly the diversity of perspectives in American cultures

---

emphasis on how well students are internalizing the thinking processes they will need to learn both in and out of school.

As more states move away from use of standardized test scores as the primary approach to evaluation of schools and school districts, it is expected that educators will feel less obliged to concentrate on simple fact acquisition and more committed to engaging students in authentic learning activities. Of course, this does not mean that standardized test scores are without value. See Figure 3.2 for an example of how such data can be used to suggest programmatic decisions.

For a more authentic and interactive means of assessing students' needs, consider the Informal Textbook Inventory. It is a means of introducing a textbook to a class, having students tell the teacher about their preparation for using it effectively, and seamlessly teaching them how to use it to full advantage. This technique sometimes is referred to as a Classroom Reading Inventory (CRI).

THE INFORMAL TEXTBOOK/CLASSROOM READING INVENTORY

Getting Acquainted with the Textbook

An Informal Textbook Inventory (ITI) essentially is a special type of open-book test designed to familiarize students with using one of education's most basic learning tools: the textbook. This "new idea" is over seventy-five years old. We have seen an excellent ten-question version of

Figure 3.2
Local high school excels in knowledge but lags in reading.

The following standardized test score information was reported for a local high school in a major city: Of thirty-four high schools recently tested in the state, this high school was

First in mathematics

First in social studies

First in science

Second in narrative (story) reading

Sixth in expository (content area) reading

These data suggest the following conclusion. If the youngsters in this school are first in the three traditional areas of knowledge acquisition but sixth in ability to comprehend (i.e., think) in these subjects, then a program to further maximize application and content area reading in the disciplines is in order.

the ITI in a 1924 edition of a fifth-year reader (Walker & Parkman). Since most texts on the market do not contain such a ready-made inventory, you probably will need to construct your own. There are several good reasons for creating and using an ITI at the beginning of the school year:

✦ It is easily administered in group, paper and pencil format.

✦ It tests and teaches simultaneously.

✦ It draws the teacher's and students' attention to the processing strategies involved in using text parts, text aids, and related resources.

✦ It provokes active awareness and discussion of text features.

✦ It lends itself well to computer (hypertext) presentation and scoring.

✦ It is purposeful and well structured but nonthreatening.

✦ It reflects the highest current standards of performance-based assessment.

When used early in the school year, while student attitudes and expectations are still being formed, the ITI provides an excellent means of establishing a disciplined, well-managed classroom tone. By simply tallying the results of the inventory, the teacher can obtain a record of each student's ability to deal with the textbook as well as indications of some of the potential benefits and shortcomings of the textbook itself.

Such assessment can take time to prepare, but it also stores well and improves with age and use. It is the type of activity that is the mark of a professional teacher. Students appreciate the help, and supervisors rarely fail to take note. The second and subsequent times you use the ITI, you will be even more pleased because you will have refined it and will know better what to expect and how to better orchestrate the full activity.

Constructing the Informal Textbook Inventory

The following outline illustrates the general form of the ITI:

I. Organization and Structure of the Text

A. Understanding the Textbook Organization

Develop three to five straightforward questions about how the text is structured and how to use the comprehension aids provided within the text.

B. Using the Text Organization Effectively

Develop three to five questions that students can answer by referring to the index, table of contents, glossary, appendices, or other text sections and/or aids.

II. Basic Comprehension

Select a short portion of the text that contains an important concept with supporting details and at least one graph, chart, or picture. (The same selection can be used in the following section on applied comprehension.)

A. Comprehending the Main Idea

Develop one or two fill-in or multiple-choice questions that direct students to state or select the main idea of the material read.

B. Noting Supporting Details

Develop three or more fill-in, multiple-choice, or matching questions about specific facts or ideas in the selection.

C. Understanding Vocabulary in Context

Develop three or more fill-in, multiple-choice, or matching questions that direct students to state or select a definition for key terms used in the selection.

D. Understanding Information Presented in Graphic or Pictorial Form

Develop one or more questions requiring students to state or select an interpretation of a graph, chart, or picture that adds information not explicitly stated in the selection.

III. Applied Comprehension

Questions in these sections can be based on the same text selection used in Part II.

A. Drawing Conclusions and Critical Thinking

Develop one or more questions that require students to draw valid conclusions based on the information presented.

B. Evaluating and Judging

Develop one or more questions that require students to evaluate and apply information from the text in terms of their own experiences, values, and existing knowledge base.

IV. Specialized Options

    A. Assess special requirements of the discipline. This could mean understanding geographical directions in social studies, a section on understanding style or mood in literature, or a section on applying symbols in mathematical formulas. Examples are found in Chapter 11, on content-specific applications.

    B. Assess pupil abilities to deal with the linguistic features of the text with a Standard Cloze Passage test (described later in this chapter).

Administering and Evaluating the Informal Textbook Inventory

Before asking students to tackle the inventory, explain some of its features and purposes: It is not a test in the usual sense of the word; every text differs slightly from every other, and this is a way to find out how. Point out further that although answers will be discussed as a group, each student will need to independently complete the inventory as thoroughly and accurately as possible.

Once all students have completed the inventory, collect and score the results. For diagnostic purposes, any error is taken as a sign of need in that category.

Much of the diagnostic value of the inventory comes from the group discussion of the items when the tests are returned to the students. Compare and contrast student strengths and weaknesses among the various categories of questions. Review and discussion of the inventory with the class can take from one-half to two full class periods depending on individual students' abilities, the difficulty of the text, and the objectives the teacher may wish to achieve.

The next assessment instrument, the Standard Cloze Passage test, also can be constructed from a class textbook. It is much easier to construct, but it yields a more general account of a pupil's ability to handle a given textbook at the linguistic, or language and syntactic, level.

STANDARD CLOZE PASSAGE TEST

The term *cloze* refers to a written passage with certain words blanked out to be filled in by the reader. Early studies of this task revealed that it is closely related to reading comprehension across age and most grade levels (Bormuth, 1965). Subsequent studies, however, indicated that cloze was not a direct measure of reading comprehension. Instead, it was a fairly accurate measure of one of the factors that contributes to comprehension, namely, familiarity with the language redundancy patterns, or repetitive sentence structures and phrases in prose (Culver, Godfrey, & Manzo, 1972; Weaver & Kingston, 1963). Technically speaking, this means that cloze and reading comprehension have relatively little in common with one another, but both are strongly related to a third thing (probably verbal reasoning), and therefore either can be used to infer the other.

This and related work added several points to our understanding of the potential values and possible shortcomings of cloze passage testing. These points are summarized in the following list:

1. Cloze is a good, quick assessment strategy for sampling students' ability to handle the language patterns common to different types of content material—and therefore is a good complement to an ITI.
2. Cloze will tend to underestimate the comprehension abilities of students with weak standard English backgrounds, since comprehension is inferred from familiarity with English language patterns.
3. Cloze tends to penalize students who are divergent thinking, impulsive, or perfectionistic, since the task is rather tedious, with an error rate higher than what students are used to.
4. Independent practice on cloze tasks does not contribute to improvement in reading comprehension; however, guided discussion of which words work best in each blank, and why, does result in improved comprehension.

The general cloze task can have many forms and purposes. The specific form of the cloze task described next, the Standard Cloze Passage test, is a useful assessment tool for content teachers.

Purpose of the Standard Cloze Passage Test

When constructed, administered, and scored as described next, the cloze test provides a fair indication of how a particular group of students will be able to read and understand a particular piece of reading material. Students' individual scores can be categorized to indicate whether the reading material used is at their own independent, instructional, or frustration level.

Preparation of the Standard Cloze Passage Test

To prepare a Standard Cloze test, select a passage of about 300 words from a textbook. The passage should be one that students have not yet read. Copy the first sentence with no deletions. Then select a word at random in the second sentence. Delete this word and every fifth word thereafter until fifty words have been deleted. Finish the sentence containing the fiftieth blank, and copy the next sentence with no deletions. The blanks should be typed as lines five spaces long and numbered from one to fifty. Students record their responses on numbered answer sheets.

Administration of the Standard Cloze Passage Test

To administer the Standard Cloze test, first talk through a few sample cloze sentences. See Figure 3.3 for suggestions about how to do this. Tell students that the task is more difficult than what they may be used to, but that even if they miss half of the items they will have done very well (actually, 40% correct is still instructional level). You may also wish to assure students that their scores will not be part of their course grades but are an important means for teachers to better understand and provide for their reading needs. This introduction should encourage most students to do their best while reducing the problem noted earlier with this type of task.

Scoring the Standard Cloze Passage Test

To score the Standard Cloze Passage test, simply count the number of words filled in correctly. Count only exact words; do not count synonyms as correct. Multiply this number by 2 (since there are fifty items) to get

Figure 3.3
Pointers on demonstrating cloze testing.

Two elements must be considered for proper word replacement, *semantics*—or meaning—and *syntax*—or grammatical function. Demonstrate these by making choices available on the first two examples that make this point. Then increase the difficulty level of the examples to the actual testing task with two or three more deletions that offer no choices.

Example
Germany today is reunited, but its people still feel the differences from the period of Soviet domination. West Germans are highly __(industrious/frivolous)__ , in the tradition of __(ancients/old)__ Germany. The East __(Germans)__ feel less industrious and __(are)__ given to reliance on __(government)__ for their support.

the percent correct. Scores below 40% mean the material is at the students' frustration level: It is too difficult for them to read and learn from even with instructional support. Scores from 40% to 60% mean that the material is at these students' instructional level: They can read and learn from the material with some assistance and guidance. Scores above 60% generally indicate ability to read and learn with no special assistance, or the independent level.

Why Synonyms Won't Do

An understandable concern of teachers is the fact that only exact replacement words are counted correct in scoring the standard cloze test. Synonyms are not counted in such testing for three reasons. First, the assessment format was standardized according to exact-word scoring; therefore, the evaluation criterion cannot be used if synonyms are accepted. Second, the rank ordering of students does not change appreciably when synonyms are accepted; everyone simply has a higher score. Finally, if synonyms are allowed, scoring for the teacher becomes a much longer and more tedious process. You may, nonetheless, wish to use a more interactive version if you feel that the standard form is inappropriate for your students.

Interactive Cloze

For a more interactive version of cloze testing, consider these guidelines for a nonstandard form: Have students score their own papers with an allowance for synonyms based on class discussion of reasonable alternatives to the exact word deleted. Increase the independent reading level score to 70%.

To further encourage self-evaluation and strategic reading, ask pupils to write a sentence or two telling what they think their score indicates about their ability to read the material and what they think they should do to read better in the particular textbook from which the passage was taken.

Next, we turn to the topic of writing. Of all the things we attempt to evaluate in school, writing is one of the more difficult to assess satisfactorily. Nonetheless, it is an area of considerable interest in modern education.

EVALUATION OF STUDENT WRITING

Teachers' enthusiasm for activities that involve student writing often is dampened by the prospect of piles of papers to be painstakingly graded. Fortunately, the recent renovation of an old idea called *rubric* evaluation of student writing cuts down on the paper load. As a result, it is making student writing a more attractive option for more teachers.

Using Rubric Evaluation to
Enhance Writing Activities

A writing rubric is a set of guidelines for holistic scoring of compositions. It is a teacher-constructed list of characteristics for ranking the quality of student papers, generally on a number scale or simply as *high, medium,* or *low.* The teacher uses a rubric to grade student compositions by simply determining which rubric level each composition best matches. Grading compositions thus becomes a speedy process of categorizing papers by level rather than a tedious chore of red-penciling each and every error and composing brief but time-consuming written comments on students' papers.

Ideally, the teacher gives the rubric for a writing assignment to students along with the topic. This encourages students to participate in self-evaluation and to internalize high standards. A student's working drafts are read by a partner student, using the rubric to make editorial suggestions. As teachers drop in on these peer editing sessions, their suggestions become more meaningful to these works in progress than conventional written comments on a final product paper. Used in this way, rubrics are a valuable way of stimulating individual and peer revisions of school compositions.

Depending on the importance of the objective of the writing assignment, the rubric may be simple or quite complex. Figures 3.4 and 3.5 provide two sample rubrics: one addressing a specific writing objective, and the other addressing content objectives of a particular writing assignment.

Figure 3.4
Sample rubric 1: Using examples and illustrations.

3	The topic sentence is clearly written and strongly supported by lucid and interesting examples. Transitions tie the paper together in a fluid manner. Mechanical errors are slight.
2	The topic sentence is present, but support from the examples needs to be stronger and better organized. Transitions are used but need polishing. There are some mechanical errors.
1	The paragraph lacks a clear topic sentence. Examples are few in number and inadequately explained. Transitions are lacking, and mechanical errors are frequent.

Note. Adapted from *The Double Helix: Teaching the Writing Process,* edited by P. Behle, 1982, Florissant, MO: Ferguson-Florissant Writers Project. Copyright 1982 by Ferguson-Florissant Writers Project.

Figure 3.5
Sample rubric 2: A specific content assignment.

Paper Topic: 1960s Approaches to Civil Rights in the United States

High-Quality Papers Contain

An overview of civil rights or their lack during the 1960s, with three specific examples

A statement defining civil disobedience, with three examples of how it was used and Martin Luther King, Jr.'s, role

At least one other approach to civil rights, with specific examples, and a comparison of this approach with King's civil disobedience that illustrates differences or similarities in at least two ways

Good organization, well-developed arguments, few mechanical errors (sentence fragments, grammatical errors, spelling errors)

Medium-Quality Papers Contain

An overview of black civil rights during the 1960s with two specific examples

A statement defining civil disobedience, with two examples of its use and Martin Luther King, Jr.'s, involvement

One other approach to civil rights, with examples, and a comparison of it with King's civil disobedience by their differences

Good organization, few mechanical errors, moderately developed arguments

Lower-Quality Papers Contain

A general statement defining civil disobedience with reference to Martin Luther King, Jr.'s, involvement and at least one example

One other approach to civil rights and how it differed from civil disobedience

Fair organization, some mechanical errors

Lowest-Quality Papers Contain

A general statement on who Martin Luther King, Jr., was, or a general statement on civil disobedience

A general statement that not all blacks agreed with civil disobedience

A list of points, poor organization, many mechanical errors

Note. From "Guidelines for the Use and Evaluation of Writing in Content Classrooms," by D. L. Pearce, 1983, *Journal of Reading, 27,* p. 215. Copyright 1983 by the International Reading Association. Reprinted with permission of Daniel L. Pearce and the International Reading Association.

Evaluating Expression and Concepts

A persistent problem in evaluating student writing is that some compositions will be organizationally, structurally, and mechanically perfect but lack originality and richness of thought, while others may have distracting errors in form but contain striking expressions and/or fresh conceptual approaches. A popular solution to this problem has been a dual-grade system—one grade for ideas and one for mechanics. A rubric that combines mechanics and content, such as sample rubric 2 in Figure 3.5, provides guidelines for students to assist one another in working toward an effective combination of both aspects of a quality composition.

The initial planning time spent in preparing a rubric tends to enhance the quality of student products as well as to simplify grading. A rubric-guided writing assignment at the beginning of the school year can provide a valuable addition to the ITI.

Next, we discuss another form assessment that is growing in popularity. It is a means of incorporating and organizing many possible forms of assessment called portfolio collection and analysis.

Portfolios: Rationale, Functions, Promise, Problems

A portfolio is a collection of works intended to illustrate a range of abilities and possible special talents over time. The idea of a portfolio is to show what one can do and how one has progressed through various stages and periods.

Portfolios for students, in effect, are based on the proposition that pupils should be involved in assessing their progress and actively selecting and keeping samples of their best work for periodic review. There are two popular types of student portfolios: show portfolios, which include only a few selected samples of work, and working portfolios, which include a wide array of works in progress (Farr, 1992). Periodically, students should be helped to select pieces from their working portfolios to place in their show portfolios. The show portfolio should include the pupil's best current works, as well as some works that are representative of earlier stages of learning. The teacher's role is largely to serve as a consultant who councils students on the works that seem to reflect their progress in reading, writing, thinking, and content learning. The process of collecting, reviewing, and maintaining student portfolios tends to create interactions between teachers and students that can lead to greater empathy and a sense of common purpose.

Contents of Portfolios

Depending on the teacher's purposes, student portfolios may include any or all of the following types of entries:

+ Quarterly writing samples from a variety of perspectives across genre: journal writing, personal narrative, fiction, nonfiction, poetry
+ Evidence of progress in aspects of communications from phrasing to grammar and spelling

+ Evidence of progress in comprehension and content knowledge
+ Results from informal inventories
+ Taped oral readings and presentations
+ Drawings and other expressive works
+ Photographs of special projects too bulky to store
+ Year-to-year photographs of self, the teacher, and other students
+ Periodic anecdotal accounts and comments from teachers

Teacher and student comments give the portfolio depth and dimension. Here are some sample comments:

Jack, your account of the religious basis for the civil war in Bosnia is enlightening. I read it to my wife at dinner the other night.

Mr. Ahkim 10/23/96

Tamica, this algebra homework assignment tells me that you can read and follow word problems quite well. However, I think you should recheck your calculations.

Ms. Toma 11/10/96

Students can be asked to write short explanations of why they chose certain entries for their show portfolios. For example:

I included this report on "Russia Today" because I think it includes my best work so far on using citations and references.

Mark 11/10/96

This is a tape recording of me in the spring play. I was the narrator, and I thought I was pretty good. I'd like to listen to it again next year, and see how much I have changed.

Nina 5/12/96

The single most important value of portfolio assessment is that it shifts the emphasis away from the errors and the false starts kids make while acquiring knowledge and skill. Instead, the emphasis is placed on preserving, and periodically reviewing, completed pieces that youngsters value. Unlike grade books and permanent record files, which few have access to, the portfolio collection may be kept in an easily accessible part of the room for others to view, with proper permission. Importantly, maintaining portfolios is something youngsters do for themselves as well as for others. As such, the portfolio system helps to build and expand interests that lead to further reading (Ediger, 1992).

Disadvantages of Portfolios

The most serious disadvantage of portfolios is that they can quickly become quite complex and cumbersome. Portfolios were originally intended to provide a means of balancing other more standardized forms of assessment with a concrete record of a student's actual work. The student portfolio itself, however, is only the raw data on which this balancing is based. Evaluating these data should be a simple, subjective, and self-evident process. It can, however, be turned into a tedious, overly objectified, time-consuming one. According to one research report, some teachers view student portfolios as too demanding, and "yet another means of increasing and controlling teachers' work while appearing to empower them" (Gomez, Graue, & Bloch, 1991, p. 621). On the other hand, electronic technology is making portfolio collection and analysis somewhat easier. Computer programs are being written that guide collection, assessment, and interpretation, all with a click on an appropriate icon. See Figure 3.6 for an example (Duckworth & Taylor, 1995) of a computerized portfolio.

Now that you know about several means of estimating students' abilities and progress in reading and writing about materials at different levels of difficulty, learn next how to estimate the difficulty level of the textual material they are asked to read. This, too, is a "new" technology that is about seventy-five years old.

ASSESSING TEXT DIFFICULTY

Readability Formulas

The difficulty level of a text is referred to as the text's *readability*. Historically, junior and senior high school texts have been written with more concern for content than for difficulty level. A tenth-grade American history text, for example, might have a readability of grade twelve. This has begun to change in recent years as members of school district text selection committees have started including readability as a major criterion by which to evaluate potential textbook purchases.

Readability depends on a number of factors, including the influence of print size, number and quality of graphic aids, and an individual's level of interest and prior knowledge in the topic area. The greatest influence by far, however, comes from two simple factors: average length of sentences and word difficulty, which largely is a function of the frequency of use of a word in popular print. The most commonly used procedures for estimating readability are formulas that employ these two factors in one way or another.

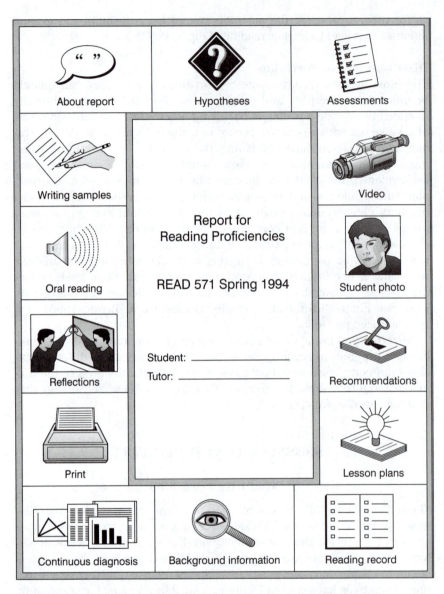

About report

Hypotheses

Assessments

Writing samples

Video

Report for
Reading Proficiencies

READ 571 Spring 1994

Oral reading

Student photo

Student: _____

Tutor: _____

Reflections

Recommendations

Print

Lesson plans

Continuous diagnosis

Background information

Reading record

Figure 3.6
Assessing literacy through hypermedia portfolios.

One of the more commonly used readability formulas is detailed next. It is presented here to illustrate the process of estimating readability level rather than to suggest that teachers should regularly undertake even these abbreviated analyses by hand. However, it can be enlightening to do a text analysis by hand, especially if no other means is available.

Raygor's Readability Graph

The Raygor procedure, illustrated in Figure 3.7, uses the number of words containing six or more letters and the average sentence length of three passages of 100 words each to estimate a text's difficulty. Baldwin and Kaufman (1979) found the Raygor formula faster than and as accurate as the original Fry formula (1968, 1977), on which it is based.

Computer Programs for Readability Checking

Even simplified formulas for estimating readability are time-consuming to do manually. Fortunately, a wide variety of computer software now is available for obtaining readability estimates on textbook excerpts. This is much more realistic in terms of time and elimination of the human error inevitable with lengthy syllable/word counting and calculating. Microsoft Word 5.0 or higher has two readability formulas built in. For more information on commercially available computer readability programs, ask your local software dealer or school librarian.

There is another approach to evaluating readability that any veteran teacher can use effectively and that new teachers can use to increase their sensitivity to factors in a text that will influence the level of difficulty for students. It is called a readability checklist.

Readability Checklists

Checklists to guide readability estimates are totally subjective and do not necessarily yield a grade-level readability estimate. They do, however, indicate whether a given book is appropriate for a particular group of students. Checklists are most effective when several teachers rate the same material and then average (or otherwise compare) their judgments. A group of teachers from a given content area may wish to develop their own checklist that addresses specific content concerns.

One list includes the following items, to which the rater responds with a particular group of students in mind:

1. Are the concepts far beyond the students' direct experiences?
2. Are abstract concepts linked to examples and situations that are familiar to students?
3. Are technical terms defined in context as they appear?

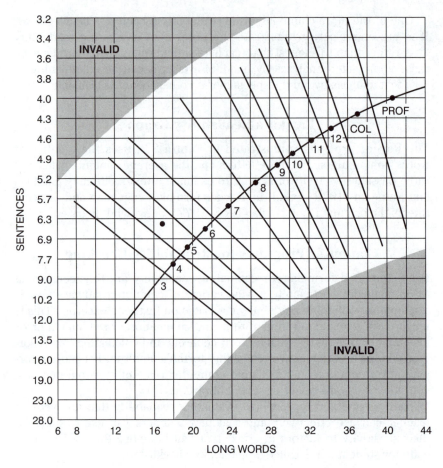

1. Count out three 100-word passages at the beginning, middle, and end of a selection or book. Count proper nouns but not numerals.

2. Count sentences in each passage, estimating to the nearest tenth.

3. Count words with six or more letters.

4. Average the sentence length and word length over three samples, and plot the average on the graph.

Figure 3.7

The Raygor procedure for estimating readability.

Note. From "The Raygor Readability Estimate: A Quick and Easy Way to Determine Difficulty" by A. L. Raygor, in *Reading: Theory, Research and Practice. Twenty-sixth Yearbook of the National Reading Conference* (pp. 259–263), edited by P. D. Pearson, 1977, Clemson, SC: National Reading Conference.

4. Does one idea lead logically to another?
5. What does the author assume about the students' previous learning experiences?
6. Are textbooks aids provided?
7. Is the material appealing, or does it look too "textbookish"?
8. Is the writing brief, concise, and to the point? (Harker, 1977)

Readability checklists can even be adapted for use by students. To help students to become more independent and strategic readers, they need a greater capacity for self-appraisal of text difficulty, text aids, and personal ability to negotiate a given textbook. One way to help them to do this is the FLIP inventory, described next.

FLIP: For Student Analysis of Text Difficulty

FLIP (Schumm & Mangrum, 1991) invites students to judge how well they will be able to read and learn from a particular reading assignment by analyzing its *f*riendliness, *l*anguage, and their own *i*nterest and *p*rior knowledge, using a FLIP chart (see Figure 3.8). Students are instructed to FLIP through the reading assignment and use the chart to record their judgments.

By adding the FLIP elements rated, students are able to evaluate the general level of the assignment. They then proceed to interpret their assessment to determine an appropriate reading rate and to budget reading and study time (see Figure 3.9)

Following is a valuable closing thought on readability. It uses the idea of student input in a way that may have occurred to you when you first read about cloze testing.

Matching Student Abilities with
Text Difficulty through Cloze

The Standard Cloze Passage test described earlier is as much a readability strategy as it is a measure of students' reading ability. It does not yield a grade level estimate of the difficulty of a given text, but it does predict how well a particular student or group of students will be able to read and learn from it. Hittleman (1978) pointed out that cloze measures readability, whereas other means predict text difficulty. He also noted that the cloze procedure is the only available procedure that can take into account, in a natural setting, the constraints of the language system of the reading matter, the reading ability and other characteristics of the reader, and the background information needed by the reader. In other words, there are two ways to compare your students' reading levels with your textbook's readability level. One is to compare some form of student reading test score to a formula-based readability estimate in the text. Another is simply to give a

Figure 3.8
FLIP chart.

Title of assignment _____

Number of pages _____

General directions: Rate each of the four FLIP categories in a 1 to 5 scale
(5 = high). Then determine your purpose for reading and appropriate reading rate,
and budget your reading/study time.

F = Friendliness: How friendly is my reading assignment?
    Directions: Examine your assignment to see if it includes the friendly elements
    listed below.

    Friendly text features

Table of contents	Index	Glossary
Chapter introductions	Headings	Subheadings
Margin notes	Study questions	Chapter summary
Key terms highlighted	Graphs	Charts
Pictures	Signal words	Lists of key facts

    1————————2————————3————————4————————5

No friendly text features	Some friendly text features	Many friendly text features

                           Friendliness rating _____

L = Language: How difficult is the language in my reading assignment?
    Directions: Skim the chapter quickly to determine the number of new terms.
    Read three random paragraphs to get a feel for the vocabulary level and
    number of long, complicated sentences.

    1————————2————————3————————4————————5

Many new words; complicated sentences	Some new words; somewhat complicated sentences	No new words; clear sentences

                           Language rating _____

I = Interest: How interesting is my reading assignment?
    Directions: Read the title, introduction, headings/subheadings, and summary.
    Examine the pictures and graphics included.

    1————————2————————3————————4————————5

Boring	Somewhat interesting	Very interesting

                           Interest rating _____

**P = Prior knowledge: What do I already know about the material covered in
my reading assignment?**
    Directions: Think about the title, introduction, headings/subheadings,
    and summary

    1————————2————————3————————4————————5

Mostly new information	Some new information	Mostly familiar information

                         Prior knowledge rating _____

Overall, this reading assignment appears to be at:
    ____ a comfortable reading level for me
    ____ a somewhat comfortable reading level for me
    ____ an uncomfortable reading level for me

Note. Flip chart from Schumm, Jeanne Shay, & Mangrum, Charles T., II. (1991, October). FLIP: A framework for content area reading. *Journal of Reading, 35*(2), 120–124. Reprinted with permission of Jeanne Shay Schumm and the International Reading Association. All rights reserved.

Figure 3.9
FLIP follow-up.

My purpose for reading is (circle one):
A. Personal pleasure
B. To prepare for class discussions
C. To answer written questions for class assignment or for homework
D. To prepare for a test
E. Other: _____

My reading rate should be (circle one):
A. Slow—allowing time for rereading if necessary
B. Medium—careful and analytical
C. Fast—steady, skipping sections that are about information I already
    know

Active reading time:
Chunk 1, pages _____ – _____ , estimated time: _____ minutes
Chunk 2, pages _____ – _____ , estimated time: _____ minutes
Chunk 3, pages _____ – _____ , estimated time: _____ minutes
Chunk 4, pages _____ – _____ , estimated time: _____ minutes
Total estimated time: _____ minutes

Note. Flip chart from Schumm, Jeanne Shay, & Mangrum, Charles T., II. (1991, October). FLIP: A framework for content area reading. *Journal of Reading, 35*(2), 120–124. Reprinted with permission of Jeanne Shay Schumm and the International Reading Association. All rights reserved.

Standard Cloze Passage test constructed from a representative portion of the text. Hence, the Standard Cloze Passage test permits a direct comparison using a single measure. To improve the quality of the match, you have only to construct more than one sample for the text.

✦ *Looking Back and Looking Ahead* ✦

This chapter offered a broad range of options for considering and conducting assessment in the context of the content area classroom. It described traditional and emerging options for assessing students' reading, text management, and writing. Finally, the chapter turned from student assessment to text assessment and provided a tour of available means for assessing the difficulty level of printed material.

The next chapter begins the core of the book. It includes four chapters on the comprehension process. Reading comprehension is one of the most complex areas of human learning. As you read more about this process and how to promote it, you likely will come to a fuller appreciation of the models and instruments that this chapter described.

✦ ✦   **TRADE SECRET**   ✦ ✦

Getting to Know You

It is an axiom of professional education that to know others, you must first know yourself. To reach this island of self-knowledge, however, one must navigate through the reefs of self-doubt and self-examination. This can be particularly formidable because, as the German writer Herman Hesse put it, "Nothing . . . is so distasteful to man as to go the way which leads him to himself."

When you are up to facing this process, you might wish to look into some of the personality and temperament inventories that are available for popular consumption in most bookstores. These may not always have the high accuracy of some of the more heavily norm-based personality tests, but they tend to be sufficiently accurate for getting a look at yourself, since most of them essentially are made up of the more telling items of traditional measures like the Minnesota Multiphasic Personality Inventory (MMPI). See Appendix A for one such inventory.

SECTION II

Reading and Learning from Text

This section is the heart of content area literacy. If you have been convinced that you should be part of this literacy effort, you will need to be especially competent in improving reading comprehension in content-specific textbooks.

Accordingly, the four chapters of this section address the specifics of how to provide support to students in comprehension at every stage of that process: prereading, during reading, and postreading. Accordingly, Chapter 4 deals with methods designed to support all three phases of reading, not that subsequent methods completely neglect these. Chapter 5 details much of what you will need to know about prereading for schema activation, or preparing students to read effectively. It contains a good deal of information about two support components, questioning and modeling. Chapter 6 tells how to help students to self-monitor and self-repair comprehension while reading. It includes a brief account of some efforts to redesign textbooks that would contain a new generation of built-in aids to readers. Finally, Chapter 7 reports on the sometimes maligned value of traditional recitation, as well as discussion at the postreading phase. It also offers a focused treatment of postreading cooperative or collaborative learning methods. Strictly speaking, this focus could have appeared earlier; however, most of what is thought of as comprehension checking and cooperative learning tends to take place following individual efforts to read.

CHAPTER 4

Guiding Learning from Text: Three-Phase Methods

Reading maketh a full person; conference a ready person, and writing an exact person.

—Paraphrased from Francis Bacon

✦ *Organizing Thoughts* ✦

Interactive teaching methods for modeling and supporting readers can be categorized according to emphasis on guiding one of the three phases of the reading process: prereading, silent reading, or postreading. The *three-phase* methods described in this section are intended to support student efforts to develop strategies for all three phases of the process. The idea is to help all students to develop the flexibility and good habits characteristic of proficient readers.

THINKING STRATEGIES OF PROFICIENT READERS

Nearly fifty years of research have revealed that readers who comprehend at high levels actively build meaning by using a variety of specific reading–thinking strategies. Proficient readers, often referred to in the research literature as *expert readers*, have developed the habit of using the active thinking strategies detailed in Figure 4.1.

The factors that the teacher needs to consider in deciding which method or combination of methods to use to impart active thinking strategies should be determined by such practical considerations as time available for instruction, the nature of student needs, and the difficulty level of the textual material. Some authorities believe that the first three-phase method presented, if used consistently, is all that a content teacher really needs in the way of methodology. Reflect on this as you read, and see if you agree.

THREE-PHASE SCAFFOLDS FOR CONTENT AREA LITERACY

The Directed Reading–Thinking Activity

The Directed Reading–Thinking Activity, or DR-TA (Stauffer, 1969), parallels the master lesson structure for many methods and programs in effective education. The DR-TA is a form of guided problem solving. Several studies have shown that it improves purpose setting (Henderson, 1963), critical thinking (Davidson, 1970; Petre, 1970), and even such collateral concerns as personal-social adjustment (Grobler, 1971).

Figure 4.1
How the experts do it.

Before reading, expert readers activate schema and set a purpose for reading. This involves

- Looking for organizing concepts
- Recalling related information, experiences, attitudes, and feelings
- Deciding how easy or difficult the reading selection is likely to be
- Setting a purpose for reading
- Trying to develop a personal interest

During silent reading, readers continuously monitor comprehension and use fix-up strategies as needed. Doing this involves

- Translating ideas into own words
- Comparing ideas to personal experience
- Trying to identify main ideas—stop and question when this is unclear
- Noting important details
- Rereading whenever necessary for clarification
- Consolidating ideas into meaningful groups
- Noticing unfamiliar vocabulary
- Forming mental pictures
- Evaluating the author's purpose, motive, or authority when appropriate
- Inventing study strategies as needed
- Managing time to sustain concentration

Following reading, expert readers check basic comprehension, build schema, and decide on relevant applications of the new information. Elements of this process include

- Checking basic comprehension by reciting ("What did I learn?")
- Organizing information into chunks of manageable size ("How can I remember it?")
- Deciding what is important ("How much should I understand this?")
- Trying to clarify ambiguous ideas ("Did I really understand this?")
- Evaluating new information in terms of previous knowledge and experience ("Does this make sense?")
- Developing study strategies according to class demands or personal purposes ("What should I do to remember this?")
- Reviewing material periodically ("How much do I remember now?")

The DR-TA is a framework for instruction that parallels the active, study reading process. Its artful construction is most evident in the balance it provides in its first and final steps. In the first step, the teacher guides students in calling up prior knowledge of, and experiences with, the topic to be read; in the last step, students are encouraged to relate the new information to their own lives and other school learnings. The procedural outline presented is based on a version developed for content area use (Shepherd, 1978).

Steps in the Directed Reading–Thinking Activity

1. Preparation for Reading
   a. Investigate and expand the background of student experience.
   b. Preview the reading material.
   c. Introduce the vocabulary pertinent to the fundamental concepts.
   d. Evolve purposes for reading.
2. Reading the Material Silently
   a. Note students' ability to adjust their reading to the purposes for reading and to the difficulty of the material.
   b. Observe students to note specific areas of need.
3. Developing Comprehension
   a. Discuss answers to purpose questions.
   b. Clarify and guide further development of the concepts and vocabulary; introduce new vocabulary if needed.
   c. Assist students in noting organization of information and in recalling pertinent facts.
   d. Determine the need for further information from the text and/or other source books.
   e. Redefine purposes; set new purposes for reading.
4. Rereading (Silent and/or Oral, in Part or in Entirety)
   a. Clarify the essential pertinent information and concepts.
   b. Give specific skills training in comprehension as indicated by student needs.
5. Following up the Information
   a. Set up problems requiring further information.
   b. Choose supplementary reading related to the topic to develop and extend interests, attitudes, and appreciations.
   c. Extend further understanding, and clarify additional concepts as necessary.
   d. Analyze the information, and help students relate it to their own lives.

Notes on the Directed Reading–Thinking Activity

Notice that the wording of the DR-TA does not state *how* each of its steps should be done (for example, the skills step in 4b) or if each substep *needs* to be done. It is not so much a method as an instructional frame-work, within which various methods might be used. Although the DR-TA parallels what expert readers do, it was developed before the realization that specific reading–thinking strategies can and should be taught through modeling and interactive teaching. You will see, later, that while other methods may follow the basic framework of the DR-TA, they tend to be considerably more specific about how to model and encourage use of reading–thinking strategies.

Three-Phase Graphic Organizer

A graphic organizer is a two-dimensional picture of the logical organiza-tion of textual material. In one standard format, called a *structured overview*, the main topic is placed in a box in the center, subtopics are arranged in boxes around it, and details related to each subtopic are noted on lines extending from the appropriate boxes. A well-planned graphic organizer can form the basis for an interactive prereading dis-cussion, an effective guide for silent reading, and for individual or small-group postreading reflection.

The essential element of the three-phase graphic organizer method described next is that, in preparation for teaching the lesson, the teacher analyzes the logical organization of the reading selection, selects an appropriate graphic format, and completes the graphic organizer to be used. With this preparation, the prereading step can be done crisply and interestingly. Recent research, however, indicates that graphic organizers have little influence on reading comprehension if they are simply given to students before or after reading. Their effectiveness lies in students' par-ticipation in creating them. For this reason, as you will read in step 2, fol-lowing, the teacher uses the preprepared graphic merely as a reference for guiding a brainstorming session on students' background knowledge about the topic.

Steps in the Three-Phase Graphic Organizer

1.   Teacher Preparation.   Analyze the reading selection to deter-mine a graphic organizer format that matches its organization. Prepare a graphic organizer that includes all important information in the selection.

2.   Before Reading.   Guide schema activation. *Without showing the prepared graphic to the class*, announce the topic, and ask students what they think they will read about in the selection. As students make sugges-tions, begin a rough construction of the graphic organizer on the board or overhead, while students copy it on their papers. Typically, the first suggestions made will be details, rather than major subtopics. For example, in a selection about spiders, one of the students' first suggestions would likely be that "they have eight legs," rather than the subtopic, "body parts." For some selections, students will be able to generate the needed subtopics or anchor information; for other selections, the teacher will need to supply some if not most of these. During this interaction, the teacher should be open to modifying the planned structure of the graphic organizer if students make reasonable alternative suggestions. For maximum support, the teacher may show students where to draw blank lines for information to find in their reading. By the end of the prereading session, students will have an incomplete graphic organizer that they have helped to develop (see Figure 4.2).

3.   During Reading.   Students read silently to complete the graphic organizer. While they read silently, students add information to their graphic organizers as they find it in the selection.

4.   After Reading.   Check comprehension and retranslate. (a) Once students have read, the teacher guides a discussion based on students' additions to the prereading graphic organizer. (b) (This step is optional.) The completed graphic organizer is divided into sections. Students are divided into small groups, four to five students to a group, and each group works together on one portion of the organizer to retranslate it from pictorial form into a connected paragraph (see Figure 4.2, part C) or to tackle some deeper level of understanding and research on the topic presented.

Notes on Graphic Organizers

Graphic organizers have been found to be especially useful in helping readers deal with what has been called *inconsiderate text*, that is, textual material that is too difficult because of poor writing and/or faulty assumptions about the reader's level of familiarity with the topic (Alvermann & Boothby, 1983). They do this by visually highlighting important ideas and playing down irrelevant and potentially distracting points.

The next method uses graphic organizers in another way. It is a good method to use after students have become familiar with the teacher-guided method described earlier.

PLAN: For Study Reading

PLAN—or predict, locate, add, note—is a four-step thinking method and a strategy that students can be taught to use before, during, and after reading (Caverly, Mandeville, & Nicholson, 1995). Much of PLAN's value is represented by this anecdote. A fifth grader three weeks into use of PLAN is reported to have said, "No, Mrs. Hirsh, you can't teach us. We teach ourselves; you just help" (Caverly et al., 1995, p. 198).

A. Incomplete Graphic Organizer Created during Prereading

Branches of the U.S. Government

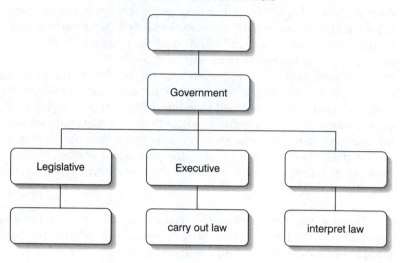

B. Complete Graphic Organizer

Branches of the U.S. Government

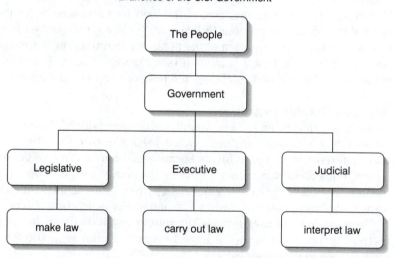

C. Retranslated Graphic Organizer

No U.S. government branch stands above the power of the people. Each of the three governmental branches has a primary legal function. The legislative branch makes laws, the executive branch carries them out, and the judicial branch interprets them.

Figure 4.2

Examples of an incomplete, complete, and retranslated graphic organizer.

Steps in PLAN

1.   Predict.   Readers begin by creating a *probable map*, or incomplete graphic organizer, of the content of the reading selection, using the title as the main topic, and using subtitles, highlighted words, and other clues to arrange additional categories on the map. See Figure 4.3 for an example of a sixth-grade student's prediction map for a social studies chapter.

2.   Locate.   Readers then place a check mark beside familiar information and question marks beside unfamiliar concepts and ideas. This enables readers to determine the degree of difficulty of the reading selection. When students become familiar with the PLAN format, they often complete the locate step while they are constructing the tentative graphic organizer in the predict step. See Figure 4.4 for a college student's locate step for a chapter from a U.S. history textbook.

3.   Add.   While reading, students add words and short phrases to the map to explain items labeled with question marks and to clarify and extend existing knowledge labeled with check marks. This step encourages the habit of metacognitive monitoring while reading. If readers cannot come up with a way to represent the information on their map, they probably have not understood it and need to use some form of fix-up strategy to clarify their understanding. The creators of this method found this step to be essential to successful application of the next step. See Figure 4.5 for an example.

4.   Note.   Finally, readers take notes of what they have learned and decide how to use it to fulfill their original purpose for reading. They may need to reconstruct their map if their predicted pattern does not fit their new understanding of the content and organization of the material. Other note activities include reproducing the map from memory if the task is to prepare for a multiple-choice or true/false quiz; retranslate the map into paragraph form if the information will be tested in essay form; or write a cognitive and affective response if the task is to evaluate and react to the text content. See Figure 4.6 for an example.

Notes on PLAN

PLAN has proven to be very effective in empirical tests and field trials at the college, high school, and middle school level (Caverly, Burrell, & McFarland, 1992; Mandeville & Caverly, 1993; Mandeville & Van Allen, 1993). The creators of PLAN suggest that once students have learned to use it, they should be encouraged to adapt it to the text and the assigned task. Repeated experiences with *mechanically* activating schema by drawing a predicted map and *mechanically* assessing prior knowledge and monitoring comprehension by marking and adding to the map even-

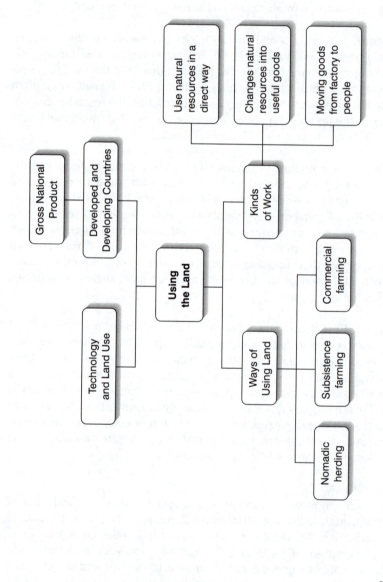

Figure 4.3
A sixth-grade student's prediction map for a social studies chapter.

The boxes in the map contain the following text:

- Gross National Product
- Developed and Developing Countries
- Technology and Land Use
- **Using the Land**
- Kinds of Work
  - Use natural resources in a direct way
  - Changes natural resources into useful goods
  - Moving goods from factory to people
- Ways of Using Land
  - Nomadic herding
  - Subsistence farming
  - Commercial farming

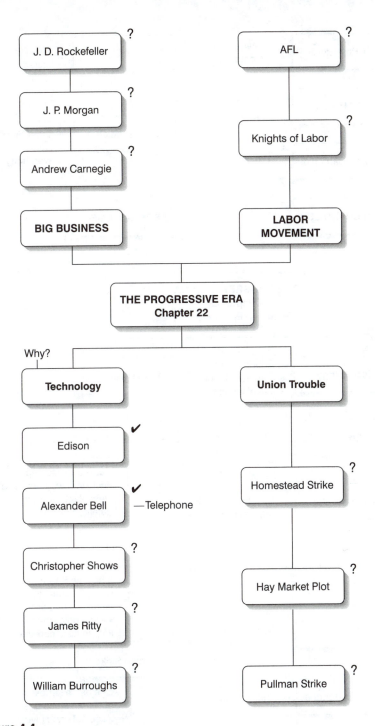

Figure 4.4

A college student's locate step for a U.S. history book chapter.

Note. This map is based on a chapter in Boyer et al., 1993. From "PLAN: A Study-Reading Strategy for Informational Text" by D. C. Caverly, T. F. Mandeville, and S. A. Nicholson, 1995, *Journal of Adolescent and Adult Literacy, 39*(3), p. 192. Reprinted with permission of David C. Caverly and the International Reading Association. All rights reserved.

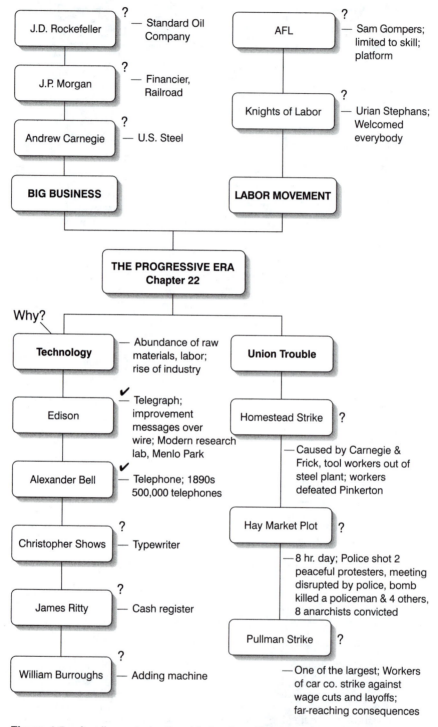

Figure 4.5 A college student's add step for a U.S. history book chapter map.

Note. This map is based on a chapter in Boyer et al., 1993. From "PLAN: A Study-Reading Strategy for Informational Text" by D. C. Caverly, T. F. Mandeville, and S. A. Nicholson, 1995, *Journal of Adolescent and Adult Literacy, 39*(3), p. 193. Reprinted with permission of David C. Caverly and the International Reading Association. All rights reserved.

Figure 4.6
A summary for the note step from a U.S. history book chapter.

> The Progressive Era was full of excitement. With that excitement came pain and suffering. As big business grew with giants like Carnegie, Rockefeller, and Morgan, so did the mistreatment of workers. Laborers were overworked, underpaid, and sometimes put into danger. Children were common victims. Labor unions were established in hopes of protecting the workers. Unfortunately, unions such as the AFL and the Knights of Labor were put into conflict situations. Three main conflicts were the Homestead Strike, Hay Market Riot, and the Pullman Strike.
>
> The Homestead Strike was the attempt by Andrew Carnegie and Clay Frick to keep laborers from fighting for an eight-hour workday at the Homestead Steel Plant. They hired Pinkerton detectives to keep workers away. Fortunately, the workers spotted the detectives during the strike outside and defeated the detectives. The fight between the detectives and workers forced the governor to bring in the militia to keep peace at the plant. The Hay Market Riot was one of the bloodiest conflicts. Laborers were striking to keep an eight-hour workday with fair pay at Hay Market Square in Chicago. Police tried to get rid of the laborers and came in direct conflict with them. The police shot in the crowd, killing innocent people. The laborers then wanted a rally in response to the attack. The rally was peaceful, but the police still wanted them to disperse. A bomb was then thrown, killing one policeman and four bystanders. Eight anarchists were blamed for the bombing and convicted with no real evidence. The Pullman Strike was one of the most consequential strikes in the era. Many companies joined the strike on behalf of the Pullman Car Company workers. This strike marked the reasons for many future consequences.

Note. This summary is based on a chapter from Boyer et al., 1993. From "PLAN: A Study-Reading Strategy for Informational Text" by D. C. Caverly, T. F. Mandeville, and S. A. Nicholson, 1995, *Journal of Adolescent and Adult Literacy, 39*(3), p. 194. Reprinted with permission of David C. Caverly and the International Reading Association. All rights reserved.

tually establish these thinking strategies as mental habits that students will apply even without the physical act of drawing the map.

The Guided Reading Procedure

The Guided Reading Procedure (GRP) (Manzo, 1975) reflects a way to read in the disciplines that is quite traditional. The simple purpose of a GRP lesson is to bring students to a firm conviction that their *personal determination* and willingness to *self-monitor and self-correct* are critical to what they can expect to comprehend and learn from time spent reading.

The GRP is highly scaffolded. Students retrace and restructure the material read in several ways, thus providing ample support for reading, organizing, and reviewing. It also creates a teachable moment for improving study and test-taking strategies (see the sample dialogue in Figure 4.7). For these reasons, this three-phase method can be especially uplifting to students with fading hopes of keeping up in their subjects.

Steps in the Guided Reading Procedure

1.   Teacher Preparation.   Identify a selection to be read, or listened to, of moderate-to-high difficulty and not exceeding 2,000 words for a senior high class, 900 words for a junior high class, and 600 words for an intermediate class. Prepare a ten- to twenty-item test on the material to be given at the end of the class period. As the lesson proceeds, make sure that the test items are given fair coverage.

2.   Student Preparation.   Two purposes for reading are established. One is content specific and arrived at with the class. The second is more of a mindset: Direct the group to "read to remember all you can, and after you have read, I will record what you remember on the chalkboard just as you state it to me."

3.   Reading and Recalling.   After approximately fifteen minutes of reading, begin asking for free recalls. Record all information on the chalkboard until students have expressed everything they can remember. Difficulties in remembering and differences in what students do remember will form implicit questions that impel the next step.

4.   Self-Monitoring/Self-Correcting.   Instruct students to review the material read and self-correct inconsistencies that arose in their attempts to recollect. Students may also wish to add information previously overlooked. Note such changes and/or additions on the chalkboard.

5.   Restructuring.   Encourage students to organize their recollection into outline form to be recorded in their notebooks. The outline can be as simple or elaborate as age and grade level permit. You may ask non-specific questions at this time, such as "What was discussed first?" "What was brought up next?" "What seems to be the main idea?" Avoid overly specific and leading questions.

6.   Teacher Monitoring and Correcting.   If students appear to have overlooked any critical ideas or inappropriately equated them with other ideas, raise guiding questions about these points, such as "What do you suppose is the most important of these five points made by the author?" "How does this information relate to what we studied last week?" Or, more

Figure 4.7
Sample dialogue, Guided Reading Procedure.

1. **Selection and Class**
   Social studies material. Title: *The Island of Japan,* six hundred words, sixth reader level of difficulty. Used with a seventh-grade class of largely average readers.

2. **Purposes for Reading (from the teacher this time)**
   A. "Read to determine why Japan leaned toward isolation."
   B. "Try to remember all that you can about this selection. I will record what you recall on the chalkboard as you state it."

3. **Following Fifteen Minutes of Silent Reading (Sample Dialogue)**
   Teacher: What do you recall of what you have read?
   Student: They got isolated by a volcano.
   Student: Japan is as big as Missouri.
   Student: They are surrounded by water.
   Student: They have a lot of typhoons.
   Student: Japan doesn't have any natural resources.
   (STOP)

4. **Self-Monitoring/Self-Correction (Sample Dialogue)**
   Teacher: Reread the selection now, and note any corrections for the board or additions.
   Student: Many volcanoes, not one, formed Japan.
   Student: It is the size of Montana, not Missouri.
   Student: There are four main islands, but I can't remember their names.
   Student: One (island) is Honshu.
   Student: Japan has about 1,500 earthquakes per year.
   (STOP)

5. **Restructuring**
   Teacher: Let's organize our information into an outline. What is a good title?
   Student: The book says *The Island of Japan.*
   Teacher: What comes next?
   Student: It was formed from many volcanoes.
   Student: It is made up of four big islands and many small ones.

Figure 4.7, *continued*

(Chalkboard)

The Island of Japan

I.   Formed from volcanoes

     A.   Four major islands

          1.   Honshu

          2.   ?

          3.   ?

          4.   ?

---

6. **Teacher-Guided Correcting and Completing**

    Teacher: Look back in your book. Reread quickly for the information that we are still missing, and let's fill it in.

    (TASK Completed)

7. **Evaluation**

    Teacher: Close your (text) books now, put away your notebooks, and answer the questions I am now putting on the board on the paper being provided.

    Sample test items:

    1.   In what ocean can Japan be found?

    2.   How many major islands are there in Japan?

    3.   What is Japan's greatest resource?

    4.   How did being an island cause Japan to be in isolation(?) or did it?

    (STOP)

8. **Introspection**

    Teacher: What did you learn about how to read better or smarter?

    Student: There is at least one key idea in each paragraph. Don't go ahead until you get it out.

    Student: I remembered a lot more than the first time we did this, just by concentrating.

    Student: Rereading and focusing really helps. I got 100% this time. I had only 40% the first time.

    (STOP)

9. **Study Step (Optional)**

    Teacher: Today we're going to see how we are progressing in developing effective study habits. Take out your notes on *The Island of Japan,* and take the next fifteen minutes to study them. Then I will put some questions on the board on that topic, and let's see how well you do. After our little quiz, we'll discuss how you studied and how to study smarter.

specifically, "Do you see any ideas here that could be connected to the article we read last week, 'Man and the Moon'?"

7. Evaluation. Give the test prepared in Step 1. A score of 70% to 80% should be required to pass the test.

8. Introspection. Discuss any insights students may have reached about their own learning processes as a result of the GRP experience. The chief point to be made is that accuracy in comprehension and recall can be improved to a good degree by an act of will.

9. Optional Study Step. Several days later, give a second test on the same material. Allow students about fifteen minutes before the test to review material from their notes.

Notes on the Guided Reading Procedure
In a typical GRP lesson, students may say little or nothing on the first invitation to recall and recite what they have read. As teachers, we tend to have great difficulty with silence. If you can force yourself to wait silently for a few (seemingly interminable) seconds, the flow of language and thought will begin. The first few—and probably labored—student responses will lead to hook-ups, self-corrections, reflections, and other associations. These will generate still more recollections and responses. Invariably, this results in a spiraling effect that often draws in even the most reticent students. See the sample dialogue in Figure 4.7 for examples of this.

The GRP has been studied by several researchers and has collected strong empirical validation (Ankney & McClurg, 1981; Bean & Pardi, 1979). Its effectiveness is most clearly established at the intermediate and junior high levels with science and social studies material. It also has achieved strong endorsements as a listening activity (Cunningham, Moore, Cunningham, & Moore, 1983) and as a suitable method for adolescents with learning disabilities (Alley & Deshler, 1980; Maring & Furman, 1985).

The final method in this chapter also could be considered a child of the DR-TA. However, it is more specific about the "how-to's." Most teachers find that it is an easy way to engage students in an interactive and productive lesson.

K-W-L Plus

The K-W-L Plus strategy (Carr & Ogle, 1987) follows the general framework of the DR-TA but also stresses summarizing and graphic mapping. The method moves from what students *know* (K) to what students *want to know* (W) to what *students have learned* (L) to the *plus*, which requires construction of a graphic organizer.

Steps in K-W-L Plus

1. Know. The teacher leads a brainstorming session on what students already know about the topic. As ideas are given, students write them in the "Know" column of their individual worksheets. (See Figure 4.8 for an example of a ninth-grade student's worksheet.)

2. Want to Know. The teacher then moves the discussion toward aspects of the topic that students do not know. Students are helped to state these as questions and write them in the "Want to Know" column of their worksheets.

3. Learned. (a) During reading, students pause to write the answers to the "Want to Know" questions in the "Learned" column of their worksheets. New questions, and answers, can be added as they read and find information they did not anticipate. (b) The teacher leads a discussion of what was learned in answers to the original questions and what additional information was learned.

4. Plus. The teacher leads students in categorizing the information that was learned and in creating a graphic organizer to represent this. (See Figure 4.8 for an example of the plus-step graphic organizer created in this way.)

Notes on K-W-L Plus

An earlier version of K-W-L that did not contain the *plus*, or mapping step, did not fare well in research comparisons. The *plus* version, however, has been uniformly supported. Teachers especially like this method because demonstration lessons are active and have clear and identifiable steps.

✦ *Looking Back and Looking Ahead* ✦

This chapter offered five possible means by which to provide three-phase, total support to students in reading to learn. Ideally, you will select and build proficiency in the one or two methods that best match your subject area and teaching style. The next chapter will offer you about an equal number of means and methods from which to select for frontloading, or prereading, instructional support. The chapter also contains some interesting buttressing information on questioning, curiosity, and modeling.

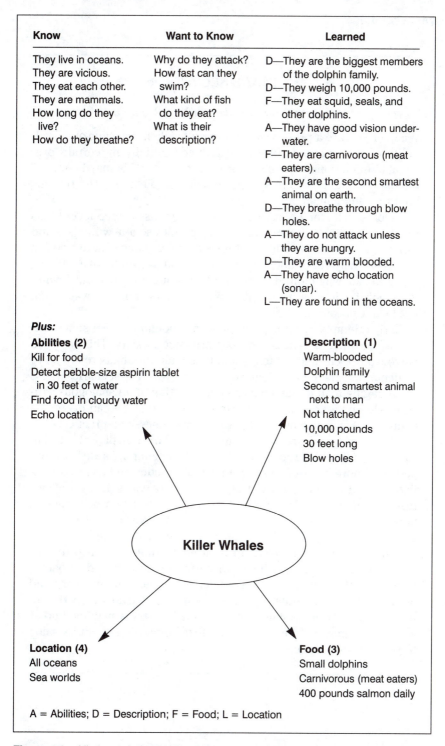

Know	Want to Know	Learned
They live in oceans.	Why do they attack?	D—They are the biggest members of the dolphin family.
They are vicious.	How fast can they swim?	D—They weigh 10,000 pounds.
They eat each other.	What kind of fish do they eat?	F—They eat squid, seals, and other dolphins.
They are mammals.	What is their description?	A—They have good vision under-water.
How long do they live?		F—They are carnivorous (meat eaters).
How do they breathe?		A—They are the second smartest animal on earth.
		D—They breathe through blow holes.
		A—They do not attack unless they are hungry.
		D—They are warm blooded.
		A—They have echo location (sonar).
		L—They are found in the oceans.

Plus:

Abilities (2)
Kill for food
Detect pebble-size aspirin tablet in 30 feet of water
Find food in cloudy water
Echo location

Description (1)
Warm-blooded
Dolphin family
Second smartest animal next to man
Not hatched
10,000 pounds
30 feet long
Blow holes

Killer Whales

Location (4)
All oceans
Sea worlds

Food (3)
Small dolphins
Carnivorous (meat eaters)
400 pounds salmon daily

A = Abilities; D = Description; F = Food; L = Location

Figure 4.8 Ninth grader's K-W-L worksheet and graphic organizer for killer whales.
Note. From "K-W-L Plus: A Strategy for Comprehension and Summarization," by E. Carr and D. Ogle, April 1987, *Journal of Reading, 30*(7), pp. 628–629. Reprinted with permission of Eileen Carr and the International Reading Association. All rights reserved.

✦ ✦   TRADE SECRET   ✦ ✦

On Acquiring and Using New Methods

Whether you are a preservice or veteran teacher, the value and credibility of new methods often are reduced initially by certain predictable inhibitions affecting your performance. This may be one of the darkest and best-kept secrets of teacher education. The reasons are basic and human.

As preservice or in-service teachers, our dissonance level tends to rise to a point of distraction when we first use a new method and especially so when we will be observed or evaluated. There also are things we may think about that can be counterproductive: "If this really works, why didn't I think of it?" "I thought of this, but I won't get credit for it even if I use it," "What if this is a better way to go, but I can't make it work?"

Early attempts to do anything new are bound to raise some self-doubt, ego defensiveness, and performance anxiety. This tends to narrow our focus and flexibility and thus limit our ability to attend to students and their individual needs. However, this scenario is less discouraging than it may appear. Consideration of an analogous situation—learning how to drive a car—suggests that we can overcome many of these problems through simple awareness and practice.

When we first learn how to drive, we dare not play the radio, carry on a conversation, or take in the scenery. As our driving becomes more habitual, both from actual practice and from visualizing, we can do all of these things and more. So it is with a new teaching method: It is important to continue to use a new method until dissonance is reduced, comfort is increased, and we once again can become sensitive and aware of student needs. A new methodology generally needs to be used no more than two to four times for the benefits to begin to outweigh the initial drawbacks. Unfortunately, there is a strong tendency to abandon new ideas and methods before completing even a single full trial. Keep this in mind, and make a commitment to yourself to try a new method at least three times before you reach a firm conclusion about its value to you and your students.

CHAPTER 5

Prereading Methods for Schema Activation and Instructional Modeling

People see only what they are prepared to see.

—Ralph Waldo Emerson

✦ *Organizing Thoughts* ✦

This chapter explains the importance of prereading and the goals of prereading instruction. It focuses on the role of teacher questioning and unlocking students' natural curiosity. It then discusses the process of *instructional modeling*, which is the fundamental principle employed in several prereading methods. Keep in mind that methods designated as *prereading* tend to include attention to silent reading and postreading as well; they merely are structured to teach and impart the so-called "frontloading" strategies.

THE IMPORTANCE OF PREREADING

Effective comprehension depends on readiness, or having and recalling relevant knowledge and experiences, and on establishing an appropriate purpose for which to read. In a survey of teaching practices (Gee & Rakow, 1987), professors specializing in content area literacy ranked prereading methods as the most vital techniques content teachers could use to help students learn from text. Through well-designed prereading instruction, unfamiliar terminology and allusions can be addressed and rectified, and students can be alerted to key concepts, facts, issues, and organizing questions that can serve as purposes for which to read.

The prereading, or readiness, phase of reading instruction helps students to establish an appropriate orientation to the reading task. This orientation has three dimensions, which are described in some detail in Figure 5.1.

Each of the components of prereading readiness can be addressed in step-by-step fashion before reading, as is done in conventional three-phase approaches such as the Directed Reading–Thinking Activity. However, this can be time-consuming and even tedious. The methods in this chapter each address some combination of the elements listed earlier but in a more focused, brisk, and interactive manner. They are designed for teachers to use selectively, depending on the particular needs of their students and the challenges presented by the material to be read. Most of these methods also contain the elements necessary for the latter phases of reading. Some, as discussed later, promote gains in comprehension that equal and even exceed some of the more time-consuming three-phase methods.

Figure 5.1
Dimensions of prereading readiness.

Attitude Orientation: For Reader Engagement

1.   Raise attention and reduce distractions.

2.   Pique interest in the topic and the task.

3.   Motivate for sustained effort.

Background Orientation: For Schema Activation

1.   Activate appropriate schema: relevant background knowledge and experiences.

2.   Correct possible misunderstandings.

3.   Provide necessary new ideas and facts.

4.   Establish a sense of the organization and sequence of the reading selection.

Reading Strategies Orientation: For Active Meaning Making

1.   Establish a purpose for reading.

2.   Remove word-recognition obstacles.

3.   Preteach key concept terms.

4.   Alert and alleviate other vocabulary, graphic, and/or syntactic hurdles.

5.   Lay the foundation for development of active reading strategies: for example, inquiry, prediction, making connections to prior knowledge and experience, and evaluative thinking.

GOALS OF PREREADING INSTRUCTION: READER ENGAGEMENT, SCHEMA ACTIVATION, AND ACTIVE MEANING MAKING

Reader Engagement

Successful reading begins with genuine attention to the task: Readers must be actively engaged in the process (Rosenshine, 1984). Thus, one goal of prereading instruction is to help students develop the attitudes and interests that build the habit of active engagement as an initial component of the study reading process.

Schema Activation

In Chapter 2 we defined *schema* as the sum of one's prior knowledge, experience, sensorimotor learnings, and inclinations. In this section, we focus on its functional value in focusing and organizing reading.

Again, the primary role of schema is to provide the grid for receiving and organizing information. However, simply having a broad background of information and experience about a topic may not ensure effective comprehension. To read with comprehension, readers must consciously recall the schema structures that are relevant to the reading selection, so that they can actively form connections between this personalized organization of facts, perspectives, and experiences, and the new information from the text. Thus, how readers *use* what they know can be as important as how *much* they know.

The final goal of prereading instruction is to demonstrate and build strategies for constructing meaning from print. Most such strategies, beginning with formulating appropriate purposes for reading, are grounded in questioning.

Active Meaning Making

Why Students Don't Ask More Questions

Research and intuition both suggest that the key to getting students to question is not as much a matter of teaching them to inquire as it is a process of enabling them to overcome several subtle social-psychological *inhibitions* to this otherwise natural inclination. Unfortunately, these inhibitions often are created or increased by teachers' actions or responses to questions. This realization has led to increased attention to what teachers should avoid doing, or how not to use and respond to questions. See Figure 5.2 for a brief account of these.

Clearly, question posing and *answering* by teachers can do much to overcome several inhibitions to student curiosity and questioning. Of further aid in teaching with questions is more knowledge about the types of questions that can be posed and the cognitive demands that each involves.

The most widely used system for characterizing questions is based loosely on a hierarchy of difficulty called the *Taxonomy of Educational Objectives: The Cognitive Domain* (Bloom, 1956). There are eight basic question types derived from this and several other authoritative sources (Aschner et al., 1962; Barrett, 1967; Manzo & Manzo, 1990a, 1990b; Sanders, 1969). See Figure 5.3 for a description of each question type.

The most effective way to help students develop the complex cognitive and affective elements of effective questioning is *not* simply to teach them about the various types of questions. Questioning is a complex cognitive and affective function that is best addressed by providing opportunities for students to interact with models of effective questioning in real and simulated reading–thinking situations. Ideally, this should be done in a hands-on, apprenticeship setting that is suitably matched to the complexity of this task.

Figure 5.2
How *not* to use and respond to questions.

The Squelch.
Teachers understandably feel obliged to squelch passive–aggressive questions that students raise when they are fearful or agitated. Before a test, for example, teachers often observe this flurry of questions: "Do we have to skip a line after every answer?" "Do you want last names first?" "Can we use notebook paper?" "Can we use pencils?" In response to such annoyances, teachers sometimes get *too* skilled at squelching student questions. This problem is not easily overcome, but it is useful to remember the advice of the Roman orator Publius Syrus: "Every question does not deserve an answer."

The Sting.
As teachers, we ourselves occasionally use questions in ill-advised, ambiguous, and even sarcastic ways. When a student persists in talking while we are trying to explain a point to the class, we might resort to saying something like, "Well, maybe you can explain this to the rest of the class better than I, since you don't seem to value my explanation." After a simple stare, and/or moving closer to offenders to quiet them down, you might try a more direct but less sarcastic statement that corrects and explains, "When you talk during class you distract yourself, me, and the class. Please try to save your enthusiasm for later."

The Void.
"Any questions?" is a popular teacher tool for inviting clarifying inquiries. When students are asked this question in this form, however, they feel, "Oh, if only I knew what I don't know!" A better approach is to say something that will guide questioning into an area where there is often confusion in the topic at hand: "Can someone ask a good question to clarify when we need to change signs in an equation?" then "What other questions could be asked about signs?" finally, "Any other questions about anything discussed today?"

Punishing Questions with a Question.
Even when students "know what they don't know," they often are (1) at a loss for the words to frame and articulate that vague thought into a question, (2) unsure of how to win the teacher's empathy with the question, and (3) wondering what needs to be done to get a response they can understand. On these points, several students have said things amounting to "I hate when the teacher answers my question with another question or says things to me that are even more confusing than my original question." Students often need assistance in how to better direct their initial questions and/or ask necessary follow-up questions.

Figure 5.3
Question types.

1. **Recognition questions**.
   Recognition questions require identifying the answers from available choices (e.g., multiple-choice questions)

2. **Recall questions.** Recall questions require remembering the answers with little prompting and no clues. ("When was the Battle of Hastings?")

3. **Translation questions.** Translation questions entail transferring something from one symbolic form to another. ("Can you describe this picture?" "Can you tell in your own words what the author said in this paragraph?" "Can you say what you just heard in your own words?")

4. **Inference questions.** Inference questions have the reader combine available textual information to reach an answer that is compellingly logical but not explicitly stated in the text. ("What is the relationship between Jack and Joseph in this story?")

5. **Conjecture questions.** Conjecture questions involve an inferential leap, because all the information is not yet, or may never be, available. ("As we read ahead, do you suppose that Jack's life will rise above his father's?")

6. **Explanation questions.** Explanation questions require verification of a previous point. They may involve reference to the text and/or to other sources. ("Why do you think Jack's life will rise above his father's?")

7. **Application questions.** Application questions require critical and constructive thinking and problem solving. ("In similar circumstances, how might a person like Jack avoid hurting his father?")

8. **Evaluation questions.** Evaluation questions are a specialized type of application question that requires critical thinking, aesthetic sense, and personal judgment. ("How do you feel about the story? The characters? The style of writing? The moral to be drawn?")

MODELING: A FORM OF APPRENTICESHIP TRAINING

Modeling is a form of teaching in which the instructor demonstrates a desired outcome and encourages the learner to internalize and imitate it. It is the traditional means of apprenticeship training in trades and crafts, where the objective is to teach complex motor skills. It is only fairly recently that learning psychologists and educators have begun to recognize and explore the power of this form of teaching when applied to cognitive, rather than motor, learning.

The human inclination to observe and imitate one another is the most familiar and frequently used mode of human learning outside of school. A prime example of its use is in natural language acquisition. Only a very small percentage of the words and language forms we know did we acquire as a result of direct instruction. Mothers may teach their children to say some important words like *mommy, hot, chair*, and so on, but children pick up an enormous number of words on their own. Parents or teachers may remind children to say "he ran" instead of "he runned," but the majority of what children learn about word order and language structures is learned incidentally. The way we speak, the words we use, and the way we feel when using these words are the direct result of the speech patterns and concerns of the models to whom we were exposed and with whom we have interacted. From the models we select to emulate, we learn motives and attitudes as well as words and actions. Thus, *inquiring minds beget inquiring minds.*

In any situation, however, various models are available from which to choose. Selection of the model to be emulated is based on subjective assessments of the degree to which those about us appear to have mastery over a given environment or situation. In school settings, students do not automatically choose the teacher or the good student as a model. There is an ongoing competition with other influential peers and adults in the home and community. Instructional strategies that employ modeling must include devices for winning students' attention to the desired models and behaviors.

Modeling of mental operations has its rational basis in social and imitation learning theory (Bandura & Walters, 1963; Miller & Dollard, 1941). Simply put, the idea is that we tend to copy and internalize a larger array of a model's character and behaviors than merely those traits that are essential to the task at hand. By taking advantage of this additional, incidental learning dimension, it becomes possible to teach very complex and subtle behaviors along with key target behaviors, and in a much shorter period. Further, the mental image of the model serves as a mental template, or set of guidelines, that the novice can use to monitor and evaluate subsequent attempts to apply and refine the new behavior in different situations. In short, internalization of the target strategy is most likely to occur only after youngsters have used a cognitive operation in situations where adults and other peer experts have modeled and given them some form of feedback on their performance (Camperell, 1982; Vygotsky, 1978).

Conditions for Effective Modeling

The efficiency of modeling as a basis for teaching and learning can be increased under certain conditions. Here are six conditions that are particularly relevant to the content area classroom:

1. When the student's attention somehow is drawn to a desired model
2. When the impression can be made that the model is doing something masterful and desirable
3. When there is a reduced social risk entailed in imitating a desired behavior
4. When the new behavior appears doable, as when students observe someone from their peer group engaged in the behavior
5. When students are permitted to interact with the model in an affective (feeling) manner as well as in purely cognitive, or school-like, ways
6. When *reciprocity,* or involved interaction, is encouraged; that is, when students have the opportunity to both influence and be influenced by the model

The last element, *reciprocity,* serves another critical purpose in effective teaching. It is empowering in the sense that it raises student competence while inviting student individuality to emerge. In this way, students learn generalized strategies for effective learning that are *personalized,* rather than continuing merely to *copy* the behavior of the model.

As you study the teaching methods ahead that feature modeling, remember to look for the specific action(s) of the teacher that might attract students' attention to, and provide active engagement with, desired models.

PREREADING METHODS FOR READER ENGAGEMENT, SCHEMA ACTIVATION, AND ACTIVE MEANING MAKING

ReQuest Procedure

The Reciprocal Questioning (ReQuest) procedure (Manzo, 1969b) is designed to permit teachers to model good questioning and question answering, to encourage students to focus on teachers and competent peers as effective models, and to teach students how to set their own purposes for reading.

Steps in the ReQuest Procedure

1. Teacher and students should have copies of the selection to be read before them. The teacher states the basic goal: "Our intent in this lesson is to improve your ability to set a logical purpose for which to read."
2. The teacher guides the students through as many sentences (or, in time, short paragraphs) of the selection as seem necessary to formu-

late a logical purpose to continue reading silently. This is achieved in the following way:

a. Students and teacher silently survey the selection and then read the title and first sentence. Students are first permitted to ask the teacher as many questions as they wish about *the title and first sentence only* (see Figure 5.4). Students are told that they should try to ask the kinds of questions the teacher might ask and in much the way the teacher might ask it.

b. The teacher answers each question as fully as possible without intentionally withholding information, asking questions back, or elaborating unnecessarily.

c. Once students have asked all their questions, the teacher asks as many questions as seem appropriate to focus attention on the purpose for which the selection was written or the key question that it answers.

d. When students encounter a teacher-generated question that they feel they cannot answer, the teacher encourages them to explain why they cannot do so.

First sentence of the selection: "The katydid is any of several large, green, American, long-horned grasshoppers usually having stridulating organs on the forewings of the males that produce a loud, shrill sound!"

Student Questions		**Teacher Answers**
S1	What color are katydids?	Green.
S2	Where are katydids found?	The type described are called American, so I suppose they can be found in America, though perhaps elsewhere as well.
S3	What family are katydids in?	Grasshoppers, though I'm sure they have some scientific name as well (Tettigoniidae!).

Figure 5.4
ReQuest procedure: Sample student questions/teacher answers (seventh-grade level).

e. The pattern used to review the first sentence—silent reading, followed by student questions, followed by teacher questions—is continued through the second and subsequent sentences of the first paragraph(s).

f. Beginning with the second or third sentence, the teacher, mindful of serving as a model of questioning behavior, begins to ask questions that require integration of units from the earlier sentence(s), for example, "Judging from the first two sentences, why do you suppose this selection about the history of architecture has been titled 'The Arches versus the Domes'?" (see Figure 5.5).

g. Throughout the interaction, students are reinforced for imitating the teacher's questioning behavior. Reinforcement can be direct or indirect: a socially approving comment ("That's a good question") or an empathetic and complete answer to the question—a natural, powerful, and often overlooked means of reward.

TQ¹
TQ²
TQ³

Comment

Strij-uh-lay-ting?

Teacher Questions/Comments	**Student Answers**
Q. What is the subject of this sentence?	Q. How do you suppose you should pronounce s-t-r-i-d-u-l-a-t-i-n-g? What does it mean?
Q. What do you suppose is meant by *long-horned*?	
C. It really doesn't explain, so I looked it up. *Long-horned* means long antennae (illustrates on the chalkboard).	C. I had to look that one up, too. It seems to be that it means making a harsh, grating sound.
	S1. Katydids.
	S2. They have long horns?
Q. What do you suppose the remainder of this selection is going to be about?	S1. Strij-uh-lay-ting? Does it mean walking or something like that?
C. Let's read and question each other on the next sentence and see if it helps us to decide what the rest of the selection will be about.	S2. Katydids or things like them?
	S2. Maybe about things they do in nature?
	S1. Maybe it's about stridulating organs?

Figure 5.5
ReQuest procedure: Sample teacher questions/comments and student answers.

3. The ReQuest procedure should continue until students can accomplish the following:

    a. Decode and derive proper meanings for all the words in the initial paragraph(s).

    b. Demonstrate a thorough understanding of the sentences read.

    c. Formulate a reasonable purpose, preferably stated as a question, for silently reading the remainder of the selection. The teacher can help with this process by first urging students to frame thoughts and speculations or hypotheses into questions, for example, "What question do you suppose this article will answer regarding the relationship between arches and domes?" Then the teacher can guide students into reading by saying, "Now please read the remainder of this selection silently, and see if we have identified a good purpose for reading." (Note: On some occasions, more than one legitimate purpose for reading may evolve. Depending on the group's ability level, all may be asked to test both purposes, or the class can be divided such that different groups of students check the correctness of each prediction.)

4. Following silent reading, importantly, the teacher's *first* question should be "Did we identify the best purpose for reading this selection?" The next question should be the actual purpose question that was to guide silent reading (Manzo, 1985).

Done in this way, ReQuest is an effective means of preparing students for a difficult home reading assignment as well as for immediate classroom reading and discussion.

Notes on ReQuest

ReQuest pioneered the use of modeling to teach mental processes. It first was developed for one-on-one teaching. However, it proved equally effective in content classrooms with heterogeneous groups (Manzo, 1973), in programs to promote personal-social adjustment in juvenile delinquents (Kay, Young, & Mottley, 1986), in mainstreaming students with learning disabilities (Alley & Deshler, 1980; Hori, 1977), and with second-language students (McKenzie, Ericson, & Hunter, 1988). It also has become the basis for a larger movement in education called Reciprocal Teaching (Palincsar & Brown, 1984), described presently.

On a more anecdotal level, a sixth-grade student named Clarence taught us a valuable way to bring about effective peer modeling during a ReQuest interaction. See Figure 5.6 for a summary of what Clarence taught us about effective questioning.

See Figure 5.7 for other questions that we learned to ask from ReQuest interactions. The questions are described with respect to the instructional objectives they seem to best serve.

Figure 5.6
Learned from Clarence about questioning.

Clarence was one of several students whom Ula Manzo had invited to participate in a demonstration lesson of the ReQuest procedure. Everyone was a little hesitant about including Clarence, because we never knew quite what to expect from him. He was a very active youngster and liked to be the center of attention. He also was characteristically disorganized and unconcerned about schoolwork.

As we began the ReQuest procedure, Clarence immediately caught on to the idea of students asking questions. In fact, we found ourselves so mesmerized by the demonstration Clarence was providing that we let the lesson go on much longer than it otherwise would have. What captivated us was the nature of the questions Clarence asked and the dramatic effect they seemed to have on the other youngsters. Here is how the lesson unfolded.

The reading selection used for the demonstration was a passage from a sixth-grade social studies text, which began as follows:

Discontent Turns to Revolution
Paris, July 1789: French people everywhere watched the events at Versailles with great interest. To most of them, the members of the Third Estate were heroes. Soon all kinds of wild rumors began to spread. Troops were gathering to murder the people of Paris! Assembly members were going to be killed!

Before beginning the ReQuest procedure, the group had been given some background related to the text, including labels for the three Estates that comprised the Estates General of Paris and the fact that at the time representatives of the Third Estate (peasants, laborers, and professionals) were gathered in Versailles for the purpose of writing a constitution for France.

Once the ReQuest procedure began, Clarence proceeded to ask five to six unusual and model questions about each sentence. The other students noticed the uniqueness of Clarence's questions: Each time he asked a question, they tended to follow with similar questions. On the first sentence, he asked, "What does *watched* mean here?" Other students then asked, "What does *everywhere* mean here?" On the second sentence, Clarence asked, "Did the king think they were heroes?" Other students asked, "Did the clergy think they were heroes?" "Did all the people in the Third Estate think they were heroes?" "Did they think they were heroes?"

From this experience, we all learned that whenever a student asks an interesting question, the teacher can reinforce it simply by responding, "Can anyone ask another question like that one?"

Figure 5.7
Other questions generated by ReQuest users.

Cunning questions designed to get students' attention and engage them in the lesson: "Now that you have carefully read the first sentence and asked me all the questions you care to about it, I have some for you. But first, are you sure that you don't want to reread that sentence or ask any additional questions? OK, turn your books face down. Now what was the fifth word in that first sentence?" or "What is the title of this piece?" and/or "Who is the author?"

Predictable questions intended to calm: Typical *what, why, who, when, where,* and *how* questions will do this. Students generally are ready for these and can feel successful and involved when they are asked them.

Mind-opening questions designed to stir wonder, make connections, and stimulate further questioning: "Turn your books face up and study that first sentence for a moment. Why do you suppose there is a comma after the fourth word in that sentence?" Hearing no answer, "Let's read it orally with the comma after the third word. Now after the fifth word." The answer may never become vivid, but the youngsters who struggled with this question seemed to come to a fresh sense, perhaps for the first time, that there is a profound relationship between punctuation and communication. Awareness and effective use of such print markings are characteristic of expert readers. (To dramatize this point, show sentences under different punctuation conditions: "A woman without her man has no reason for living" can become "A woman: without her, man has no reason for living," or "Call me fool if you wish" can become "Call me, fool, if you wish.")

Next we discuss another approach to teaching that attempts to take full advantage of the byplay between modeling and reciprocity.

Reciprocal Teaching

Reciprocal Teaching (Palincsar & Brown, 1984) is an attempt to amplify and elaborate on the fundamental elements of the ReQuest procedure into a more broadly based educational approach. It begins with a class discussion of why we sometimes experience difficulties in reading text. The processes of *questioning, summarizing, clarifying,* and *predicting* are introduced as helpful strategies for attending, understanding, and remembering.

The next phase in Reciprocal Teaching is direct instruction in each of the four processes. This is done in isolation but through teacher modeling and examples based on a meaningful text. When students are comfortable with the four processes of questioning, summarizing, predicting,

Introspective questions, which tend to induce metacognitive or intro-spective-type thinking. "Did we raise a good question (purpose) to guide our reading of this selection?" "What have you learned about proper reading from this lesson?" "What meaning did you give to the word _____?"

Common-knowledge questions, which tap into and develop cultural literacy by cultivating awareness of the information that surrounds us: "What kinds of buildings typically are of Gothic design in American cities?" This was followed by these prompts: "Picture in your mind some older courthouses and state buildings you have seen. Can you describe some of their features?"

Elaborative knowledge questions designed to stimulate a taste for additional potentially relevant information: "Do you know how architectural arches are supported? . . . Well, I just happen to have read that. . . . "

Provocative questions for which neither the teacher nor the selection has a right answer but nonetheless are worth discussing: "Why do you suppose certain forms of architecture have developed and flourished in some countries rather than in others?"

Personalized questions of the evaluative types that only the student can answer: "Do you think you would enjoy being an architect?" or "What style of architecture do you suppose you would lean toward if you were an architect?"

and clarifying, they and the teacher begin to take turns assuming the role of teacher. The one playing the role of teacher is responsible for leading the dialogue examining the reading selection. Figure 5.8 presents an example of the questioning, summarizing, and predicting aspects of Reciprocal Teaching. This script is taken from an actual classroom dialogue with a group of children whom Palincsar and Brown (1986) trained in this strategy.

In this content area version of Reciprocal Teaching, students are grouped by twos in peer dyads and are instructed to ask each other questions about the material to be read. The content area variation has the following steps:

Reciprocal Teaching for Content Area Reading

1. Students convert subheadings in text into two written predictions of what they think they will read about.
2. The class discusses these.

Figure 5.8
Illustration of Reciprocal Teaching.

Student 1 (in role of teacher): My question is, What does the aquanaut need when he goes under water?

Student 2: A watch.

Student 3: Flippers.

Student 4: A belt.

Student 1: Those are all good answers.

Teacher: Nice job! I have a question, too. Why does the aquanaut wear a belt? What is so special about it?

Student 3: It's a heavy belt and keeps him from floating up to the top again.

Teacher: Good for you.

Student 1: For my summary now: This paragraph was about what aquanauts need to take when they go under the water.

Student 5: And also about why they need those things.

Student 3: I think we need to clarify *gear.*

Student 6: That's the special things they need.

Teacher: Another word for *gear* in this story might be *equipment*— the equipment that makes it easier for the aquanauts to do their job.

Student 1: I don't think I have a prediction to make.

Teacher: Well, in the story, they tell us that there are "many strange and wonderful creatures" that the aquanauts see as they do their work. My prediction is that they'll describe some of these creatures. What are some of the strange creatures you already know about that live in the ocean?

Student 6: Octopuses.

Student 3: Whales?

Student 5: Sharks!

Teacher: Let's listen and find out. Who would like to be our teacher?

Note. From "Interactive Teaching to Promote Independent Learning from Text," by A. S. Palincsar and A. L. Brown, 1986, *The Reading Teacher, 39,* pp. 771–777. Reprinted with permission of A.S. Palinscar and the International Reading Association. All rights reserved.

3. Following reading of a segment of material (usually four paragraphs), students write two questions and a summary reflecting the information in that segment.

4. Students write examples of any information that require clarification.

5. The class discusses the written questions, summaries, and clarifications.

Notes on Reciprocal Teaching

Positive outcomes have been reported from studies using Reciprocal Teaching with students who were classified as good decoders but poor comprehenders (Reeve, Palincsar, & Brown, 1985). *Time* magazine (circa 1988) called Reciprocal Teaching the most important development in instructional theory in the twentieth century. Bruer (1993) further referred to it as a primary example of the revolution that has taken place in instruction and that few outside education are aware of. Ironically, reciprocal teaching has appeared in fewer and fewer textbooks for teachers in recent times. A possible reason for this diminished interest may be found in the fact that Reciprocal Teaching requires considerable teacher and student training before use, whereas its predecessor ReQuest ideally is used by novices to learn how to reciprocally interact.

The next two methods are among those obvious things that are easy to overlook. See if either of these would have occurred to you.

Reading before Reading

The idea of reading before reading started as a popular movement in the 1950s with *Cliff Notes*, or book digests. In due course, comic-book versions of the classics became a familiar "underground" means of making the classics more palatable and giving readers a head start on reading unabridged versions. Not surprisingly, these mechanisms received a black eye when many students began using them as substitutes for, rather than supplements to, the original books. Open resentment against digests and abridged materials was reversed shortly thereafter, however, when a theory called *advance ideational organizers* restored credibility to the intuitive value of some type of reading before reading. Here are two means of taking advantage of this traditional idea, without sacrificing academic rigor.

Advance Organizers

In a now classic study, learning theorist David Ausubel (1960) had students read a prestructured statement (500 words), or advance ideational organizer, before reading a longer (2,500-word) selection in science. The advance ideational organizers clearly and significantly improved student comprehension. Subsequent studies by several other researchers produced results that sometimes replicated this finding but at other times did not. The difference in these outcomes was traced primarily to the quality of the prereading passage. Ideally, an organizer had to impart a sense of structure but not be too abstract. Some findings indicate that short literal accounts, usually used by the control group treatment, also had a positive effect on comprehension.

Accordingly, we recommend combining abstract and literal organizers (Manzo & Manzo, 1990a). One way to do this is to paste an abstract organizer to the inside front cover of a book and a literal organizer to the inside back cover. Then encourage students to use both organizers as a prereading strategy and as frequently as they wish while reading the larger work. Figures 5.9 and 5.10 provide examples of a literal and an abstract organizer for *The Old Man and the Sea.*

Figure 5.9
The Old Man and the Sea: Literal organizer.

The Old Man and the Sea tells of an extremely poor old fisherman, Santiago, who fishes along in the Gulf stream, and of Manolin, a boy who had fished with him until the man's luck had gone bad. The boy still had deep respect and affection for him, however, and brought him food and other things he needed.

The book opens in September as the old man decides to go far out into the Gulf stream to take advantage of a strong current. He rowed out in the dark, lowered his bait, and began drifting with the current. When the sun was high, the bait was taken by a large fish. The man tried to pull the fish up, but it was too big and simply began towing the boat out to sea. All afternoon and all night the fish pulled the skiff, with the old man resolutely straining against the line to ensure that the fish did not break it.

About sunrise, the fish gave a lurch, which cut the man's hand. Santiago ate strips of raw tuna to keep up his strength, and he wished the boy were with him. Finally, the fish surfaced, and it was the biggest fish the man had ever seen—longer than the skiff. But it dove again and continued towing the boat the rest of that day and into the night.

The old man was suffering greatly by now but was still resolved to bring the fish in. He tried to sleep, still standing and holding the line, but woke as the fish again surfaced and pulled him down into the boat, where the line cut into his hands and his back. He got up and fought the fish to try and tire it. As the sun rose on the old man's third day at sea, the fish began to circle, and the man was able to pull in some line. After several hours, feeling dizzy and faint, the old man pulled the fish near enough to the boat to harpoon it. Since the fish was larger than the boat, the man lashed it alongside, rigged the sail, and, exhausted, set sail for home.

But it was too good to last. Sharks had caught the scent. From sunset until after midnight, the old man fought the sharks, first with his harpoon, then his knife, and finally a club. But it was no use—they had cleaned his fish, and he was beaten.

He arrived in the harbor and managed to reach his shack before he collapsed with fatigue. In the morning, the fishermen were astounded at the 19-foot skeleton lashed to the boat. When the old man awakened, the boy heard of his ordeal and tried to console him.

Notes on Advance Organizers. Apart from the preceding more literary use, abstract and literal advance organizers also can be made and provided for difficult content textbook chapters. Students can be encouraged to read these and ask questions about them before reading the text and reminded to refer to them as needed during reading. We are attempting to make advance organizers created by other readers available through an interactive system on the InterNet. For more information, see the description of the REAP procedure in Chapter 9.

Figure 5.10
The Old Man and the Sea: Abstract organizer.

> *The Old Man and the Sea* tells of a fisherman's struggle with the elements
> while trying to hook and kill a huge fish, only to have it eaten by sharks.
>   The story basically is a testament to humankind's unconquerable
> spirit—to our ability to achieve dignity in the face of defeat. Humans are
> shown to be noble because of their willingness to struggle and preserve
> against the hardships in life. The man tells the fish, "I will show him what a
> man can do and what a man endures" (p. 66) and "Man is not made
> for defeat . . . a man can be destroyed, but not defeated" (p. 103).
>   The book also shows the author's view of humankind in relation to
> the physical universe. The fisherman refers to both the stars and the
> fish as "my brother." This is taken to mean that we should respect and
> love our natural environment even as we strive to carve existence out
> of it and conquer it.

Reiterative Reading

Reiterative Reading (Crafton, 1983) is based on the proposition that students can independently acquire relevant background information through
the reading process itself. In one study of this approach, it was found that
simply having eleventh graders read two different articles on the same
topic "dramatically improved students' comprehension of the second article and the cognitive level at which they processed it" (Crafton, 1983, p.
587). The researcher concluded that her study supports three assertions:
(1) "the common view of reading as a natural knowledge-generating activity"; (2) the belief that "text on an unfamiliar topic can serve as cognitive
preparation for the next"; and (3) the observation that experimental subjects who read two forms of the same material "were more *active* during
the reading process and personalized information to a greater degree than
did subjects who read unrelated materials" (Crafton, 1983, p. 590).

Notes on Reading before Reading

An anecdotal validation of reading before reading, and some new and
easy ways to accomplish it, are illustrated in Figure 5.11. Today, reading
before reading can be easily accomplished in several newer ways. Con-
tent-rich electronic text on most any topic is available from on-line services or the InterNet. In addition, there is viewing before or after reading. A monthly look at public and cable television offerings provides
numerous opportunities for such nontextual reiteration or previewing
and reviewing of films, documentaries, and programs on topics in literature, science, social studies, and the arts.
    The next and final method for facilitating the prereading stage of com-
prehension arose from earlier studies on the rise and decline of curiosity

Figure 5.11
Anecdotal evidence for reading before reading.

A. V. Manzo once taught world geography to a difficult, sometimes unruly class of low-achieving ninth graders. The class had a new, slick, black-covered text that was impossible in almost every way: The print was small, information was dense, and sentence structures were complex beyond reason. In short order, Manzo found twenty copies of a very old geography text in the district's attic. The class read both books, alternating the order according to fancy more than to any deep analysis of textual value. In addition to the obvious benefits of seeing most things twice, and in different words, the students often were challenged and amused by diverse perspectives, sometimes contrary information, and changing and often bewildering facts. For example, the students puzzled over how a then obscure and backward Iran could have been the seat of the great Persian Empire. There were many times when both teacher and students wished they had a third or fourth text to explain some things in even greater detail. They never could quite get a conceptual fix, for example, on how maps were made in the past when map makers could not get up high enough to see.

in school-age children. The method that evolved from these studies is very robust and slightly unorthodox.

Question-Only

Whenever students read or listen in school, questions are being answered. The problem is that students often don't know what those questions are, and hence they cannot read or listen actively. Even when they have some level of awareness of an important organizing question, students tend to be inexperienced in framing their question in such a way as to allow focused reading, or to invite appropriate help from a speaker/teacher when they are listening. In due course, natural curiosity begins to suffer, and soon most inquiry grinds to a halt. The Question-Only method can reverse this trend.

Steps in the Question-Only Method (Manzo, 1985)

1. The teacher announces a topic to the class and explains that they must learn about it solely through their questions and will be tested on the topic. The test will cover all the information the teacher considers important, whether or not the students actually extract the information with their questions.

2. The class questions, and the teacher answers fully but without telling more than anyone logically would need to know and at the same time taking care not to miss a teachable moment for telling all that the question logically entails.

3. The teacher gives the test.

4. Class discussion follows. Here teacher and students note which questions were raised and which should have been raised.

5. Students are directed to read their texts carefully or listen to a short lecture to discover what they failed to learn through their initial questions.

Example

Teacher:	The topic today is the Jura. Any questions?
Student:	You said "the"—does that mean Jura is a thing?
Teacher:	Yes.
Student:	This is geography, so is it a country?
Teacher:	No.
Student:	A river?
Teacher:	No.
Student:	Mountains?
Teacher:	Yes.
Student:	It sounds foreign. Is it in India?
Teacher:	No.
Student:	South America?
Teacher:	No.
Student:	Eastern Europe?
Teacher:	No, but close.
Student:	Western Europe?
Teacher:	Yes.

Ten minutes later, students will have deduced facts such as that the Jura is between Switzerland and France and its highest peak is 6,000 feet. The quiz that follows should teach the class more about the topic but also more about how to inquire.

Quiz Questions

1. Does the Jura serve as a natural boundary?
2. What does it divide?

3. What happened to the valuable forests that once covered the mountainsides?

4. What do you suppose is the relationship between mountains and rivers?

Check your text now for answers to those questions you didn't anticipate.

Question-Only Options

1. The teacher can add a five-minute period of comments only, encouraging students to say what they feel they learned about the topic and/or about asking questions from the Question-Only format.

2. The teacher can have students use the Question-Only strategy to interrogate other students on a report or term paper previously prepared as a class requirement.

Notes on Question-Only

Research and field experience have revealed that Question-Only helps students from kindergarten through medical school to raise incisive and systematic questions on difficult and mundane topics (Legenza, 1978; Manzo & Legenza, 1975). The enthusiasm students have shown for this method probably arises from the fact that it offers them an assertive but nonbelligerent means of "poking back," or reciprocally influencing lesson activity. It also helps students to incidentally discover and provide for their own learning needs by stimulating them to ask questions about the things that most befuddle them in an upbeat and ego-protective atmosphere.

Ironically, the only time this highly analytical activity may go stale is when the teacher becomes overwhelmed by the rapid pace with which material is covered. The teacher may react by slowing down the lesson and, in the process, taking the winds of enthusiasm out of the students' sails; therefore, be prepared to cover a good deal of information quickly and with considerable depth. Quick-paced instruction of this type is proving to be a powerful way to simultaneously teach slower and gifted learners (see Manzo & Manzo, 1993, for further details).

✦ *Looking Back and Looking Ahead* ✦

This chapter presented some important ideas regarding frontloading, or helping the reader to maximize prior knowledge and experience before reading. It advocated for teaching students to do this for themselves through interactions with teachers and peers and by seeking easier texts and computer-based and multimedia assistance. The next chapter discusses several means of keeping interest and attention focused during independent silent reading and viewing. See if you can find a method that best suits your subject and teaching style for guiding silent reading.

✦ ✦ **TRADE SECRET** ✦ ✦

*Dealing with Nonproductive Questions,
Answers, and Comments*

There are numerous ways for students to question, answer, and comment during classroom interactions. Some of these are facilitating and productive, and others are quirky and difficult to handle. Start a personal journal of useful verbal protocols, or "things to say when. . . . "

Here are some typical problem situations that tend to arise during questioning, answering, and commenting and some techniques we have seen veteran teachers use to deal with them.

Problem. The students who can't seem to think without talking. They are not really disrespectful but garrulous or irrepressibly talkative. They begin to answer every question whether or not they know the answer.

Remedies

1. Avoid eye contact with them.
2. Occasionally turn your back to them, and ask a question while walking away from them so that they can't quite hear it, thus preventing them from answering before others can.
3. Call a name or a row before asking a question.
4. Strictly enforce a rule of raising a hand before talking.
5. Find a reason to talk about the different ways people think and talk. Be sympathetic, but point out that compulsive talkers tend to disrupt the teacher, dissuade others from speaking up, overly dominate a discussion, close out opportunities to listen and learn, appear boorish, and anger others. Stress that this is a problem that can plague people for the rest of their lives if not curtailed early.

Problem. The students who raise the same question that has been raised and answered.

Remedy. Ask "Does anyone recognize this question?" If no one responds, you have strong evidence that you need to raise and probably answer the question again. If the question or the answer has more than one part, write out key words on the chalkboard.

Problem. The students who characteristically speak too low to be heard.

Remedy. Begin walking to the other side of the room so that these students must project to you, and in the process speak loudly enough for others to hear.

Problem. Disruptive sounds, such as heating or cooling systems, prevent class members from hearing one another.

Remedies

1. Have students arrange desks so that they face one another.
2. Repeat students' questions and answers (despite the usual prohibition against doing so).
3. Explain the problem to the class, and say that you frequently will be calling on someone else to repeat questions and answers to ensure that everyone hears. This also can keep students more alert the first time.

Problem. Students who fail to participate in responding to recitation-type questions.

Remedies

1. Examine your questions. You might be asking "guess what I'm thinking" questions. All teachers occasionally lapse into this routine.
2. Provide more "wait time": Count to five to yourself before saying another word, then ask students if they want the question repeated or explained further.

Problem. Students who do not pay attention or participate in discussions or other class activities.

Remedies

1. Reassess what you are asking students to do. Is it meaningful, clear, and doable in the time you are allowing?
2. Use a polling technique to warm up your audience and get them involved. The most popular method is to ask questions that require one of two choices, such as those asked in television polls in which one calls a given phone number for each choice. You can also offer more elaborate, content-related choices. Here is an example: "Some people think 'The Merchant of Venice' is a put-down of Jews, others think it is a put-down of Christians. Who thinks it is a put-down of Jews? Who Christians? Who is unde-

cided? Who has no idea? Let's continue to analyze this play and see whether Shakespeare tips his hand one way or the other."

Problem.   The student who asks a question, gives an answer, or makes a comment that is "out in left field."

Remedies

1. Simply say, "I don't quite see the relevance of that. Can you explain further?" Where such responses clearly are characteristic of a certain student and it is clear to the class that you are not being arbitrary, omit the request for further explanation.
2. Ask if another student can help explain or clarify the question, answer, or comment.
3. Try to get things going in another direction by simply accepting the response and saying, "OK, does anyone else have a different point of view or way of answering this question?"
4. When such a response seems to be intentionally irrelevant, don't forget the power of a stare—or simple silence in response.

CHAPTER 6

Guided Silent Reading Methods and Strategies

Reading taste and ability are always tethered to past experience.
But reading itself is one way of increasing this capital fund of past
experience.

—Edgar Dale

✦ *Organizing Thoughts* ✦

The aspect of reading instruction we know *least* about is that of guiding students *while* they read silently. This chapter presents the methods and ideas now available for doing so. These range from attempts to teach readers to follow the structure of a text to means of restructuring the text to readers' needs. Read to see which method(s) best suit your subject specialty and personal style of teaching.

TEACHING STUDENTS TO
THINK WHILE THEY READ

Once students begin to read silently, something is needed to keep the process going and to keep it focused and productive. In silent reading, students must sustain attention, draw on prior knowledge and experiences, translate new information into familiar terms, monitor comprehension, and, most of all, sustain these efforts in a sea of other competing interests, needs, and distractions. Teachers cannot physically follow students on this silent incursion into print. Nonetheless, teachers can help, though not very easily, and certainly not for all students all of the time. This is important to remember, because teachers can easily get discouraged about trying to help with reading needs, especially when faced with other pressing demands, such as the need to cover the curriculum.

One thing teachers can do to remain focused is to keep some manageable targets in mind. Targets can be selected from what highly proficient, or expert, readers have been found to do while reading. It has been learned that expert readers do the following:

- ✦ Clarify and focus their purposes for reading.
- ✦ Identify the important aspects of a message.
- ✦ Separate relevant from irrelevant details.
- ✦ Monitor their ongoing efforts to comprehend.
- ✦ Engage in self-questioning to determine whether they are meeting their goals.
- ✦ Take corrective action, that is, use fix-up strategies, when their failure to understand becomes evident (Baker & Brown, 1984).

The previous chapter described prereading activities intended to prime effective reading, largely by calling up relevant background information and experiences, establishing appropriate purposes, and converting word obstacles into meanings that facilitate comprehension. Realistically, however, teachers know that within moments of guiding students into their own silent reading, each student's unique personal mental agenda can begin to add some static interference to the author's voice and to the teacher's instruction. Hence, the objectives of guiding silent reading are to counter these obstacles to comprehension and to permit the author to be heard, allow curriculum objectives to be met, and even encourage students to actively pursue personal interests and objectives. For these reasons, a combination of means and methods are needed in silent reading that will tend to suppress static while somehow permitting the voices of the teachers, the author, and the reader each to be heard.

STRATEGIC CUES TO AID SILENT READING

Strategic cues are teacher-taught but student-controlled means for increasing self-monitoring and self-fixing. In other words, they are things to do when reading comprehension begins to falter. In this section, we consider two classes of such strategies. The first—and simplest to use— is various forms of guiding questions, designed to get students to think along certain lines while they read. The second is marking systems, intended to keep reading even more active and alert.

Guiding Questions

The wise teacher always looks for the easiest way to meet student needs. Several researchers have shown that students can easily be trained to ask themselves some simple guiding questions while they read (Baker & Brown, 1984; Meichenbaum & Asarnow, 1979; Singer & Dolan, 1980). Here are three simple questions that students have been taught for guiding story-type reading:

1. What is the main idea?
2. What are the important details?
3. How do the characters feel, and why? (Meichenbaum & Asarnow, 1979)

The first two questions also can be used to guide the reading of expository textbook material. This simple approach can be enhanced by having students pause after about ten minutes of reading and asking them these questions. This reminds students to ask these questions on their own so that they might more actively try to clear up misapprehensions that might be impairing comprehension.

The next method has been called a *universal content area technique*. It is applicable to most any content subject requiring textual reading and is easily used by any subject teacher. It is a think-aloud method.

Oral Reading Strategy

In the oral reading strategy (Manzo, 1980), the teacher reads a brief portion of the selection to the class, making a conscious attempt to think aloud—that is, to model the metacognitive thought processes good readers might use to focus attention, develop and maintain interest, and monitor comprehension. The oral reading strategy calls for the teacher's oral reading to be brief and for students to have an immediate opportunity to emulate the model as they continue to read silently.

Steps in the Oral Reading Strategy

1. *Teacher Preparation.* Preview the selection students will be assigned to read. Imagine that you are reading this material for the first time, from your students' perspectives. On a photocopy of the first page or so (depending on print formatting), make notes of questions and comments to model for students as you read the first several paragraphs aloud just before their independent silent reading of the assignment.

These think-alouds, as they have been called (Davey, 1983), should focus on recollection of background information, identification of the main point of the selection, clarification of key terms, and translating phrases and sections into one's own words. Davey suggests using guiding questions such as these:

+ What is this going to be about?
+ Do I know anything about this already?
+ Do I know what that means in this context?
+ Can I summarize so far in my own words?
+ Can I predict where this is going?

2. *Teacher Oral Reading.* Tell students that you will read a little of the beginning of the reading assignment aloud to show them how to read actively when they are reading silently. Using the notes you have prepared, read and think aloud. Encourage students to answer your think-aloud questions.

3. *Release Responsibility to Students.* At a reasonable stopping point (after no more than about five minutes), tell students to continue immediately to read silently, trying to use the same self-questioning processes you have just demonstrated. See the example in Figure 6.1 to get a sense of how the teacher can use this think-aloud process to demonstrate active reading strategies in a direct and interactive way.

The next method also is helpful in teaching youngsters to read and think. In some ways, it is even simpler than the Oral Reading Strategy and therefore is possibly more suitable to a younger group of students and/or a less experienced teacher.

About-Point

About-Point (Martin, Lorton, Blanc, & Evans, 1977) is an easy to remember guide for silent reading. Students are instructed to pause at logical points, such as at the ends of paragraphs or text subsections, and complete the following two phrases:

> *This section is about _____ ; and the point is _____ .*

Example
This section is about the characteristics of plains; and the point is that while plains may have different weather and vegetation characteristics, the key characteristics are their altitude and their flatness.

Options for Using About-Point
Preparation.   Teach students the basic About-Point format, using several short paragraphs. Explain that an *about* statement should be more than a single key word but less than a summary. A *point* statement should include the most important elements of the section. It is useful to demonstrate a few examples and talk through the process of expressing good *about* and *point* statements. Once students have the idea, the simple format can be used in several ways.

Option 1:   When giving a reading assignment, have students put pencil checks beside particular paragraphs for which they are to write About-Point statements.

Option 2:   Assign paragraphs for About-Point statements as option 1, but have students work in pairs or cooperative learning groups to develop the About-Point statements collaboratively.

Option 3:   When giving a reading assignment, instruct students to select on their own a certain number of About-Point statements on paragraphs of their choice.

The Oral Reading Strategy and About-Point are good examples of how strategic teaching—that is, matching teaching methods to student needs—

Figure 6.1
Example of oral reading (think-aloud) method.

The teacher's think-alouds are shown in bracketed italics in the following example of a teacher's oral reading:

In the unit "Force and Motion," you made a force meter using a rubber band. *[What is this going to be about? Oh, it's right here in the title that I skipped, "Elastic Responses".]* As the force increased, so did the length of the rubber band. *[So, when you pull harder, the rubber band gets longer.]* The stretching was the response of the rubber band to the tensile force on it. *[What's "tensile force" again? Hmm, I can't remember right now. Does anyone know? No? We could read ahead and hope to figure it out, or look it up in the index. I think I'll read ahead. There are only two more paragraphs and if I still haven't a clue, I'll look it up.]* This stretching is said to be an elastic response. Why? Because when the force was renewed *[Can anyone say in your own words what that means—"when the force is renewed"? Right, Jan, "when you pull on the rubber band again." OK, when you stretch it again . . .]*, the rubber band relaxes and returns to its original length. Most construction materials are made to respond in the same way. *[OK, this passage seems to be about "elastic response." It probably will say more about why it's important to know the specific (hmm tensile?) strength and elastic response of materials used in construction . . . and maybe how to determine these. Can anyone tell me now what "tensile force" means? Fred, "how hard something pulls back after it is stretched"? That sounds close to me. Now, continue to read the rest of this section. Remember to keep asking yourself what the author is saying, the way I have been doing.]*

---

promotes strategic reading—that is, students selecting the best strategy by which to read and learn. The next method is another example of a teaching procedure that engages students in active reading behavior often demonstrated by expert readers.

Comprehension Monitoring System

The Comprehension Monitoring System was field tested with high school teachers in home economics, social studies, and biology (R. J. Smith & Dauer, 1984). In this approach to guiding silent reading, teachers create a coding system for students to use to record their cognitive and affective responses while they read. The code may vary according to the characteristics of the material and the curriculum objectives. A coding system that is suggested for social studies reading follows:

A	=	Bored
C	=	Confused
D	=	Disagree
M	=	Main idea

A suggested coding system for science reading follows:

C	=	Clear
D	=	Difficult
I	=	Important
S	=	Surprising

Students are given the code on a handout sheet before reading and asked to record their responses as they read on narrow strips of paper affixed to the margins of the pages they are reading.

Now that we have considered several ways to cue strategic thinking during silent reading, we'll address another need. This one is based on the controversial proposition that teaching students how text is structured will enhance their text comprehension. Before reading too far ahead, try to anticipate why this might be a controversial approach.

Text Structure

Some reading educators contend that an effective way to improve silent reading comprehension is to teach students about text structure and expository patterns (see Figure 6.2 for a listing of the twelve most common paragraph patterns). This belief is based on the frequent research finding that there is a strong correlation between reading comprehension and knowledge of text structure (Meyer, 1975). This was thought to imply that teaching poorer readers about the structure of writing would result in improved comprehension. Those who interpret the research in this way propose that the form and format of a communication are integral parts of its message. The lukewarm belief in this is evident in one study where reading specialists ranked text structure instruction fourteenth of twenty-three teaching practices for comprehension improvement (Gee & Rakow, 1987). Further, it has been pointed out that elaborate instruction in classification schemes such as of different paragraph patterns is not only unnecessary but potentially counterproductive. The reason is simple: The number of paragraphs that follow a clear-cut pattern is low, but the number of paragraphs that combine a variety of patterns into one paragraph is high (Niles, 1965). In short, when students are taught to read for meaning, their awareness of text structure increases, but when they are taught to identify text structure, comprehension growth does not follow to the same extent.

Figure 6.2
Expository paragraph
patterns.

> 1. Introductory
> 2. Definition
> 3. Transitional
> 4. Illustrative
> 5. Summary
> 6. Main ideas supported by details
>   or examples
> 7. Chronological order
> 8. Comparison/contrast
> 9. Cause and effect
> 10. Problem/solution
> 11. Descriptive
> 12. Narrative

Consider next the interesting topic of adjunct aids to silent reading. You may know of one type of these as reading guides or study guides.

ADJUNCT AIDS TO SILENT READING

When coaches shout commands during an athletic event, they are attempting to remind the athletes of what has always been taught and practiced in a less competitive situation. Such coaching from the side-lines would be distracting were it not for extensive prior training. The same general principle applies to written aids to text comprehension, or adjunct aids. These aids work best when students have been explicitly taught to use them and are given ample opportunity for guided practice.

Adjunct aids fall into two classes: those that are external, or supplementary to the text, and those that are built into the text. Research findings on the merit of both types generally are positive. The problem, however, is that there is no theory structure to provide a set of simple guidelines for constructing adjunct aids that will always be effective. Essentially, it is a matter of hit-or-miss engineering. This would be tolerable in the case of a teaching method being delivered extemporaneously and therefore easily adaptable to the situation. Adjunct aids, however, require considerable preparatory work and expense, so teachers will want to be careful when constructing them to ensure that their quality is equal to their quasi-permanence and cost in energy and time.

EXTERNAL AIDS TO SILENT READING: READING GUIDES

Reading guides essentially are teacher-made instructional materials that accompany reading assignments. Such guides somewhat resemble old-fashioned workbook exercises, but they are designed to be used throughout the reading process, rather than merely on a postreading basis.

The idea of reading guides, according to Herber (1978), their chief contemporary proponent, is to simplify difficult material. Reading guides are designed to teach reading processes as well as to improve information acquisition. Students are expected to refer to the guide while reading, then back to the text, then back again to the guide (Manzo & Garber, 1995). Often, a guide amounts to a written-out version of the Directed Reading–Thinking Activity described in Chapter 4. It can contain vocabulary and concept preparation as well as guiding questions. The most significant advantages of guides, in our judgment, are that they permit the teacher to focus student attention on key elements in a passage and that they require *every* student to attempt some type of active and reflective response to at least the points referenced.

Despite mixed findings on guides, their popularity still is evident in the numerous versions that have been developed. Some of the most traditionally used formats for reading guides and some recent innovations are described next.

Three-Level Guides

A Three-Level Guide is designed to lead students from basic to more advanced levels of comprehension of textual material (Herber, 1978). Part 1 of a Three-Level Guide contains questions at a literal level: What did the author say? Part 2 contains interpretive questions: What did the author mean? Part 3 contains application questions: How can you *use* this information?

Guidelines for Constructing a Three-Level Guide

1. Begin by deciding which *applications* are appropriate to the material, and develop questions for part 3 of the guide. If you start by developing these questions/activities first, you will better know which details and inferences to focus on in writing parts 1 and 2 of the guide.

2. Next, determine what information is needed to make these applications, and whether it is explicitly stated in the text or must be inferred. Information that must be inferred to make the level-three applications is used to develop questions for part 2 of the guide.

3. Finally, write questions for part 1 of the guide, directing attention to the necessary literal information in the reading selection (Vacca & Vacca, 1986).

Typically, students are directed to answer the literal questions in part 1 while they are reading and to complete the interpretive and applied questions in parts 2 and 3 after reading. A useful variation is to have students complete part 1 independently, and then form cooperative learning groups to complete parts 2 and 3.

Process Guides

Typical teacher-made reading guides focus on fact identification. A Process Guide is intended to teach the active thinking strategies needed to construct meaning from text. Following is an example of a Process Guide from a social studies textbook:

---

1. Identification of Key Terms
Directions: Check off the terms listed below as you come to them in reading. Review them after reading to see what you can remember about each.

Page	Reading Vocabulary	Social Studies Terms	People, Places, Events
166	stealthily summit	regulars redcoats	Bunker Hill Breed's Hill
175	ill-matched	tactics Tories tarred and feathered	Continental Army man-of-war

2. Categorization
Directions: Use the context in which you encounter the above terms in your text to place them in one of the categories listed below.

- A. Categories (not all words fit these categories):
    1. Words that describe an action or state of being (verbs)
    2. Words that modify (adjectives and adverbs)
    3. Words that name persons, places, or things (nouns)
- B. Should you finish early, try recategorizing the above terms in the following ways:
    1. Words related to war
    2. Words that describe strong feelings
    3. Words that describe the English and their sympathizers

3. Text Structure
Directions: Chapter 9 answers three basic questions. The first and third are listed below. What is the second question this chapter addresses?

- A. Why did the Thirteen Colonies decide to declare their independence?
- B. _____
- C. How did the Thirteen Colonies win their independence?

4. Identification of Important Details
Directions: As you read, mark each statement as true (T) or false (F).
Where a statement seems false, cross out the incorrect information and
replace it with the correct information.

_____A.   The Battle of Bunker Hill actually was fought on Breed's Hill.
_____B.   Breed's Hill is in Pennsylvania.
_____C.   The Continental Army was made up largely of Europeans
          against England.

There is no single format for a Process Guide. As the preceding examples show, the sections and questions need to be matched to the demands
of the subject and the particular reading selection. The best way to learn
how to construct one is simply to try it. Following are some suggestions
to guide your efforts.

Guidelines for Constructing a Process Guide

1. Pick an important section of text. Process Guides are time-consuming to construct, so you will want to spend your efforts on something
   of conceptual value.

2. Read the selection carefully, putting yourself in the students' place:
   "If I didn't know much about this, what would I need to do?"

3. Refer to the preceding sample activity types to determine which
   activity or combination of activities is best suited to the material.

4. Remember that the purpose of a Process Guide is not to elicit facts
   but to engage students in active thinking and reading about possible
   interpretations and implications of new information.

The next type of reading guide breaks with traditional routines. It
departs from the usual expectation that students need to begin at the
beginning and read every word through to the end.

Reading Guide-O-Rama

The Reading Guide-O-Rama (D. Cunningham & Shablak, 1975) is
another form of reading guide. It is a set of written prompts to students
as to the best way to read and think about a given reading selection. In
constructing a Guide-O-Rama, teachers should determine which concepts and information they expect students to learn from the reading.
Next, teachers should consider how they, as an expert reader, would
approach the selection. An effective Guide-O-Rama points out unimpor-

tant as well as important information and forewarns readers about what to expect in class discussion. It may direct students to read portions of the material out of sequence, such as reading a final summary first. It may instruct students to read a short section of the assignment and then summarize the key points or facts. Here are some sample items from a Reading Guide-O-Rama:

Example 1: Page 93, paragraphs 3 to 6. Pay close attention to this section. Why do you think Hunter acted in this manner? We will discuss your ideas in class.

Example 2: Page 94. See if you can rewrite the bold print at the top of this page as a question. You should pick up five ideas under this topic very quickly. Jot these down.

Example 3: Read page 179, column 1. The author has provided us with some interesting information here, but it isn't important to our course of study. Just skim it, unless, of course, it is of special interest to you.

Graphic Organizers as Reading Guides

As described in Chapter 4, on three-phase approaches, graphic organizers provide another way to guide silent reading comprehension. These may be used as part of a structured reading guide (see Figure 6.3) or partially constructed in a whole-class brainstorming session as described in Chapter 4.

Additional Notes on Creating and Using Reading Guides

Composing any type of reading guide can be an insightful experience for teachers. It draws one into a careful analysis of the textual material and a deeper understanding of the processes that students must call on to read in a given discipline. It also can get the creative juices flowing; teachers often are surprised at the insights into students' reading and learning needs that can be gained in this way. Furthermore, problems related to producing, revising, and storing guides have been virtually eliminated with the increasing availability of computers with word processing, graphics, and storage capabilities.

The next and final section of this chapter describes a way to give students ready access to the other kind of guidance for silent reading. These are the guides that are built directly into the reading selection and optimistically are a harbinger of things to come.

The first main idea to be dealt with in this chapter may be called "The Thirteen Colonies Decide to Declare Their Independence." If you think of this statement as the rim of a wagon wheel, it will help you find the supporting details or the sequence of important events. These are represented as the spokes. Complete the remaining spokes by discovering the events that led the colonists to seek their independence. (Each of these supporting details will be a major category and will most likely appear in darker print in your text.)

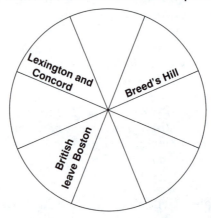

Make similar illustrations for the nine spokes, or subtopics. Fill in the supporting details for each (see following illustrations). When you are finished finding the supporting details for each main idea (in boldface print), you will have a good outline of this entire chapter.

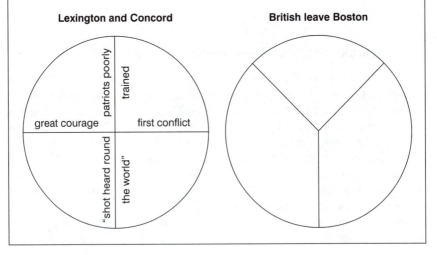

Figure 6.3
Wagon wheel graphic organizer for main idea and supporting details.

BUILT-IN GUIDES TO SILENT READING

A logical alternative to teacher-prepared reading guides is a textbook with *built-in* guides. These essentially are hard copy versions of what now is called *hypertext* in computer lingo. These internal guides have been called *imbedded aids* (Manzo, 1977) and *marginal gloss* (Otto & Hayes, 1982). Both typically include help with word analysis, word meaning, basic comprehension, remembering, and even thinking beyond the text to greater depth, elaboration, and critical analysis. Aids can lend assistance at all levels of reading and to readers at all levels.

The idea of built-in guides is that they are woven into the actual textbook itself during the production stage. A. V. Manzo produced the imbedded aids prototype shown in Figure 6.4 for a chapter from a high school world history text, *Man's Unfinished Journey* (Perry, 1971), as part of a research and development project.

Despite the high marks that the built-in guides received from teachers and students, it was/is a hard sell to publishers to assume the additional costs involved in producing such books on a regular basis. However, books with semblances of built-in guides are beginning to appear. This may be due to our growing collective exposure to hypertext. This software innovation, which permits additional explanatory detail by clicking on an idea or sentence, seems to be increasing our expectation that such things can be achieved in some measure with conventional print. Relatedly, the field of study called *text technology* (Jonassen, 1982, 1985a, 1985b) continues to grow to meet this rising demand.

✦ *Looking Back and Looking Ahead* ✦

This chapter reviewed several options for guiding silent reading from text. To decide on the one or two that you might employ in your teaching, select one or two that you might personally use or that you wish were available for you in reading the next chapter. It describes the options available for making the most of the postreading phase of learning from text.

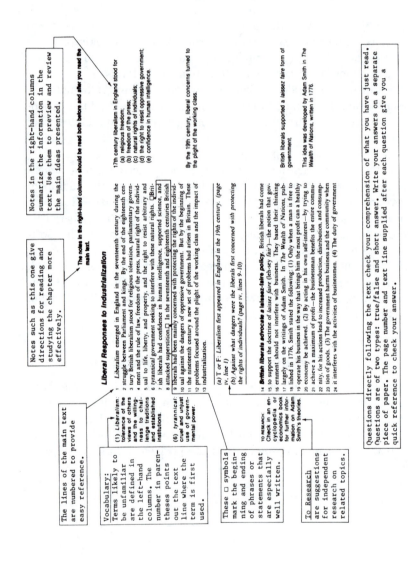

Figure 6.4
Example of imbedded aids.

Occasionally a word is missing from the text. You should be able to fill in the missing word with little trouble. Failure to do so may mean your attention is drifting. The correct word can be found in the lower left-hand margin.

1 is to maintain peace and order within the community and not to meddle
2 with the affairs of business.
3 The supporters of _____ insisted that poverty is natural. Since
4 some are meant to be wealthy and some poor, government can do nothing
5 about poverty. Any governmental reforms might hurt business and make
6 things worse.

Was the liberal idea of laissez faire limited to business? See Reader Helper Note 78.

7 ***Malthus blames poverty on overpopulation.*** Another English thinker
8 who helped shape the liberal attitude in the early days of the Industrial
9 Revolution was T. R. Malthus. In his *Essay on the Principle of Population*
10 (1798), Malthus declared that the population always increases faster than
11 the food supply. As a result mankind is always threatened with starvation.
12 The real cause of poverty, according to Malthus, is overpopulation. Until
13 the poor learn to keep down the size of their families, poverty will never be
14 eliminated. Malthus concludes:

TO THINK ABOUT: What possible connections can you see between the growth of liberal thinking in Britain and the success of the American Revolution?

15 When the wages of labor are hardly sufficient to maintain two children, a
16 man marries and has five or six. He of course finds himself miserably
17 distressed. . . . He accuses the [greed] of the rich. . . . He accuses the
18 [prejudiced] and unjust institutions of society. . . . The last person that he
19 would think of accusing is himself.

MINI NOTE: Adam Smith and T. R. Malthus each had the ability to see things differently from others around them. This is called divergent thinking.

20 Malthus also argued that as the population increases, the supply of workers
21 becomes greater than the demand. This leads to unemployment, low wages,
22 and perpetual poverty. For Malthus, lowering the birth rate was the only
23 effective way to combat poverty.
24 In effect Malthus was saying that, since the misery of the worker is his
25 own doing, no laws passed by the state can eliminate poverty. Factory
26 owners were delighted with Malthus' view. It soothed their consciences to
27 be told that they were not responsible for the sufferings of workers.

28 ***Democratic liberals propose reform legislation.*** The problems of the
29 working class persisted. Convinced that a laissez-faire policy was not ac-
30 ceptable, a growing number of liberals in England and elsewhere urged the
31 government to introduce reforms to aid the working man. They wanted
32 legislation that would improve conditions of work in the factory, allow the
33 growth of labor unions, eliminate property requirements for voting, and
34 increase educational opportunities for the poor. Whereas the older liberals

(3) laissez faire

Reader Helper Notes stimulate you to think beyond the basic information covered in the text. Notes at the end of the chapter (pages 32–34) provide additional information and suggest possible answers to the questions raised.

Another idea popular with British liberals came from T. R. Malthus in *Essay on the Principle of Population* (1798).

Malthus said excessive population growth was the real cause of poverty, not greedy business practices.

Mini Notes provide enrichment information related to the text.

To Think About are questions which have no one correct answer. They are intended to raise broad generalizations or to provide topics for discussion and debate.

Note. The text used to demonstrate these imbedded aids is from the Experimental Edition of Chapter 2 of *Man's Unfinished Journey, a World History,* by M. Perry, 1971, Boston: Houghton Mifflin. Copyright 1971 by Houghton Mifflin Company. All rights reserved. Reprinted by permission.

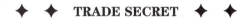

✦ ✦ TRADE SECRET ✦ ✦

Reduce Parent Involvement

As educators, we sometimes can overdo our efforts to enlist parental involvement. In your own efforts to involve parents, keep in mind that parents don't work for us—we work for them. Several common practices deserve to be rethought. Most of them turn out either to be assignments for parents rather than for students or to exceed our authority. Here are some examples:

✦ Requiring that parents sign students' homework

✦ Requiring that parents sign students' assignment pads each day

✦ Requiring students with no means of transportation to go to a public library on their own

✦ Requiring students to order and purchase books or special supplies

✦ Requiring students to view a certain television program

✦ Requiring rather than inviting parents to pick up student report cards, meet teachers, or attend school functions

In all likelihood, many evenings are spoiled and dinners ruined because students must bring up homework and other obligations and school problems to their parents. Evenings and dinnertimes ought to be a time for family members to interact with one another in personal ways. Even a seemingly small assignment can be brought to a parent on the heels of a long and stressful day or a difficult home situation. Instead of demands, consider offering options, invitations, and help to parents. In this way, you can satisfy parents who wish to help students with homework and such without presuming to tell all parents what to do and when to do it regardless of what they have planned or what is happening on a particular evening. If we can reduce the help we ask of parents and increase the help we provide them, it is a good bet that they will value us and what we have to offer more fully.

CHAPTER 7

Postreading Questioning and Cooperative Methods

Great discoveries and improvements invaluably involve the coopera-tion of many minds.

—Alexander Graham Bell

✦ *Organizing Thoughts* ✦

Successful silent reading sets the stage for verifying, clarifying, elaborat-ing, exploring, and further developing confidence as a strategic reader. These processes are advanced largely through recitation, discussion, writing, and vocabulary enrichment. This chapter focuses on the most traditional of these, recitation or teacher questioning, as a basis for guided discussion. The chapter then turns to cooperative learning mod-els that can be used to assist comprehension through peer collaboration.

RECITATION-BASED APPROACHES FOR CHECKING COMPREHENSION

Human progress has been likened to a footrace in which reason, knowl-edge, and invention are pitted against fear, ignorance, and uncertainty. Every classroom teacher coaches a team that will, like it or not, run a leg in this race. The methods and equipment available to teachers for build-ing winning teams through reflective postreading recitation and discus-sion play a critical part in this process.

Figuratively speaking, prereading is planting and cultivating, silent reading is budding and blooming, and postreading is fruit bearing and harvesting. In postreading, prior knowledge is combined with recent incoming information and transformed into usable new knowledge for continuing the process.

The postreading step of most three-phase reading methods is the point at which teachers help students to check comprehension, broaden schema, and extend certain skills, most particularly that of verifying answers and conclusions with reference to the textual material. Most of the tools for nurturing these outcomes are familiar: recitation, discus-sion, writing, and practice in comprehension and applied thinking. The focus here is on the more literal-reconstructive aspects of comprehen-sion and knowledge acquisition.

Postreading Recitation

Recitation generally is marked by teacher-directed questioning or old-fashioned drill. As a method of teaching, it has gone from overvalued to undervalued. The dialogue in Figure 7.1 illustrates a typical postreading

Figure 7.1
Postreading recitation.

> Students in an eighth-grade health class read a portion of [a] chapter on poison control the day before the videotaping [of the following discussion]. In the beginning segment of the transcript, which was typical of the entire lesson, Ms. Sneed quizzed the class on their assigned reading.
>
> *Ms. Sneed:*   All right, Vinny. Would you try to identify the poison for all victims or only the ones that are conscious?
> *Ms. Sneed:*   All victims. Good. Roger? Would you call the poison center for all victims or only the ones that are conscious?
> *Roger:*   All of them.
> *Ms. Sneed:*   All of them. Good. Lee? Would you treat for shock only those victims who are conscious or all victims?
> *Lee:*   All victims.
> *Ms. Sneed:*   All victims. Good. Would you watch to be sure that all victims keep breathing, Jeri, or only the conscious ones?
> *Jeri:*   All.

recitation lesson. Notice that the teacher's questioning tends to be at the text-explicit, or literal-reconstructive level.

Some educators believe that such postreading quizzing and reviewing is not comprehension teaching at all but simply another form of testing (Durkin, 1978–1979). We respectfully disagree. Simple questioning following reading is a reasonable means of inducing a retrospective analysis of what has been read. It provides feedback on what the teacher deems important and lays the foundation for further group analysis. If every reading and homework assignment were followed with just this much attention, we could expect a fair degree of improvement in students' reading and learning from text. It wouldn't be correct to call a recitation session a discussion or conversation, but it is not an unreasonable way for teachers and students to interact when the object of reading is to acquire certain discipline-specific information.

Support for recitation–questioning can be traced back to Thorndike's (1917) seminal study of comprehension. That study demonstrated that reading is an act of reasoning and therefore is better served by silent reading and recitation–questioning than by oral reading and phonics instruction. As defined here, recitation–questioning tends to be characterized by three types of literal level questions: recognition, recall, and translation. Recognition questions require finding information; recall questions require remembering information; and translation questions require paraphrasing, or converting information from one form to another. Research on the questions teachers ask following reading provides insight into patterns that can be compared to teaching objectives. Two types of questions are especially relevant to content teachers: translation and evaluative-type questions.

Patterns of Teacher Questioning Following Reading

It has been found that teachers tend to ask too few translation and evaluative-type questions. Generally, translation questions account for fewer than 1% of the total number of questions asked in instructional situations (Guszak, 1967; Manzo, 1969a). This is unfortunate, because translation questions provide several advantages in comprehension checking.

1. They urge students to listen to one another ("John, can you tell in your own words what Mary just said?").
2. They offer another way to keep students engaged and attentive.
3. They generally are necessary for discussion based on higher-order questions.

Importantly too, postreading recitation need not be limited to such questions; in fact, good teachers long have known that it is much more engaging of young people to *begin* with an evaluative- or "what did you think?" -type question. Unfortunately, again, observational studies reveal that teachers ask too few evaluative-type questions; less than 10% of total questions (Durkin, 1978–1979; Guszak, 1967; Manzo, 1969a, 1969b). This is regrettable, since this type of question, as previously noted, places a high value on student judgment and tends to draw pupils into learning in a more thoughtful and personal way. Evaluative questions also are valuable means of helping two groups of learners: those who are classic underachievers and certain overachievers, or higher illiterates, as Francis Chase, former dean of the University of Chicago, once called them.

Underachievers tend to have weak literal comprehension and to depend on others to tell them what they think. This is evident in the frequency with which they reply "I don't know" even to simple personal judgment questions. More frequent use of evaluative questions tends to stimulate such underachievers to fall back on their own resources, that is, to accept more responsibility for reading more carefully and thoughtfully. Overachievers have an analogous problem. They tend to have good literal and inferential comprehension; however, they too can be dependent, though in a different sense. They read and absorb well but do not seem to relate what they read to prior knowledge and experience. Evaluation questions coax this type of student into a more reflective mode. This causes such students to draw on their own life experiences and to incorporate more of their academic learnings into their social-emotional and intellectual growth.

The bottom line is that teachers need to add more translation and evaluative questions to their postreading inquiries. It also aids student thinking and engagement if the teacher asks these questions with enthusiasm and interest, rather than with an attitude of rote drill.

Peer Recitation

To get students more actively involved in the analysis and extraction of information from text, it helps to add a certain measure of peer involvement. The chief way to do this is to divide the class into competitive teams for a cooperative learning purpose. Each team can be made responsible for leading a postreading, or peer recitation, session. Here are some techniques to stimulate such recitation:

+ Five-question format: A team leads the class in filling out a "who-what-when-where-why-how" outline

+ Inverted questioning: An answer team tries to ingest and digest everything they can on a given section of text. The class then questions the team, and the team tries to answer the class questions as best as they can. For fun a beeper or buzzer can be added. We observed one eighth-grade science teacher who gave the questioning group a child's toy that made a deep buzzing sound when a button was pushed. The class used it to signal a wrong answer. No one seemed disturbed by the competition, and several otherwise low-participating students were quite caught up in the "in-your-face" humor that young teens seem to enjoy.

+ Written questions: Everyone prepares a few questions on the content to be mastered. Going around the room in a certain order—up and down rows or across aisles—students read questions not previously asked, and the class must answer. The teacher might collect the best questions for use on a unit test. This enhances students' motivation to construct quality questions and to listen carefully for the answers.

In our experience, recitation–questioning can build a fast-paced tempo, which raises attention and engagement, and even an aura of academic discipline and learning. Contrary to what one might first think, bright students do not seem to resent it, and slower ones really profit from it. More importantly, it routinely lays a foundation in group situations for further, more reflective discussion. This is no small accomplishment, since one of the biggest problems in any group discussion, whether in the classroom or at a faculty meeting, is just getting everyone on the same page.

Handling Incorrect Responses

Given that one of the primary purposes of recitation is to get things straight, it does present some nagging social problems in how to handle incorrect responses. Apart from the buzzing sound previously noted, which clearly is tongue-in-cheek, there are several other research-based means of turning incorrect answers into positive learning experiences (Collins, 1987; Rakes & Smith, 1987). You probably use or would use several of these techniques intuitively, but it is good to have your intuition validated when teaching is your profession.

Fixing Incorrect Answers in Recitation

1. *Think again.*   The greatest source of incorrect responding is an impetuous response. If you think a student who gave an incorrect answer has the background to answer correctly, ask that student to think again, "I'm sure you'll think of it if you just give yourself a little more time."

2. *Give a prompt.*   When students give a partial answer, or need you to provide more structure, offer a small piece of information: "The person whose name we are looking for also died prematurely in a duel with Aaron Burr."

3. *Differential reinforcement.*   Tell the part of the answer that was correct: "You're right, bears are mammals. Do you recall whether mammals are warm blooded? Are human beings warm blooded?"

4. *Paraphrasing the question.*   If it appears no one knows the answer, yet you judge that they learned the information, rephrase the question: "When you go west, do you gain or lose time?" "OK, then where does the sun rise?"

5. *Provide help but make students accountable.*   If a student gives two incorrect answers to the same question, or if two students answer incorrectly, give the answer and tell them they will need to remember it. (This gives them incentive to remember the questions and the answer.) Return to the student(s) again before the period is over, and ask the same question, "Now, before you go, who can tell me again where New Hampshire is?"

6. *Asking for clues.*   Ask fellow students to give clues, or ask the student who missed the question to call on a classmate to help by giving either a clue or the answer, "Charlie, who would you like to ask for help in naming the other three Great Lakes?"

7. *Incorrect "if" statements.*   If you recognize why the answer was wrong, supply the question for which the answer would have been correct. For example, if you asked, "What is the capital of New Zealand?" and the student answered "Canberra," you could respond, "Canberra

would be the answer if someone asked what the capital of Australia was. How about the capital of New Zealand?"

8.   *Examples of possibilities.*   Use oral multiple choices at the close of a lesson or unit or as a review: "Who was the first European to see the Pacific Ocean? Balboa, Cortez, or Cabeza de Vaca?"

9.   *Nonexamples or opposites.*   If students don't raise their hands to answer a question, tell them what the answer is not: ("Which country in South America has the oldest tradition of democracy?") "The answer is not Brazil or Chile."

10.   *"One thing I learned today."* Toward the end of class, call on some students to tell one thing that they learned that day without repeating any item previously stated by another student. Done frequently, this question can be fun as well as motivational, since it seems to welcome a little parting humor as well as attention to subject matter.

11.   *Expanding the answer.*   Ask students to tell why they answered the way they did or why they believe their answer to be correct: "*Why* do you think it is two hours earlier in Los Angeles than it is Kansas City?"

The last technique typically offers a good bridge from recitation to discussion—the next topic.

From Recitation to Discussion

Class discussion is distinguishable from recitation in several ways, most notably by the following:

1. Different points of view are welcomed.
2. Students interact with one another as well as with the teacher.
3. Responses are longer and more elaborate than in recitation.
4. Talk becomes more conversational and marked by comments as well as by responses to questions.
5. Discourse creates conflicting perspectives, and a dynamic tension within as well as among individuals.
6. Discussants, including the teacher, are expected to be willing to change their minds, or be transformed in response to points made.

Meanings shared in class discussion are not merely a collection of individual meanings but a new set of meanings developed as members talk and listen to one another and to themselves (Benge-Kletzien & Baloche, 1994; Pinnell, 1984). *Classroom discussion* does differ from *social discussion* in that its expressed purpose is to orchestrate group talk in ways that are topic relevant, analytical, and toward some educational objective or insight. Ideally, classroom discussion provides a mechanism for fine tuning the internal conversations that everyone engages in so that these are raised to a higher standard of thinking and reflection (Calfee, Dunlop, & Wat, 1994; Tharp & Gallimore, 1989).

Discussion-based teaching is highly thought of in democratic societies. Nonetheless, it is not without its problems. For example, although the daytime talk shows discuss some controversial topics with input from many people, many still tend to fall short of the objective of improving thinking and knowledge. The backbone of effective classroom discussion remains the presence of persons capable of reaching, and thereby modeling, insightful and alternative perspectives. This point is better illustrated than explained.

A. V. Manzo once observed a group of teachers in a workshop designed to demonstrate the use of reading guides for analysis of poetry. A discussion of a sample poem could have occurred in any secondary school literacy class. The teachers were asked to read a poem and develop question guides on three levels. These guides easily generated questions that drew out these literal facts: A man was sitting on a park bench in New York City, watching and reflecting on the innocent play of children. Next, the group was asked to create questions that required interpretive-level thinking of the poem. These were more difficult to develop, but the teachers with guidance from the two trainers came to see that man's reflections were of the halcyon, or happy and carefree, days of youth before the adults somehow learned to be cross and cunning with one another. On an applied level, most everyone seemed satisfied that this was what the "universal truth" in this poem was about. That is, that unlike childhood, adult life is filled with cunning and deception. But this analysis was just about the level that would have been reached on a TV talk show, until one person suggested that he saw something else in the poem. As he listened to the group's analysis, he began to think that the man in the poem could have wandered out of a nearby office building where he had been caught in a cross fire of office politics. In need of a reprieve, he attributed peace and cooperation to the children's play because he needed to believe that there was a freer time in life. After a long pause, someone else said, "Is there really such a thing as carefree, halcyon days?" Then someone else added that only recently she had read about the enormous cruelty that children can bestow on one another and how some seem to derive an innate pleasure from being bullies.

This more cynical bit of counterpoint created the dynamic tension needed to move the discourse from a fairy tale to a slice-of-life insight into the human condition. In another situation, the dynamic tension might have been stimulated by a softer, less cynical view. In either case, however, the "universal truth" may lie not in the author's words or apparent intentions but in some reader's schema, or prior knowledge and experience. In this case, it lay in one reader's insights into stress and its effects on human perception and behavior. This was constructive reading at its best. While there probably is no one correct interpretation, in this case, the discussants learned something about how to conjecture about an author's subconscious as well as conscious intentions. They learned this because some one was able to squeeze more out of his personal experience and background knowledge than the relatively superficial perspective that was consensually arrived at. This is why minority views, if reasoned, must be not only heard but welcomed. For an exercise in such inferencing, see Figure 7.2.

Now consider a basic method for promoting the dynamic tension necessary to ignite discussion, focus differences, and foster insight.

Three-Question Format for Effective Discussion

Discussion by nature can be an unpredictable and unwieldy event. It depends in large measure on the group's willingness to pursue unplanned avenues of thought and the leader's accompanying ability to

Figure 7.2
Between the lines: A sample of higher-level inferencing in discussion-based teaching.

To get a more vivid idea of the powerful role personal perspective plays in constructing meaning from text, consider what meanings, inferences, and conjectures you would make if you examined one week's worth of trash from three different homes. Develop a short description of each family.

Home 1: Large white-wine bottle; gourmet frozen dinner boxes; remnants of fresh vegetables; envelopes from Merrill Lynch, Exxon, Dreyfus Fund, and American Express; empty laxative and skin moisturizer bottles; *Travel* and *Modern Maturity* magazines

Home 2: Frozen french fries package, meat packages, several large soda bottles, chips and cookie packages, gallon-size milk containers, brochures for summer camps and after-school activities, *Time* and *Mad* magazines

Home 3: Yogurt containers, bran cereal boxes, packaging from a computer component, two pairs of still usable ladies' shoes, *National Geographic* and *Modern Life* magazines

As you build a schema for each of these families, you may feel that you can describe one family easily but need more information on the others. Like the ability to construct meaning from text, your ability to build new schema depends largely on actively comparing your existing knowledge to new information and other perspectives.

bring them together toward some meaningful insights. This requires both flexibility and restraint. There is a Three-Question Format that can be a useful tool for striking this balance. This method reminds discussion leaders in school to ask each of three guiding questions in some way during the course of the discussion:

1. What did you think, or what do you suppose, influenced the writer?
2. What did the writer say?
3. What might one learn from this?

A good example of a "What do you suppose?" question can be drawn from the poem discussion referred to earlier. The question that could have stimulated more people to reach a higher level of possible insight might have been something like, "What do you suppose prompted the writer to see things as this writer did?" In the situation just described, appropriate follow-up questions might be

+ What do you think of the value of a walk in the park as a way to deal with the stress the writer may have been feeling?
+ In what other ways might the writer have dealt with his stress?
+ What might business and industry do to reduce stressful conditions?
+ Can stress really be avoided, or is it part of the human condition?

The next two methods rely on cooperative learning, or jigsaw, theory. They are presented here as postreading methods rather than three-phase methods because the information provided in the previous two chapters is essential to following their purpose and organization.

COOPERATIVE LEARNING METHODS FOR COMPREHENSION

Jigsaw Theory

A variety of approaches to teaching reading and content mastery rely on cooperative groups, or jigsaw theory (Aaronson, Blaney, Sikes, Stevan, & Snapp, 1975; Slavin, 1980). Based on this theory, students are taught that they each can play a role in bringing about a greater whole. Cooperative learning was designed as an alternative to competitive and individualistic learning (Deutsch, 1962). In cooperative learning situations, each student's achievement depends on the achievement of the group. This creates a classroom learning environment that is less competitive than the typical learning situation where achievement often is defined in relation to someone else's lack of success.

Cooperative learning, as the term suggests, occurs in small groups. However, it entails more than simply sorting students by age, interest, or compatibility. It is group activity for the purpose of encouraging students to support and depend on one another and to develop a group identity. Cooperative learning creates positive interdependence (D. W. Johnson, Johnson, & Holebec, 1993; R. T. Johnson & Johnson, 1985). It gives students the opportunity to share what they have learned, to hear the opinions of their peers, and to teach and be taught by fellow students. It is viewed by many as essential to a lifelong process of learning and to socialization. Metaanalyses—that is, studies of studies (D. W. Johnson, Maruyama, Johnson, Nelson, & Skon, 1981; Lehr, 1984; Pepitone, 1980)—reveal that cooperative learning approaches can result in modest-to-good gains in achievement but substantial improvements in factors such as the following:

1. Students develop greater confidence and self-esteem.

2. Students tend to like one another more.

3. When groups include students of different ethnic backgrounds, both prejudice and disparagement practically disappear.

4. Students develop a higher regard for school, the subject learned in the cooperative setting, and their teachers.

5. Students come to depend less on the teacher.

6. Students develop greater motivation to learn.

The core of all cooperative learning efforts is group process. Figure 7.3 provides guidelines for effective group work for teachers and students.

See now how these guidelines are reflected in the cooperative content area literacy methods offered next. Note that these methods also emphasize individual effort and personal responsibility.

The Group Reading Activity

The Group Reading Activity (GRA) (Manzo, 1974) combines several elements of the Directed Reading–Thinking Activity (DR-TA) (see Chapter 4) with the values and benefits of cooperative learning. The GRA also fosters more effective speaking, writing, and reading among students of diverse backgrounds. The method focuses on helping youngsters to learn how to critique and be critiqued by one another and to work harmoniously in groups.

Steps in the GRA

1. The teacher identifies a unit of text to be analyzed. Then the teacher poses a larger question or directive to guide reading and problem solving.

Figure 7.3
Guidelines for group work: For teachers and for students.

Guidelines for Teachers

1. Provide specific goals and objectives for each group. It is important for the students to know exactly what they are to do and why they are doing it.
2. Provide written instructions for each group, particularly when tasks for various groups are different. Written instructions should be clear, explicit, and easy to follow step by step.
3. Establish and enforce some commonsense guidelines for student behavior in the group situation (see Guidelines for Students).
4. Establish procedures to evaluate both individual and group work.
5. Time allocation for group tasks is an important factor. Some groups will need more time than others, but teachers should be alert for those who are wasting time.
6. Plan your own time in detail. Decide what groups you will work with; what the other students will be doing; and how much time you will spend with each group. Be active. Circulate, monitor, assist, direct, and evaluate.
7. Use a variety of types of groups. Do not let your groupings become permanent and static.

Guidelines for Students

1. *Conversation:* Conversation must be on the topic. Keep your voice low. Communicate with your own group, but do not disturb other groups.
2. *Stick to the Task:* The work you do with your group is just as important as your individual work. It is important that you learn to stay on the job, to work hard. Group work is not an excuse to goof off! Time is all we have; we must use it well.
3. *Responsibility:* All your life you will have to work with others. You have a responsibility to yourself, but also to others in your group. You should help, not hinder, the progress of your group toward its goal.

Figure 7.3, *continued*

4. *Movement:* Your movement around the classroom must be restricted to movement necessary to get the job done. For example, if you need material, get it quickly and quietly, without disturbing others. On the other hand, do not visit other groups to see what they are doing.

5. *Cooperation:* Working in groups requires you to be independent, mature, and cooperative. Group tasks are designed to help you learn. The teacher will not always be at your shoulder. You must be mature enough to cooperate with others in your group to ensure the orderly progress of the group toward completing the task.

6. *Evaluation:* You will be evaluated not only on the product of your group's efforts but on the process your group uses. In other words, the teacher will constantly check to see if you are on task, cooperative, mature, and responsible. The degree to which you measure up to the guidelines for good group work will be reflected in your grades.

7. *Sharing:* Since the group process is a cooperative one, you must learn to share. You should share materials, ideas, tasks, and responsibility.

8. *Listening:* You must learn to be a good listener. Everyone in the group has something to contribute. Listen carefully and respectfully to others in the group and to the teacher. A good listener is a mature person.

9. *Self-Discipline:* Working in groups demands accepting responsibility for your own behavior. You must learn to accept this responsibility, especially when your teacher is occupied with other students. Your goal, remember, is to become an independent, self-directed learner who makes the best possible use of class time.

10. *Respect:* Any cooperative endeavor is based on respect. You must respect yourself, the other students, and the teacher. This respect is reflected in your quiet, diligent, determined efforts to do your best on every learning task assigned.

Note. From "Small Group Instruction: To Make It Work" by J. Lordon, 1981, *The Clearing House, 54,* pp. 265–266. Reprinted with permission of the Helen Dwight Reid Educational Foundation. Published by Heldref Publications, 4000 Albemarle St., N.W., Washington, DC, 20016. Copyright © 1981.

Example
Let's see if we can learn from our textbooks how plants grow.

Let's see how our textbook described the historical events that have come to be called the Age of Exploration and Discovery.

2. The teacher divides the text into subsections of a few pages each and assigns each selection to a small group.

3. Initially, group members are required to read silently and individually record their findings and thoughts on the larger directive. A worksheet should be provided with guiding questions and statements such as the following:

   a. What question does this section answer?

   b. Write a statement of the main idea(s) of this section. Support it with direct quotes or paraphrased facts and points found in the text.

   c. Comment on the quality of the ideas and supporting statements: Do these seem true? Complete? Biased?

   d. What other things, ideas, and facts have you learned in the past that seem to relate strongly to what you have read?

4. As members of the group become ready—though not before at least fifteen to twenty minutes—they should begin to share their individual thoughts with one another and to create a single group rendition on a separate sheet.

5. As each group becomes ready, a student critic chosen by the teacher from one of the other groups is sent to see and hear the group's collective rendition. The student critic is expected to react with constructive criticism, such as "That sounds fine," "That doesn't seem to make much sense," "Perhaps you should have. . . ."

6. The group is permitted time to rework their rendition, drawing on the feedback provided by the student critic.

7. The teacher consults with each group for a few minutes, helping them resolve remaining conflicts, and then schedules them to present their findings to the class.

8. The class and teacher comment and question during group presentations. The teacher or a designated member of the group lists important findings on the chalkboard.

9. To build a sense of reading with power and fluency, the class is told to rapidly read each section covered with an eye toward verifying details and main points.

Notes on the GRA

Our own anecdotal reports (Manzo & Manzo, 1990a) indicate that students involved in the GRA tend to assume required roles in a surprisingly adult manner. Their language, thinking, and even social grace seem to rise to the occasion. The keenest benefit seems to be that students tend to criticize each other in constructive and intelligent ways, probably to reduce the likelihood of being treated sharply when they are critiqued in turn.

The last method of this chapter also focuses on the value and structure of the DR-TA. This cooperative method provides more scaffolding, especially in the prereading stage.

Cooperative Directed Reading–Thinking Activity

The Cooperative DR-TA achieves most of the benefits of the DR-TA but through a cooperative learning approach (Uttero, 1988). The method promotes active comprehension through prereading connections, guided independent reading, and follow-up (see Figure 7.4). However, it is largely a postreading method after the first phase. Familiar options are described for carrying out each phase.

Phases in Cooperative DR-TA

Phase 1:   Connection.   In this prereading phase, students work cooperatively in small groups to activate and extend their prior knowledge. Sample options include

1. *Brainstorming:* Students generate ideas and questions related to a few key terms provided by the teacher. They do this first in small groups, then as groups to the class.
2. *Semantic mapping:* The ideas generated in response to the words provided by the teacher are arranged into a semantic map. Each group presents their map on the chalkboard or an overhead.

Phase 2:   Guided Independent Reading.   In Phase 2, students work cooperatively as they finish silently reading smaller sections of print. Sample options include

1. *Guiding questions:* Students answer guiding questions, prepared either by the teacher or generated by students from previewing the material and formulating questions in groups.
2. *Outlining:* Students complete partial outlines prepared by the teacher or available from the text publisher.
3. *Paraphrasing:* Each student translates a section of text. Then the groups coordinate the results to produce a new rendition of the entire selection in their own words.

Phase 3:   Follow-up.   Phase 3 involves summarizing, application, and test preparation. Sample options include

1. *Summarization:* Students collectively construct a summary from the original text and/or the paraphrased renditions.
2. *Memory training:* Students apply memory strategies to mastery of the content.
3. *Test making:* Each group constructs a test on the material. Groups can be required to take one another's tests and then discuss differences in their questions, question types, and responses.
4. *Inferring:* More like conjecturing than inferencing, this invaluable critical-thinking activity encourages students to speculate about the thoughts, motives, and personalities of people connected to the information, including the authors.
5. *Semantic remapping:* Students construct a postreading semantic map that reflects new information acquired and corrected misconceptions.

Notes on Cooperative DR-TA
Anecdotal reports of field trials of the Cooperative DR-TA include the important observation that students seem to internalize the value of cooperative learning. Some students progress to the point where they independently "formed study groups which met during recess or after school" (Uttero, 1988, p. 394). This is a very significant outcome, since it suggests that students not only have been engaged momentarily but remain motivated and eager to reengage in and out of school.

Teachers working in content-specific groups have made several recommendations to us regarding differential and combined uses of the GRA and the Cooperative DR-TA. Some of these are summarized in Figure 7.4.

It should be noted that this endorsement of cooperative learning (Figure 7.5) does not mean that there is no value in certain aspects of competition as well. Effective teachers will look for ways to harness the human craving for competition as well as for cooperation.

✦ *Looking Back and Looking Ahead* ✦

This chapter attempted to reaffirm the potential values in postreading recitation. It did so, however, by supporting this traditional practice as only one part of a program that includes other methods and means. These include encouraging discussion, or instructional conversation, and cooperative learning approaches designed to reduce dependence on the teacher and to increase reliance on individual effort and group process. Chapter 9 describes more about using discussion and cooperative learn-

Figure 7.4

Uses of the Group Reading Activity and the Cooperative Directed
Reading–Thinking Activity suggested by content teachers.

1. **English teachers:** When using the GRA, add the Cooperative DR-TA
   step for inferring that encourages speculations about thoughts,
   motives, and intentions of the writer and of characters in narratives.

2. **Science teachers:** Use the Cooperative DR-TA with a heavy accent
   on the semantic mapping option. It offers a solid way to help students
   to overcome misconceptions, or what they *think* they know about
   something.

3. **Speech teachers:** Work with other teachers and their students to
   develop guidelines for students on how speech and comportment
   should differ in various phases of either the GRA or Cooperative
   DR-TA. For example, what guidelines should be followed when
   critiquing others, when contributing to class discussion, or when
   leading a group summarization?

4. **Social Studies teachers:** Put heavy emphasis on the constructive
   critiquing step of the GRA and the inferring step of the Cooperative
   DR-TA, since these closely resemble the critical thinking emphasis
   that is a primary objective of the social studies curriculum.

5. **Physical Education and Health teachers:** Stress that part of the
   third step of the GRA that basically asks, "What have you learned
   here that connects to healthy living?" Also, use the GRA with textual
   material on physical training, and continue step 5 on students'
   critiquing one another on the physical efforts to do something
   suggested by a manual or book.

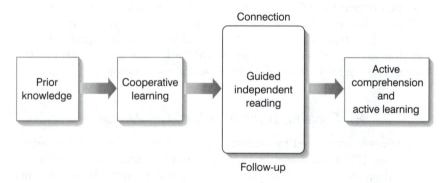

Figure 7.5

Active comprehension through the cooperative learning model.

ing techniques to promote higher-order reading and thinking. However, Chapter 8 attempts to reclaim an important intermediate link. It speaks to helping students to internalize strategies for lifelong vocabulary acquisition. Few schools have vocabulary enrichment as a specific objective, so you will want to be especially attentive to why this ought to be done, as well as how.

✦ ✦ **TRADE SECRET** ✦ ✦

Favoring One Side of the Class in Recitation and Discussion

The brain is very efficient: It forms patterns and habits easily. One such habit of mind is to favor the side of the class that conforms to your handedness. If you're right-handed, you will look at, speak to, and ask more questions of those to your right than you will those to your left. Here are two simple ways to overcome this unrecognized bias.

1. Where desks can be turned easily, make it a point to position yourself at a different side of the classroom periodically, especially when leading recitations and discussions.
2. Write students' names on a set of index cards, shuffle these occasionally, and call on the students whose names come to the top.

Students' hemispheric dominance patterns also sometimes are revealed by where they seat themselves. Those who sit to your left as you face the class are likely to be right-brain dominant. Those to your right are probably left-brain dominant. Those in the center typically will not have a strong preference. The value of permitting students to sit on the side they prefer, versus urging them to exercise their less dominant side, is as yet unresolved.

SECTION III

Higher-Order Literacy in the Disciplines

There is not much point in teaching youngsters to read, and even to acquire knowledge, if there is not an equal effort to teach them to think. *Thinking* in literature and the disciplines means being able to actively evaluate, connect, apply, and even pose and solve problems using discipline-specific print sources and related personal experiences.

The chapters in this section focus on meeting these higher-order literacy demands. Chapter 8 tells how to build language and concept development through vocabulary enrichment. Chapter 9 concentrates on using literary and expository writing, classroom discussion, and global telecomputing to advance analytical and constructive thinking. Chapter 10 is about study habits. It is intended for teachers who agree that students need to be taught how to study, since much failure to learn can be traced back to poor understanding of what study means and/or to lack of training and effort to form these habits of mind.

Of course, all of this has been talked about before, but frankly, we've been a little light on implementation. This is why these objectives may be the great challenge to the current and coming generations of teachers.

The budding democracies, and older ones, are looking forward to seeing how this generation of teachers redefine themselves in the current tele-computing environment so as to turn higher-order reading, writing, thinking, and study into global facts rather than vague ideals.

CHAPTER 8

Vocabulary, Language, and Concept Development Across the Disciplines

The most powerful thing that can be done is to name something.

—Albert Einstein

✦ *Organizing Thoughts* ✦

This chapter explains the need and purpose for vocabulary enrichment in terms of its impact on thinking, reading, and concept development. It explains how a good deal of vocabulary instruction is done in the content areas as a natural function of teaching the discipline but that teachers can greatly magnify outcomes by placing a high priority on vocabulary development and selecting appropriate methods for doing so. The remainder of the chapter details vocabulary teaching methods that can be converted into independent strategies for word learning. These are organized around each stage of the reading process.

THE NEED FOR VOCABULARY INSTRUCTION

The vocabulary level of college-bound 18-year-olds has dropped sharply in recent years. In 1940, these students typically knew the meanings of 80% of the words on a standardized reading test. By the mid-1990s, the typical student scored only 30%, which is just a little better than random guessing (Research Foundation, 1995, cited in *UMKC Insider,* 1996). This picture is even more distressing than it first appears, when full account is taken of its implications for thinking, reading, writing, and learning. Vocabulary size regularly is found to be the single best predictor of a person's (academic) IQ, level of reading comprehension, and grade-point average.

PURPOSE OF VOCABULARY INSTRUCTION

The purpose of vocabulary instruction is not merely to teach more words but to build greater precision in thought, comprehension, and expression. In other words, "The most powerful thing that can be done [to a concept and for a learner] is to name something" (Albert Einstein). The questions, then, become, (1) Where and when should instruction be given? (2) What are the best ways to teach "about things and the words that signify them?" (Kibby, 1995) and, implicitly, (3) Are there weak or ineffective ways to do so?

GUIDING PRINCIPLES FOR VOCABULARY INSTRUCTION IN CONTENT CLASSES

Vocabulary acquisition, like improvement of reading comprehension, is an ongoing, lifelong process. There is an extensive body of research on how we learn words and how to best promote vocabulary development. Figure 8.1 provides an abridged list of principles derived from several reviews of this research.

THE PLACE FOR VOCABULARY INSTRUCTION

The vocabulary methods presented here were selected because they are interactive but also incidental to content and literacy instruction. Accordingly, the methods are organized around their place in the pre- , during,

Figure 8.1
Principles of vocabulary instruction.

1. The difficulty of the vocabulary in text affects students' ability to comprehend. Preteaching selected vocabulary terms greatly improves comprehension.

2. Students develop a lifelong interest in learning new words primarily through interaction with teachers who are intrigued with words and are themselves students of language.

3. Effective vocabulary instruction demonstrates strategies for learning word meanings, rather than requiring rote memorization of definitions.

4. Vocabulary is best taught at a teachable moment; that is, when need arises. However, it also must be taught regularly and systematically for significant growth to occur.

5. It is necessary to develop a rich community of language within the school to encourage continued vocabulary reinforcement and use outside the classroom.

6. Vocabulary instruction is best anchored in relevant experiences and associations.

7. The study of morphemes—prefixes, suffixes, and roots—has a positive effect on learning the many words in our language with Greek and Latin roots.

8. Effective vocabulary instruction includes integration, repetition, and meaningful use of new words.

Note. Based on Bauman and Kameenui (1991), Kibby (1995), Manzo and Manzo (1990a), Manzo and Sherk (1971–1972), Nagy (1988), and S. A. Stahl and Fairbanks (1986).

and postreading phases of content area literacy instruction. Most of these methods, however, are suitable for a variety of other uses, including concentrated vocabulary instruction.

PREREADING METHODS FOR VOCABULARY INSTRUCTION

Preteaching the meanings of difficult words in a reading selection is a traditional part of the prereading phase of content and reading instruction. The interactive methods presented here, however, are quite different from most traditional approaches to vocabulary instruction. Instead of giving students a list of words to look up and memorize, these methods are designed to demonstrate a variety of strategies for associating new word meanings with existing knowledge and experience. These interactive methods tend to permit the teacher to model strategies for learning new word meanings and to establish a low-risk environment in which students can experiment with these strategies for word learning.

Note. From *The Study Readers—Fifth Year* (p. 85), by A. Walker and M. R. Parkman, 1924, Upper Saddle River, NJ: Merrill/Prentice Hall. Copyright 1924 by Merrill/Prentice Hall. Reprinted by permission.

Typical to Technical Meaning Approach

Common words often have special technical applications in a particular content area. For example, the word *true* is used in mechanics to indicate that gears are well synchronized; hence, *not true* means poorly synchronized. In the Typical to Technical Meaning Approach (Welker, 1987), the teacher prepares a worksheet exercise that provides practice in using a term in both its typical and technical meanings. While these practice sheets require considerable preparation time, once students have become familiar with the format, the teacher simply can ask, "Do we have any terms in today's material for which there is a common as well as a technical meaning?" and the rest of the lesson will unfold from previous practice.

Steps in the Typical to Technical Meaning Approach

1. Discuss a term's common meanings, then introduce its technical meaning.
2. Have students complete a word-to-meaning exercise, matching each term with both its common and technical meaning (see Part 1 in Figure 8.2). Then have students complete a cloze-type exercise, filling in the blanks where the terms are used in either the typical or technical sense (see Part 2 in Figure 8.2).
3. Briefly discuss students' responses before presenting information based on technical uses of the terms.

The next method has long been popular for concentrated vocabulary study. It is shown here for use on those occasions when key subject area vocabulary terms are composed of familiar prefixes, suffixes, and/or roots.

Incidental Morpheme Method

Eighty percent of the words in the English dictionary contain Greek or Latin prefixes, suffixes, or roots. These word parts, called *morphemes*, are units of language that cannot be further divided without losing meaning. Some morphemes have meanings only when attached to other word parts. Examples of such bound morphemes include *ed, ing, tele,* and *cide.* Other morphemes, such as *cover, graph,* and *stand,* called free morphemes, can stand alone, that is, are words in themselves.

Most expert readers and language users use morphemes to make sense out of and remember new words. The Incidental Morpheme method (Manzo & Manzo, 1990a) teaches students to apply existing knowledge of morphemes to new words encountered in content reading. It is important to note that this method does not seem to work as well with students of below-average intelligence.

Figure 8.2

Typical to technical meaning exercises.

Part 1

Directions: For each term below, write the letter of its common meaning and its technical meaning under the headings given.

Terms	Common Meaning	Technical Meaning
acute	_____	_____
supplementary	_____	_____
complementary	_____	_____
angle	_____	_____

Meanings

A. A person's point of view
B. Making whole, or completing something
C. Something additional to the basic requirements
D. Space between two lines or surfaces that meet
E. Having a sharp point
F. Either of two angles that combine to equal 90 degrees
G. An angle that is less than 90 degrees in value
H. Either of two angles that together form exactly 180 degrees

Part 2

Directions: Select the best word from the word bank to complete each sentence below. Each word will be used twice.

Sentences

1. The sword had a very _____ cutting edge.

2. The _____ angle for a 50-degree angle is a 40-degree angle.

3. Our reading textbook comes with _____ materials such as workbooks and ditto sheets.

4. If an angle is 53 degrees, it is called an _____ angle.

5. A black tie with a white shirt would be considered a _____ match.

6. Now that I have my thoughts on the subject, what is your _____ (or opinion) on the matter?

7. A pie can be sliced into pieces with many different _____ .

8. Two angles that together equal 180 degrees are _____ angles.

Word Bank

complementary   acute   angle   supplementary

Steps in the Incidental Morpheme Method
As preparation for using the Incidental Morpheme method, watch for
words in reading assignments that probably are unfamiliar to students
but contain familiar word parts, or morphemes. Use the following steps
to *preteach* these terms.

1. Write the term on the chalkboard or overhead, and underline meaningful word parts, or morphemic elements, that might help students
   understand the word's concept base.

   Example: *seis*   mo   *graph*

2. Ask students if they can use the underlined parts to grasp the word
   meaning, and why. If the word meaning is predicted correctly, write
   the meaning under the word and *proceed with steps 3 and 4 as
   reinforcement.*

3. Tell students you will give them additional clues for predicting (or
   remembering) the word meaning. Beneath the underlined word
   parts, write "level-1 clues," which are other, easier words using those
   morphemes. If students have not yet correctly predicted the word
   meaning, continue to ask for predictions.

Example:	seis	mo	graph
Level-1 clues:	seizure	telegraph	
			graphic

4. Beneath the level-1 clues, write "level-2 clues," which are word part
   meanings, and continue to ask for predictions until the correct definition is reached and written below the clues.

Example:	*seis*	mo	*graph*
Level-1 clues:	seizure		telegraph
			graphic
Level-2 clues:	to shake	written	
Meaning:	An instrument that records the direction, time, and intensity of earthquakes		

See Figure 8.3 for a sample listing of common Latin roots. Many dictionaries provide lists of Latin and Greek prefixes, suffixes, and roots.

   The next method illustrates a way to introduce key vocabulary terms
more quickly, while showing students one of the most effective natural
strategies for learning and remembering new words. Unlike the two
approaches just illustrated, this method is based on connecting word
meanings with the *affective*, or feeling, emotional, and attitudinal, dimension of personal experience.

Figure 8.3
Common Latin roots.

Root Meaning	Derivatives	
-aud-, -audit-	hear	auditorium
-avi-	bird	aviation
-caput-	head	capital
-ced-, -cess-	move, yield	recede
-clar-	clear	clarify
-clin-	lean	incline
-clud-, -claud-, -clus-	shut	seclude
-cord-	heart	cordial
-corp-	body	corporal
-cred-	to believe	credible
-curr-, -curs-	run	current
-dic-, -dict-	say	predict
-domin-	master	dominate
-duc-, -duct-	lead	conduct
-fac-, -fic-, -fact-, -fect-	to make, do	factory
-fer-	bear, carry	transfer
-fin-	end	finish
-fort-	strong	fortitude
-jun-, -junct-	join	junction
-laud-, -laudat-	praise	applause
-let-, -lect-	gather, choose, read	collect
-legis-, -lex-	law	legislate
-lux-, -luc-	light	elucidate
-magn-	great	magnificent

Subjective Approach to Vocabulary

The Subjective Approach to Vocabulary (SAV) (Manzo, 1983) builds on what students already know by urging them to find personal experiences or other associations with which to anchor the sometimes ethereal definitions of new terms found in dictionaries. The method helps students remember meanings of important content-related terms while illustrating how they might use the same strategy in self-directed word learning. In SAV, the teacher engages students in a highly interactive talk-through designed to teach students how to use their own and other students' experiences and tellings as a foundation for acquiring new word meanings. In this way, the biographies of individual lives become connected to the stories of the words and ideas offered in school. SAV can be particularly useful for providing multicultural outlooks and for working with second-language students. It gives teachers and students access to the alternative ways students may be processing and interpreting the world around them.

Figure 8.3, *continued*

Root	Meaning		Derivatives
-mal-	bad		malevolent
-man-	hand		manual
-mit-, -miss-	send		missile
-mov-, -mot-	set in motion		motor
-nov-, -novus-	new		renovation
-pac-	peace		pacific
-pel-, -puls-	urge, drive		propel
-pend-, -pens-	hang, weigh		pensive
-plic-, -plex-	bend, fold		plexiglas
-pon-, -pos-	place, put		postpone
-sci-	know		science
-scrib-, -script-	write		describe
-solv-, -solut-	loosen		solution
-spec-, -spect-	look		spectator
-sta-	stand firm		stable
-stru-, -struct-	build		construct
-tend-, -tens-	stretch		tendency
-tort-	to twist		distort
-ven-, -vent-	come		convention
-ver-	true		veritable
-vert-, -vers-	turn		reverse
-viv-, -vit-	live, life		vitality
-vid-, -vis-	see		evident
-voc-	call		vocation

Steps and Options in SAV

1. The teacher identifies two to four words to be pretaught before reading.

2. The teacher explains the contextual meaning of a word up front, then writes it on the chalkboard with an example or two, much as one would find in a dictionary. In this way, the teacher establishes the objective, or dictionary, meaning of the word.

3. The teacher asks the students, "What does this word remind you of?" The class briefly discusses and clarifies these experiences, thoughts, or images.

4. The teacher directs students to record the word, the objective meaning given, and some subjective association, either students' own or one offered by another class member that they find particularly vivid.

5. The teacher asks, "Now that you have a dictionary definition and a first reaction or association, what new associations or meanings do you have for this term?"

6. The class reads the selection to build further contextual meaning of key words. Also, the teacher asks students whether they encountered other words of which they were unsure. The class lists and discusses such words as the need arises using the same basic approach.

To add an element of concentrated vocabulary enrichment to SAV, students can keep a glossary of objective, subjective, and new meanings for words covered in this way. Students should start their glossaries in the backs of their content class notebooks and work forward so as not to interfere with other class notes and to keep terms separate and easily available for study and reference. Figure 8.4 presents an example from a SAV lesson.

Notes on SAV

It is hard to tell how readily a class will take to a SAV lesson on its initial presentation. Group size may be an important factor. For example, U. C. Manzo once used SAV with a tenth-grade English class of only nine students. When asked for associations with five words (*adipose, adage, accrual, agape, alimentary*), the students stared blankly. The very next

Figure 8.4
Subjective Approach to Vocabulary: Sample lesson.

> The word was *arboreal.* It was in a seventh-grade science text. The teacher gave the meaning: "The word *arboreal* means 'having to do with trees or living in trees.'" A few examples were given: "Monkeys are arboreal animals." "The word *arboreal* comes from the word *arbor,* as in Arbor Day, the day put aside to plant trees." The subjective-based aspect of the lesson began at this point. Explaining her question, the teacher added, "It will be easier for you to learn and remember this new term if you can think of some personal images or experiences that you can picture with it."
>
> One student suggested, "The word reminds me of how my mother killed my peanut tree that we brought home from Georgia by overwatering it." To this, another student added, humorously, "That sounds like a tragic arboreal experience." In that same humorous vein, another student asked, rhetorically, "Did you say that *arboreal* means 'living and swinging in trees'? Because I think my little brother is arboreal!"
>
> The teacher then asked if anyone had formed a new meaning for *arboreal.* "It sounds to me like 'anything to do with trees,'" one student volunteered. The teacher then directed the class to record the word *arboreal* in their notebooks with the objective meaning she had provided and a parenthetical note on their initial and subsequent personal associations with the word.

hour, with a little trepidation, Manzo used the same five words with another tenth-grade class of 15 students and was off and running. Soon they were composing as well as associating: "I picture Royal Stadium [home of the Kansas City Royals] when we were down but not out and came back to win the pennant and the Series; it's not over 'til the 'adipose' lady sings." A large group sometimes may be necessary to increase the chance of at least one extrovert stirring the class's imagination and responding.

In a study with sixth-grade subjects (Casale & Manzo, 1983), SAV was found to be considerably better than traditional (dictionary look-up and sentence-writing) approaches to vocabulary instruction. However, it was slightly less effective than the approach described next, Motor Imaging, which urges teacher and students to employ physical, or motor, associations to a greater extent than is usual in the sedentary context of schooling.

Motor Imaging

Motor Imaging (Casale [now Manzo], 1985) draws on the physical-sensory as well as cognitive and affective domains of learning. The underlying principle of this method is akin to the expression "Nothing is in the intellect which was not first in the senses."

Developmental psychologists have observed that infants first respond to a stimulus with gross motor movements that signify (i.e., stand for) that stimulus. Over time, the motor movements become increasingly refined until the motor meaning is internalized as a symbolic meaning, as Jean Piaget refers to it. Apparently, our initial ways of learning consist almost exclusively of tactile and sensorimotor experiences. While this is no great surprise, since that is all babies can do, we seem to have overlooked the fact that this aspect of learning may remain active long into human development.

Steps in Motor Imaging

1. The teacher takes a difficult word from the text, writes it on the chalkboard, pronounces it, and tells what it means.
2. The teacher asks students to imagine a simple gesture or pantomime for the word meaning ("How could you 'show' someone what this word means?").
3. When the teacher gives a signal, students do their gestures or pantomimes simultaneously.
4. The teacher selects the most common expression observed. The teacher then demonstrates it to all the students, who then say the word and make the corresponding movement.

5. The teacher repeats each new word, directing the class to do the gesture and simultaneously recite a brief meaning or synonym.
6. The students' next encounter with the word is in the assigned reading material.

Figure 8.5 presents some examples from a Motor Imaging lesson.

Notes on Motor Imaging
The same comparison study cited earlier, of a cognitive (dictionary), affective (subjective association), and physical-sensory, motor approach to vocabulary, showed the Motor Imaging method to be significantly better on four of five vocabulary measures (Casale & Manzo, 1983). It appears that the highest forms of learning have a most humble, if not primitive, foundation.

The promising implication of this point is that students at every level of intellectual ability seem to share a common capacity for physical-associative learning. This makes Motor Imaging, and possibly other motor-based methods yet to be devised, especially promising possibilities for heterogeneously grouped students.

Figure 8.5
Motor imaging examples.

New Word	Language Meaning	Motor Meaning
Appropriate	Right or fit for a certain purpose	Both palms together, matching perfectly
Convey	Take or carry from one place to another	Both hands together, palms upward, moving from one side to the other
Woe	Great sadness or trouble	One or both hands over the eyes, head tilted forward
Dazzle	Shine or reflect brightly	Palms close together, facing outward, fingers spread
Utmost	The very highest or most	One or both hands reaching up as far as possible
Abode	Place where you live	Hands meeting above the head in a triangular roof shape

METHODS FOR VOCABULARY DEVELOPMENT DURING READING

Prereading vocabulary methods can focus on only a very limited number of words and therefore tend to be limited to a few key concept terms. However, there also are methods that permit the teacher to provide assistance with more general vocabulary needs during this silent incursion into print.

Cooperative Glossaries

A glossary is a handy dictionary of terms used in a given book or field. Definitions are context specific and therefore more concrete. Readers especially appreciate these when wading into a new field. If there is no glossary in the class text, or the particular book or novel being read, there is a relatively easy and instructive way to create one cooperatively.

Steps in Constructing a Cooperative Glossary

1. The teacher constructs a simple glossary to a few pages of a longer selection or book.
2. Students are urged to use the Cooperative Glossary as they read.
3. Students are urged to read a few pages beyond those covered by the guide.
4. Discussion develops about how the guide helped and which additional words and/or phrases might need definition.
5. Each student is assigned to prepare a glossary for a few pages of the remainder of the text. Students should be told to note the page number for each word they select and to record *only* the dictionary definition that applies to the way the word is used in the selection.
6. Glossaries are compiled and reproduced for the entire class.
7. (Optional) The teacher adds a pronunciation guide. This step is optional because it is difficult to do; however, most students like— and need—one.

Figure 8.6 presents an example of a Cooperative Glossary.

Contextual Redefinition Strategy

Typically, new words are encountered in the following sequence: context, isolation, context (Putnam, Bader, & Bean, 1988). What this means is that when readers encounter a word they don't know, they try to figure out its meaning from the context, and then, if unsuccessful, seek meaning from another source, such as a dictionary or another person. Finally,

Figure 8.6
Cooperative glossary for *A Tale of Two Cities.*

Page	Chapter	Word	Definition	Pronunciation
67	3	Inscrutable	Cannot be understood	in-screw-ta-ble
68		Lamentation	Cry out	la-men-ta-shun
70		Opiate	A drug to help a person sleep	o-pee-ut
71		Perpetuation	Continuing	per-pet-chu-a-shun
72		Specter	Ghost	speck-tur
81	4	Consignment	Delivery	cun-sine-ment
83		Disconcerted	Confused	dis-cun-sir-ted
84		Oblivion	Complete forgetfulness	o-bli-vee-un
85		Sonorous	Loud praise	sah-nore-us
87		Supplicatory	Begging	suh-pli-cu-tory

they return to the original context to make better sense of both the word and the context. The Contextual Redefinition method (J. W. Cunningham, Cunningham, & Arthur, 1981) applies this natural process to a simple format for classroom instruction (Tierney, Readence, & Dishner, 1990).

Steps in Contextual Redefinition
To prepare for using the contextual redefinition method, the teacher first selects target words from the reading selection. Then, for each word, the teacher writes one or more sentences that provide reasonable clues to the word meaning. The sentences may come from the selection itself, if these provide reasonable clues.

1. Write each target word on the chalkboard or overhead, and ask students to guess the word meaning. Students should be encouraged to discuss their ideas and try to come to a reasonable consensus on their predicted meaning for each word.

2. Present each target word in the context sentence(s) you have prepared. Have students revise their predictions for each word meaning, again encouraging them to provide the reasons for their ideas, and building on one another's thoughts to come to a consensus.

3. Ask a volunteer to look up the word in the dictionary and to compare the dictionary definition with their predictions. This step can stir a very productive instructional conversation, since dictionary defini-

tions can sometimes be too abstract for easy interpretation, or the word could have been used in some unusual or ironic way.

Notes on Contextual Redefinition
The Contextual Redefinition method teaches youngsters that context can provide clues to word meaning (Gipe, 1978–1979) but cannot securely reveal word meanings. Teaching students to overrely on context clues is one of the great errors that tends to be made in vocabulary strategy instruction.

METHODS FOR TEACHING
VOCABULARY AFTER READING

Once comprehension is locked up tight, two other aspects of postreading can be, but seldom are, pursued: further concept development and vocabulary enrichment. This section presents some popular activities for enhancing both.

Subject Area Vocabulary Reinforcement

Learning is a process of placing new information into existing categories until a special feature that does not fit is encountered. Then a new category must be created to expand schema. Semantic feature analysis (D. D. Johnson & Pearson, 1984) is a method designed to permit students to engage in this process in a conscious and focused way. A variation on this method, called subject area vocabulary reinforcement (SAVOR) (Stieglitz & Stieglitz, 1981), is designed specifically for content area use.

Steps in SAVOR
1. Identify a category of words. Then have students brainstorm words that fit in this category, and list these examples in a column on their own paper.
2. Have students brainstorm specific features of the words they have listed. These features are listed as column headings across the top of their paper (see Figure 8.7 for an example of how the chart is constructed).
3. Next, have students fill in the charts individually, using plus (+) or minus (–) signs to indicate whether each word has a particular feature.
4. After students have completed their charts, the teacher encourages discussion about the patterns of pluses and minuses and to discover the uniqueness of each word.

As students gain more experience with the semantic feature analysis format, the teacher may wish to switch from a plus/minus system to a

Figure 8.7
SAVOR in mathematics.

Shapes	Four Sided	All Curved or Rounded Lines	Line Segment	Sides Equal in Length	Right Angles
Triangle	−	−	+	+	+
Rectangle	+	−	+	−	+
Parallelogram	+	−	+	+	+
Circle	+	−	−	−	−
Trapezoid	+	−	+	−	−
Semicircle	−	+	+	−	−
Square	+	−	+	+	+

numerical system (0 = none, 1 = some, 2 = much, 3 = all). The method is viewed as a culminating activity for reinforcing and expanding concepts introduced in the conventional content area lesson or following reading. It is particularly suitable for clarifying frequently confused terms. Figure 8.7 is an example of its use in mathematics.

Notes on SAVOR
Semantic Feature Analysis has been found to be significantly more effective than traditional methods for this purpose (D. D. Johnson, Toms-Bronowski, & Pittelman, 1982). It also has been shown to effectively improve content area reading vocabulary and comprehension in adolescents with learning disabilities (Anders, Bos, & Filip, 1984).

Vocabulary Self-Collection

The Vocabulary Self-Collection method (Haggard-Ruddell, 1982) requires that each student and the teacher search their television viewing, reading, and home environments weekly and bring to class two content-related words for the entire class to learn. Students are told to write their words on the chalkboard when they enter the classroom. The list is narrowed by eliminating duplications and words that most students know. The student who submitted each remaining word defines that word, and discussion ensues to clarify and extend meanings. During this process, students record words in a vocabulary journal along with definitions. Ideally, word manipulation exercises for embedding meanings are employed at this point. Students can develop these exercises for one another, using examples found in conventional vocabulary workbooks.

The next method is a logical link to this method. It provides a cooperative and competitive climate for further finding and using new words.

Cultural-Academic Trivia

The Cultural-Academic Trivia (CAT) game (Manzo, 1970, 1985) refers to common cultural learnings and associations that are found in our language as frequently used metaphors and allusions to explain feelings, facts, and concepts. In initial field tests of this method, students felt it was quite appropriate that the word *trivia* appeared in the title. In time, however, as their connections and fund of academic information, vocabulary, and allusions grew, they concluded that it is minds that can be trivial, not information. This prompted the idea that the game should be called "cultural-academic treasures."

Steps in CAT

1.   The class is divided into two groups. A chairperson is assigned to each group and given a set of index cards initially prepared by the teacher. On the front of each card is a word or phrase with a number from 1 to 3 designating its relative difficulty. On the reverse side is an explanation or definition of the word or phrase.

2.   The chairperson of one group chooses and writes a word or phrase on the chalkboard and then asks students in the other group if they know that word or phrase. All the information gained from the members of a group constitutes that group's total response. If that information amounts to merely an identification or recognition of the word or phrase, only the number describing the level of difficulty (from 1 to 3) is awarded to the group. If any worthwhile elaboration, as determined by the teacher, also is contributed, the score is doubled. Conversely, if the students on one team cannot respond successfully, the opposing team is given the opportunity to win points.

Example

In a high school class, the word utopia might be assigned a difficulty level of 2. If one team volunteers that the word means "a perfect political and social system," they gain the two basic points. If team members add that utopia is also the title of a book by Sir Thomas More, or that its origins are Greek, they receive two additional points.

3.   After the first round of the game, the teacher asks students to submit terms they have selected from their reading, viewing, and living environments.

Notes on CAT

Students' contributions are essential if students are to be resensitized to the language they encounter about them but tend to block out because the unfamiliar can cause undue dissonance. In the particular setting in which this game was first played, A. V. Manzo treated the cards as admission tickets to class. Students who arrived without one were sent scurrying to the library to find an appropriate term. Today, we urge students to browse the InterNet for new and poignant terms.

Of course, not all words are created equal. The success of this game hinges on the terms used. Well-selected words, and phrases, should key students to central, or schema-enhancing, academic ideas and allusions (e.g., *hieroglyphics, communist manifesto, citizen's arrest, Chaucer*). If the teacher intends to develop students' sophistication in just one area, the name of the game can be altered accordingly, for example, BAT (biological-academic trivia/treasures) or HAT (historical-academic trivia/treasures).

Themed Vocabulary, Webbing, and Semantic Clustering

One of the most rational means of vocabulary enrichment is based on grouping words by themes. Themed vocabulary study, also called webbing and semantic clustering (Marzano & Marzano, 1988), permits students to take well-known, partially known, and barely recognized words and link them together into a semantic web that will catch and hold yet newer words as well as *nuances* of meaning and connotation for familiar words. Paradoxically, it helps students understand that words do not always have precise, distinct, and unchanging meanings (Anderson & Nagy, 1989). Most importantly, themed vocabulary study imparts an effective strategy for lifelong word learning.

Steps in Themed Vocabulary Study

1. Identify a theme. See *talk* in Figure 8.8. The inner cluster reflects words that might be known by a second grader; the outward clusters, words that are known by most sixth graders; and the outer clusters, words that should be known by college students.

2. Ask students to state words they think are related to the theme.

3. If necessary, use dictionaries to check word meanings and to find additional synonyms, antonyms, and subtly different meanings.

4. Link the relevant words to one another (with brief definitions) in the form of a semantic map or web as shown.

5. Reinforce and evaluate by testing students' recall of word meanings and distinctions by having them write sentences or descriptive pieces designed to elicit the new words.

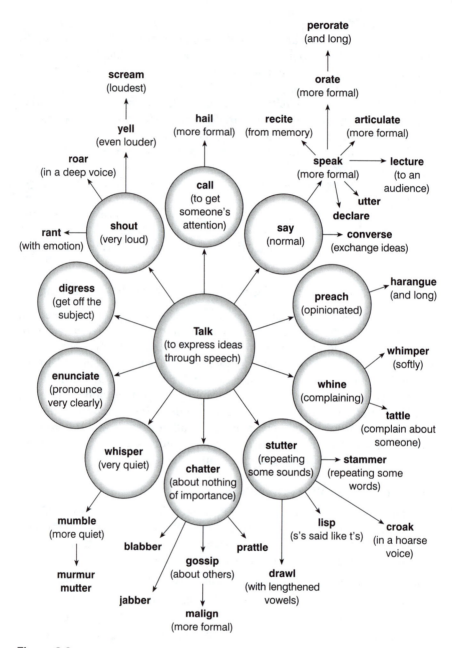

Figure 8.8

Themed vocabulary study: Semantic cluster web for *talk*.

Note. Figure from *Teaching Children to be Literate: A Reflective Approach* by Anthony V. Manzo and Ula Casale Manzo, copyright © 1994 by Holt, Rinehart and Winston, Inc., reproduced by permission of the publisher.

Notes on Themed Vocabulary Study

Themes for vocabulary study can be selected based on the guiding concept of instructional units. The possibilities are as broad as one's imagination. Here are some themes to consider for general word study that we have found to be of particular interest to middle and senior high school students:

+ Uncomplimentary but nonvulgar terms (*pesky, brusque, prissy, scattered, antsy, bawdy, addlebrained*)

+ Behavior-related terms (*manners, antsy, comportment, deportment, inappropriate, maladaptive, poised, irascible*)

+ Character traits (*endurance, restraint, perseverance, reflection, tolerance*)

+ Thinking terms (*abstract, concrete, rational, irrational, creative, critical, cognitive, diffusive, constructive, coherent*)

+ Temperament labels (*sanguine, industrious, hyper, choleric, mercurial, pensive*)

+ Attitudes (*positive, negative, hostile, aggressive, assertive, constructive*)

The impact of themed vocabulary study can be greatly amplified by combining it with other vocabulary methods previously described. It also can be linked to the next method as an incidental means of building word power.

The Keyword Vocabulary Method

The Keyword Vocabulary method is based on an ancient memory improvement technique that dates back to the time when unschooled messengers had to recall long and explicit details. It links relatively unfamiliar things to familiar things that are similar in some way and then combines the two in some thematic way into an odd and therefore memorable mental image.

Using Keyword Vocabulary

To use Keyword Vocabulary, the teacher reminds students of the meaning of a new term that has been studied and then asks them to come up with a visual image that will help them to remember the word meaning. To teach the meaning of the word *plateau*, for example, the word could be linked with the image of a huge upside-down dinner plate forming a grassy flatland; the meaning of the word *collage* could be linked to an image of a word spelled with the letters overlapping; or, to recall the meaning for *amicable*, it could be pictured as *ami* walking hand-in-hand with *cable*.

Notes on Keyword Vocabulary

The Keyword Vocabulary method has been reported to be effective in learning content material (Konopak & Williams, 1988; Levin, Morrison, McGivern, Mastropieri, & Scruggs, 1986) and with students with learning disabilities (Condus, Marshall, & Miller, 1986; Guthrie, 1984). Those who have studied Keyword the most extensively maintain that it helps students learn how to form connections and to develop elaborations on concepts (Pressley, Johnson, & Suymons, 1987; Pressley, Levin, & MacDaniel, 1987; Pressley, Levin, & Miller, 1981).

Keyword seems to create an interesting instructional conversation in which the teacher and students come to the word workbench together in an attempt to capture and represent word meanings in some memorable ways. It also tends to incidentally reveal students' thought processes, thus making it a useful diagnostic teaching tool.

The final method of this chapter offers a means to build on the most common way in which language is used and learned, through authentic life experiences. It offers a simple means by which to transform the school culture into one of a community of able language users.

Community of Language Approach

One of the easiest and most effective things that can be done to improve reading, word learnings, and oral written language is to elevate the vocabulary used in a class, subject, or, ideally, school. We know of at least one situation in which all of the teachers in a junior high school adopted a list of thirty very difficult words from a test preparation manual. Rather than teaching these words explicitly or assigning them to students, each teacher made a conscious daily effort to use the words whenever and wherever possible. Teachers watched for opportunities to use the words in appropriate contexts and sometimes even created contexts as an excuse to use the words. Throughout the spring semester, students heard these thirty words in math class, science lab, shop, art, gym, and even on morning announcements. In only a few weeks' time, students could be heard using the words in casual conversations in the hallways and cafeteria. The teachers effectively had created an elevated community of language (Manzo & Manzo, 1990a).

The impact of a simple incidental learning plan like this one cannot be exaggerated. It builds student respect for teachers as models of language, reinforces reading vocabulary, raises word consciousness and precision in thinking, and boosts standardized test scores. This seemingly incidental approach can have an even more important and far-reaching effect: Students will take their new oral language home and, in turn, incidentally share it with their family and friends. This can elevate the levels of language and precision in thinking in students' families and in the community at large, thereby reaching children who have not yet started school and among parents who have long since left it.

✦ *Looking Back and Looking Ahead* ✦

This chapter detailed how to build better thinking by teaching students a variety of strategies for continuing to do so, one word and concept at a time. The next chapter tells how to create active, expressive ways to use new words and concepts in writing to further build critical/constructive thinking in the disciplines.

✦ ✦ TRADE SECRET ✦ ✦

Teachers as Second-Language Users

Although we do not always realize it, as content teachers we tend to form ourselves into ethnocultural groups. We speak our own language, have our own cultural referents, and share similar goals and a certain kinship. For students, going to English and math classes can be like going to "Englishland" and "Mathland." Throughout a typical day, students embark on a world trip with bewildering changes in language, culture, and orientation, and all at the sound of a bell. We should keep this in mind and try to be more thoughtful and accommodating hosts when our "American-speaking" guests arrive.

One way to be a good host is to physically walk up close to your "guests" as they enter your "land" and greet them. Another is to ask questions outside the strict course of study, such as "What do you find most curious or different about this subject from the way you typically think and do things?" or "What would you most like to know about or be able to explore in this subject?" or "Are there some words that you would like me to define for you?" They will probably want to know what the choices are, which will offer an excellent opportunity to give enlightened overviews of your field and its ways of labeling things. Remember, much of a culture's orientation and way of thinking is revealed in what it cares enough about to distinctively and variably label.

CHAPTER 9

Writing, Reading, Thinking, and Telecomputing Across the Curriculum and the Globe

When teachers and students are connected, they create a community of learners in which everyone, including the teacher, learns.

—Donna Ogle (1989, p. 278)

✦ *Organizing Thoughts* ✦

This chapter is about "rousing minds to life" (Tharp & Gallimore, 1989), or critical/creative writing, reading, and thinking. Ideally, these are not separate subjects or efforts but are themes that need to be reflected throughout the curriculum. Nonetheless, there are certain specific actions that contribute greatly to this objective. This chapter focuses on integrated or interdisciplinary study; dialogical, or debate-type, discussion; and writing in response to text. Recently, electronic means of print communication such as CD-ROM and InterNet resources are offering some new and exciting means of stimulating critical/constructive reading, writing, and thinking. The InterNet is doing this largely through interactive global systems that are cross-age, cross-cultural, and cross-disciplinary. However, the potential in these new interconnected communities still rests largely on effective reading and training in the writing process, since writing still is the medium of choice and one of the best means known for promoting active learning.

RATIONALE FOR TEACHING WRITING IN CONTENT AREAS

Writing is never easy to teach or to learn. It is a habit of mind and often hard work. The prolific writer and economist John Kenneth Galbraith has said it most sincerely, "[T]here are days when the result is so bad that no fewer than five revisions are required. In contrast, when I'm greatly inspired, only four revisions are needed" (interview, CNBC, May 1996).

Writing serves at least two practical purposes in improving higher-level reading, thinking, and content mastery. Each effort to write following reading requires considerable reconstruction of text and thereby increases sensitivity to the text's content, logic, and organization. Further, each effort to write in reaction to or evaluation of text constitutes a plunge into the unknown and therefore is an exercise in using language and thought to discover and organize the "inchoate lump of meanings" (Henry, 1974) we are left with following typical passive reading. Simply put, a routine requirement to write something—almost anything—following reading ignites more active thinking before, during, and following reading. Before you read about some fundamental ways to teach writing and thinking across the curriculum, you might be interested in being brought up to speed on some underlying issues.

REFLECTIONS ON WRITING

Writing: Values and Limitations

In general, good writing tends to dignify the human experience. To teach youngsters to write is to provide them with the tools necessary for defining and describing their lives and circumstances for others to understand and consider. It isn't always apparent, but there is an ongoing competition for public empathy and support for one's personal and cultural perspectives. For this reason it is especially important to teach those least likely to write—the economically and socially disenfranchised—the how and the why for doing so.

There are many ways and no one way to teach writing. Any reasonable approach that draws attention to words, phrasing, and punctuation will result in some improvement, but no single method is likely to impart all the nuances of this complex craft. The writer's personal commitment, inclination to practice and revise, and intellectual development are just a few of the many factors involved in growth in this aspect of language mastery. Writing is a most difficult craft to teach because it entails a profound paradox: It is not simply a matter of clearly and cleverly saying what one thinks but more a way to discover what one is thinking and might better think. Nonetheless, some rebalancing of real versus imagined benefits of writing needs to be addressed.

In recent years, the writing process has been raised to an almost mystical level of power and importance. If it were equal to that inflated billing, you would expect most all who write well also to be our greatest thinkers. A perusal of history and literature suggests otherwise: Jesus Christ never wrote a word, but his message of "love thy neighbor" is the centerpiece of civilized life; on the other hand, Adolph Hitler wrote an entire book that is the antithesis of civilized life. There also have been many great writers, such as Shelley, Keats, and Coleridge, who wrote narratives and poetry of dazzling beauty but whose messages and personal lives reflected an overly romanticized, if not spoiled and self-indulgent, view of life. So then, writing needs to be combined with other elements of the curriculum and with a proper perspective so as to influence not merely how youngsters write but, to a degree, what they write in response to what they read and experience.

READER-RESPONSE THEORIES

For some educators, the primary purpose of reading in school is to achieve cultural and historical *transmission* (Hirsch, 1987), or the transferring of knowledge from those who have it to those who would then be sufficiently informed to do likewise. For others, response to text largely should be a *transaction* (Harste, 1994; Rosenblatt, 1938), or a personal construction of meaning that is highly subjective and unguided by the teacher or some other higher authority. For a growing number, however, response to text should be both, and more: The response to text should be transformation as well as information acquisition. Students therefore will be more willing to reformulate as well as formulate ideas through what have been called reflective turnabouts (Santa, Dailey, & Nelson, 1985), or changes, in personal view that may follow from receiving sound arguments and evidence contrary to their initial views (Manzo, Garber, Manzo, & Kahn, 1994; Manzo & Manzo, 1995).

A recent comparison study of the effects of each of these three methods on measures of complexity of thinking and socioemotional adjustment showed that *transmission-type* teaching was the least effective, *transactive* was next best, and *transformative* teaching was by far the most effective (Garber, 1995). For a clearer picture of the distinctions between these three perspectives in terms of the perceived role of the text, the reader, and the teacher, see Figure 9.1.

In simpler terms, the key element in transformative theory is a commitment to providing youngsters with some of the basic values that are part of democratic life, without preaching a religious creed or serving up unnecessarily biased views of life's options. The alternative that has been tried and found wanting in schools is nicely expressed in the poem "Points to Ponder":

> *What! No star, and you are going out to sea?*
> *Marching, and you have no music?*
> *Traveling, and you have no book?*
> *What! No love, and you are going out to live?*

> —Translated from the French (author unknown)

There are several versions of the transactional perspective. Some tend toward a highly subjective interpretation of what is read. Other transactional views, including the original formulation of this view expressed by Louise Rosenblatt (1938), contain elements that bring it much closer to the view that is referred to here as the *transformative perspective*.

Critical Literacy

There is a new global trend called *critical literacy*, or teaching for critical-creative reading, writing, and thinking, that is relevant here as well. This movement, which dates back to John Dewey, has been spurred on lately by the Brazilian educator Paulo Freires (1985, 1987) and his colleague Ira Shor (1987), who openly take the philosophical view that education must be taught so that it is a liberating force, rather than one used merely to train pliable workers.

Figure 9.1
Transmission.

Transmission

Role of the Text: The text is a means of transmitting society's dominant historical, literary, and cultural canon. It has fixed meanings and values irrespective of the reader. The text remains virtually static over time.

Role of the Reader: The reader is expected to acquire the precise facts and ideas being conveyed by the author and reproduce these in the same formats in which they were presented. Little attention is given to the reader's personal or critical examination of the text. The reader is simply responsible for reconstructing the author's ideas.

Role of the Teacher: The teacher focuses classroom discussion on the author's biography, the historical and political context of the author, and the traditional literary elements.

Transaction

Role of the Text: The text means unique things to different readers regardless of what the author may have intended to communicate. There is no static or inherent meaning incorporated within the text itself. Instead, the text is viewed as dynamic and subjective.

Role of the Reader: The reader brings a host of associations and inferences to every reading experience. These reader-based conceptions are a chief consideration as the reader attempts to build meaning from the written words. The reader makes fresh and unmediated interpretations, which may reflect the emotional and aesthetic needs of the reader.

Role of the Teacher: The teacher focuses classroom discussion on the reader's feelings, associations, and personal interpretations of texts.

Transformation

Role of the Text: The text is a tool for critical and constructive thought. It not only reflects the ideas and contexts of the author but also invites the thoughts and feelings of the reader. The text is a stimulus for critical-evaluative, or formulative, thinking.

Role of the Reader: The reader examines the text critically with the goal of becoming a constructive thinker and solution creator/implementer in the context of the surrounding society. The reader approaches each text consciously, separating what the author says from the reader's own thoughts and feelings. The reader suspends final judgment until the reader has developed legitimate and rational positions through a process of rigorously examining multiple interpretations. The reader sometimes reformulates thinking and/or becomes a producer of new knowledge and new texts as a result of this examination.

Role of the Teacher: The teacher focuses classroom discussion on generating and supporting varied interpretations with examples of multiple reader-response options. The teacher may ask students to make judgments about the author's intent, purpose, accuracy, logic, reliability, and literary form, or about others' responses to the same text.

Note. From *The Effects of Transmissional, Transactional, and Transformational Reader-Response Strategies on Middle School Students' Thinking Complexity and Social Development* by K. S. Garber, 1995, unpublished doctoral dissertation, University of Missouri, Kansas City. Adapted by permission.

By this view, education must focus student learning on problem posing, social issues, and power sharing (Reutzel, Larson, & Sabey, 1985). Accordingly, even the youngest of children now are being educated to think dialogically (Commeyras, 1993; Reutzel, Larson, & Sabey, 1995). Again, however, dialogical thinking is not meant to be totally without a point of reference. Where schooling is concerned, it generally means thinking critically from a certain philosophical base that openly values—that is, attempts to transmit—ideas such as freedom, equity, and respect for cultural diversity. Accordingly, the teaching methods described later selectively support and incorporate the transmissional and transactional perspectives as well as the transformative one that has been found to be beneficial to higher-order thinking and social-emotional adjustment (Garber, 1995).

THE WRITING PROCESS: AN INSTRUCTIONAL FRAMEWORK FOR WRITING ACROSS THE CURRICULUM

Traditional efforts to teach writing have focused on the final *product*. More recently, however, an instructional framework for guiding student mastery of the *process* of writing has evolved. This instructional framework was designed to parallel the process one would reasonably go through in writing. Therefore, it has come to be called simply the *writing process*. The writing process is analogous to the Directed Reading-Thinking Activity framework for planning prereading, guided silent reading, and postreading instruction. It indicates what should be done at each stage in general terms but leaves considerable latitude in just how to do it.

Steps in the Writing Process

Before Writing
Content and Idea Building: "Getting It Out."   In the content and idea-building phase, the teacher tries to prepare students for writing by

1. Raising motivation and interest
2. Encouraging exploration of the topic
3. Calling up relevant prior knowledge and experiences

Content and Idea Clarification and Organization: "Getting It Together."   The teacher's role in the content and idea clarification and organization phase is to

1. Encourage idea development by eliciting additional details, reasons, or examples.

2. Provide basic expectations for the final product, usually in the form of a rubric (see Chapter 3 for examples).

3. Assist students in identifying an audience they can keep in mind to guide the form and character of the composition.

During Writing

Composing: "Getting It Down."   In the composing phase, students attempt to relate the simultaneous din of ideas, purposes, facts, personal feelings, and biases into the linearity of words and structure. This includes finding out what you really think and then whether you can, or dare, say it. Typically, the teacher's role in this phase is to

1. Help students express initial thoughts and ideas on paper.
2. Urge students to use prewriting notes and experiences.
3. Encourage the free flow of ideas, even where they seem to contradict one another.
4. Build personal conviction that learning and clarity of thinking are desirable and attainable goals.

Revising: "Getting It Organized."   Revising is an appraisal and reconstructive phase. It requires a good deal of introspection and willingness to critique oneself, to be critiqued, and, in several strategies described later, to think like an editor and to critique the work of others. In this phase, the teacher

1. Encourages students to reorder, rewrite, and revise as needed for fluency and coherence
2. Guides discussions that clarify and thereby point to specific areas of composition that require rewriting
3. Encourages redrafting as needed with an eye toward initial purpose and audience
4. Helps students to learn how well others have understood and interpreted their writing

Editing: "Getting It Right."   In the final, editing, phase, the composition is reviewed for correct mechanics such as spelling, grammatical usage, and punctuation. The teacher assists by

1. Encouraging students to fine tune their work
2. Noting common mechanical problems and providing class instruction in these areas

After Writing
Publishing: Going Public.   In the publishing phase, a final copy is shared with an audience. The teacher aids in this process by

1. Employing methods that ensure that there will be readers for students' efforts
2. Offering opportunities for the work to serve as a foundation for reading, discussion, or study
3. Offering evaluative feedback based on a rubric for the assignment

The methods that follow offer further means of fleshing out the writing process. These methods also were selected because they support the goal of gaining an enriched understanding of the information and ideas presented in textual material. In general, you will find that the methods and activities presented will conform to guidelines based on contemporary research on writing (see Figure 9.2).

WRITING TO PROMOTE HIGHER-ORDER LITERACY

Read-Encode-Annotate-Ponder

Read-Encode-Annotate-Ponder (REAP) (Eanet & Manzo, 1976) was one of the two basic methods used in the previously mentioned study on transformational teaching (Garber, 1995). It also was among the earliest

Figure 9.2
Guidelines from contemporary research on writing.

Contemporary research indicates that writing should be
- Daily rather than infrequent
- Done whenever possible for real audiences and purposes
- More student directed than teacher directed
- Allotted sufficient time for stages of thought and editing to occur
- Set in a writing community environment
- Done to connect content, conversation, reading, and composition
- Teacher *and* peer guided, reviewed, and supported
- Done with an initial emphasis on reacting and responding to the intended message rather than on proofreading and editing

Note. From Hittleman (1984) and Reutzel, Larson, and Sabey (1995).

strategies developed for students to use to improve writing, thinking, and reading. REAP, as a teaching method, is intended to teach students a number of possible ways to respond to text. It does so by introducing them to a variety of brief and poignant ways to critique or *annotate* what they have read. Annotation types range from simple summaries to highly challenging critical-constructive responses.

Research on writing suggests that efforts to improve this type of critiquing, when taught concurrently with analytical reading and discipline instruction, result in enriched factual knowledge, conceptual development, writing improvement, vocabulary growth, and personal-social adjustment (Applebee, 1981; Bromley, 1985; Cunningham & Cunningham, 1976; Doctorow, Wittrock, & Marks, 1978; Eanet & Manzo, 1976; Garber, 1995; Tierney, Sorter, O'Flahavan, & McGinley, 1989).

Today, annotating is part of several on-line services whereby readers can chat on a variety of subjects and books. See Figure 9.3 for a list of these.

Steps in REAP

1. R: Read to discern the writer's message.

2. E: Encode the message by translating it into your own words.

3. A: Annotate by cogently writing the message in notes for yourself or in a thought book or on an electronic response system.

4. P: Ponder, or further reflect on what you have read and written, through discussion and by reviewing others' responses to the same materials and/or your own annotation.

REAP Response Types

There are many possible ways to respond to text. You will find, however, that these tend to be combinations of the eleven types illustrated next. These may be categorized into two groupings: those that are essentially

Figure 9.3
InterNet chat corners and annotation for readers.

Reader Exchange (http://cctr.umkc.edu/user/rbi/Foundation.HTML) is a nonprofit operation that uses the REAP system.

AMAZON (http://www.amazon.com/) is a bookstore where 1.1 million titles are searchable by author, awards, and customer reviews.

Chapter One (http://www.psi.met/chapter one/) is a cozy corner bookshop that invites one to read a book's first chapter before buying it.

Book Stacks Unlimited (http://www.books.com/) is called a campus bookstore with symposiums on books.

---

reconstructive, requiring literal-level responding, and those that are largely *constructive*, requiring reading and thinking between and beyond the lines.

Reconstructive Responses

1. *Summary response.*　States the basic message of the selection in brief form. In fiction, it is the basic story line; in nonfiction, it is a simple statement of the main ideas.

2. *Precise response.*　Briefly states the author's basic idea or theme, with all unnecessary words removed. The result is a crisp, telegram-like message.

3. *Attention-getting or heuristic response.*　Restates a snappy portion of the selection that makes the reader want to respond. It is best to use the author's own words.

4. *Question response.*　Turns the main point of the story or information into an organizing question that the selection answers.

Constructive Responses

5. *Personal view or transactional response.*　Answers the question "How do your views and feelings compare with what you perceive the author to have said?"

6. *Critical response.*　Supports, rejects, or questions the main idea, and tells why. The first sentence of this type of response should restate the author's position. The next sentence should state the writer's position. Additional sentences should explain how the two differ.

7. *Contrary response.*　Attempts to state a logical alternative position, even if it is not one that the student necessarily supports.

8. *Intention response.*　States and briefly explains what the responder thinks is the author's intention, plan, and purpose in writing the selection. This is a special version of the critical response that causes the reader/responder to try to think like the author or from the author's perspective.

9. *Motivation response.*　States what may have caused the author to create or write the story or selection. This is another special version of critical responding. It is an attempt to discover the author's personal agenda and hence areas of writing or unwitting biases.

10. *Discovery response.*　States one or more practical questions that need to be answered before the story or facts can be judged for accuracy or worth. This type of response to text is the mode of thinking that leads to more reading and research and occasionally to a reformulated position or view.

11. *Creative response.*   Suggests different and perhaps better solutions or views and/or connections and applications to prior learning and experiences. Students usually need some guidance and/or examples to produce this type of response. Once they begin thinking in this way, however, the results can be remarkably constructive.

REAP Responses as an Evaluation Rubric

If you wish to monitor students' progress toward higher-order literacy, you can use the preceding annotations listing as a rubric for reviewing student writings. The rubric can serve as a means of appraising the characteristic way in which a student or group of students respond to text. To use the REAP annotation types in this way, simply compare a student's writing to the preceding descriptions, and decide which annotation type it most closely resembles. The annotations already are roughly in order of difficulty: lower numbers indicate more concrete thinking, and higher numbers more personal and abstract patterns of responding. Again, the first four annotation types tend to reflect reconstructive thinking and the latter seven more constructive thinking. See Figure 9.4 for examples of reconstructive and constructive response types to a traditional fable.

Further Thoughts on Encouraging
Higher-Order Responding

One of the simplest ways to teach students to write constructively is to elicit quick personal reactions, or transactional responses, to a piece they have read. Then, the teacher should work with the class to form these initial highly subjective responses into more cogent critical and constructive ones. One of the key means of accomplishing this is simply to ask students to support their positions and/or to reconcile their initial responses with the ethical and values-based positions that are fundamental to their communities and to democratic institutions. Again, students should not be forced to conformity here but should be encouraged to reprocess the rationale for societal norms. Where students' responses differ markedly from one another, divide them into groups that produce critiques of their varied viewpoints. See Figure 9.5 for an anecdotal example from an eighth-grade social studies class we observed.

Another means of stimulating cogent writing in response to text is to refer students to good approximations of it in the form of model letters to the editor in newspapers and magazines. Notice how the sample letters to the editor in Figure 9.6 help one get a better grip on one's own thoughts and feelings about problems in China.

Figure 9.4
Sample REAP responses to text.

Travelers and the Plain Tree: A Fable

Two travelers were walking along a bare and dusty road in the heat of a midsummer's day. Coming upon a large shade tree, they happily stopped to shelter themselves from the burning sun in the shade of its spreading branches. While they rested, looking up into the tree, one of them said to his companion, "What a useless tree this is! It makes no flowers and bears no fruit. Of what use is it to anyone?" The tree itself replied indignantly, "You ungrateful people! You take shelter under me from the scorching sun, and then, in the very act of enjoying the cool shade of my leaves, you abuse me and call me good for nothing!"

Reconstructive Annotations

1. *Summary* response
   Travelers take shelter from the sun under a large tree. They criticize the tree for not making flowers or fruit. The tree speaks, and tells them that they are ungrateful people for taking shelter under her leaves and then criticizing her.

2. *Precise* response
   Travelers stop for rest and shade under big tree. Travelers say tree is useless. Tree tells them off.

3. *Attention-getting* response
   In this story, a tree talks back to people. The tree says, "You ungrateful people! You come and take shelter under me . . . and then . . . abuse me and call me nothing!"

4. *Question* response
   What tales might be told if inanimate objects could talk?

Constructive Annotations

5. *Personal view* responses
   a. We use resources like coal without thinking. Then we criticize the resource for damaging our lungs and dirtying our air.
   b. Kids sometimes use their parents the way the travelers used the tree—and then criticize them for letting themselves be used.

6. *Critical* response
   Not every word spoken in criticism is meant that way. The travelers were just a little grumpy from the long hard trip. The tree is being too sensitive.

---

7. *Contrary* response
   The travelers could be right. There are other trees that could produce something, as well as just provide shade.

8. *Intention* response
   The author wants us to be more sensitive to the people and things we depend on—especially those we see and use most often.

9. *Motivation* response
   It sounds like the author may have felt used, after having a bad experience with friends or family.

10. *Discovery* response
    I wonder how many of us know when we are being users. It would be interesting to take an anonymous poll to see how many people secretly feel that they have been used and how many honestly see themselves as users.

11. *Creative* response
    Teacher guidance: What are some analogous situations this fable reminds you of?
    a. This fable reminds me of how Dobie Gillis uses and then abuses that nice but plain girl who always hangs around him.
    b. This fable made me think that teachers are sometimes used unfairly. They give us so much, and then we put them down if they make little mistakes. They're only human!

    Teacher guidance: Having gotten the point of this fable, what should we do?
    c. We should put this fable on the bulletin board where it will remind us not to be ungrateful users.

    Teacher guidance: How would you retitle this fable if you were writing it?
    d. I'd call this fable "Travelers in the Dark," to show that we go through life without appreciating the many small gifts that come to us, while we're busy grumbling about what we don't have.

Figure 9.5

Encouraging higher-order responding.

> Following silent reading of a selection on the exploits of Hernando de Soto, an eighth-grade teacher, rather than first seeking a summary of facts, asked the class, "What did you think of de Soto?" Reactions included "sick," "cruel," and "loser." When asked to explain why they felt this way, students recited a litany of facts and events that amounted to a summary. Then the teacher asked them to get together in groups and form their reactions and reasons into personal comments on the selection. The following critique was typical of the results:
>
>> Hernando de Soto was a loser. After bringing gold back from Peru, the Spanish king encouraged him to go back to the new world by making him governor of Florida in 1539. He and 550 men looked for more gold. Even though some of them were priests, they mutilated and killed Indians in their search. After three years of this, de Soto died with nothing, and his men returned to Spain empty-handed.
>
> In this case, students' visceral and somewhat cranky responses seemed to help them distinguish de Soto from other explorers of his time and recall important information. In this way, the purpose of writing following reading was well served: Information was carefully processed, personalized, and stored for long-term recall. Further, the concept of *de Soto* and the context of the times replaced a collection of random facts about a vague historical figure named de Soto.

Figure 9.6

Letters to the editor exemplify cogent response to text.

> How tragic it is that, to cope with change, China's leaders felt they need to kill their young.
>
> The people of China will triumph. Deng Xiaoping and followers have forgotten their own history. It is impossible to repress an idea whose time has come!
>
> China had to crush the democratic resistance. The blood spilled in Tiananmen Square is a small price to pay to prevent a civil war that would consume thousands, if not millions.

Better than Book Reports

Brief response-type annotations, like letters to the editor, offer a challenge to sift through information and feelings and to struggle to take a thoughtful position. To this extent, such critiques can be more valuable than formal term papers and conventional book reports because they align more closely with student experiences and the faster pace of modern life.

Additionally, this type of writing, because it is brief, provides more frequent opportunities to read, react, and write. On a very pragmatic level, such annotations can more easily be read and shared with peers and occasionally reviewed by a secondary teacher with an average load of more than 100 students per semester.

Other Means of Promoting Higher-Order Thinking

Dialectical thinking, or back-and-forth, pros-and-cons–type reasoning, is fundamental to all human progress. That which was referred to previously as *dialogical thinking* largely is an attempt to incorporate dialectical thinking into the culture of contemporary schooling (Commeyras, 1993; Manzo, Garber, & Warm, 1992; Reutzel, Larson, & Sabey, 1995; Tishman, Perkins, & Jay, 1995).

The next three methods are variations on how to accomplish this important objective in the content area literacy class. These methods are good complements to REAP, and together with it form a solid foundation for a thinking-based curriculum.

The first method nicely pulls together the teaching of writing and critical thinking. It also teaches some of the most basic functions of how to actually express critical comments.

Opinion-Proof

The Opinion-Proof (Santa, Dailey, & Nelson, 1985) method requires students to engage in four important aspects of higher-order literacy:

- ✦ Evaluative thinking—forming an opinion
- ✦ Verification—supporting the opinion
- ✦ Persuasive articulation—writing about the opinion convincingly
- ✦ Forming a consensus, or cooperative critiquing and reviewing of opinion

Steps in Opinion-Proof

1. Provide students with an Opinion-Proof guide, either written on the chalkboard or as a handout (see the example in Step 2).
2. Have students write an opinion and supporting evidence for it from the text.

Following is a guide for the short story "Old Horse," a popular selection about an elderly algebra teacher by Oliver Andersen:

Example

Opinion Statement	Evidence to Prove My Opinion
Old Horse was sensitive.	He was patient with Rabbit. He wanted Rabbit to belong. Old Horse forced Rabbit to dislike him. He put himself down for the sake of Rabbit.

3. Students write a connected essay using their opinion and evidence as topic sentence and supporting details, respectively. If further structure is required, the teacher can use framed paragraphs (Adler, 1974; Fowler, 1982), as illustrated next.

Example

Old Horse was _____ . *One reason I feel this way is* _____ . *In addition,* _____ . *Finally,* _____ .

Here is one possible student response:

Old Horse was a very sensitive teacher. One reason I feel this way was because of his ability to understand Rabbit. Rabbit was not liked by the other students in his class because he was a friend of Old Horse's. In addition, Old Horse understood Rabbit's need to become a part of a group of friends, and Old Horse knew that he was part of the problem. Finally, Old Horse forced Rabbit to dislike him so much that he could become accepted by the other students. Therefore, Old Horse was a very sensitive man. He even sacrificed himself for the sake of his student.

4. The final step is peer editing. In this step, students (1) develop specific criteria for evaluating their writing, such as the questions "Does my paragraph contain a main idea statement?" and "Do I have evidence to support my main idea?"; (2) divide up into pairs or small groups and read and react to one another's paragraphs; and (3) edit and/or revise their own paragraphs before submitting a final draft for teacher evaluation.

Additional to its role in reading and thinking, the Opinion-Proof process provides a useful sequence for organizing persuasive speeches, another important language art. It accomplishes this by having students state opinions and write out supporting and nonsupporting points. This often leads to the reflective turnabout that makes Opinion-Proof a good framework for teaching in the transformative mode. The next strategy, Devil's Advocate, does this as well.

Devil's Advocate

A simple and direct means of improving dialogical thinking is to get students into a discussion that evokes this type of reasoning. Devil's Advocate is an issues-based discussion that has a rich heritage (Alvermann, Dillon, & O'Brien, 1987; Roby, 1983). It was used by Socrates and Plato and is a common convention at synods of several religions around the world.

One of three things may happen in a Devil's Advocate discussion: Positions may be strengthened, modified, or abandoned. In any case, students involved in such a discussion tend to have a great many experiences with reflective turnabout. They learn about the enormous complexity of issues that initially appear clear-cut. They learn about the paradoxes involved in trying to solve a problem only to find that the best solution can sometimes be more disruptive than the existing problem. Finally, they learn to use language not merely to state what they believe but to discover what they *might* reasonably believe.

Steps in Devil's Advocate

1. The teacher poses an issue to the class.
2. Students are paired but asked to individually prepare written arguments using the text for essential information. Sometimes there are more than two positions.
3. Students are instructed to describe to their partners their best arguments for each position. They should discuss each argument to determine whether it contains faulty reasoning.
4. Still in pairs, students are asked to discuss with their partners whether the positions they originally supported have changed as a result of this activity and, if so, why and in what way. Then they revise their individual written statements accordingly.
5. A class discussion follows based on students' arguments for each side of the issue, any changes in attitude that occurred as a result of the activity, and sources of further information related to the issue.
6. Students are offered a final opportunity to revise and prepare a final form of their position statements.

See Figure 9.7 for an example of the Devil's Advocate method. Notice how this method emphasizes critical examination of the issue with the possibility of changing one's mind, or reformulating a position, rather than winning a debate.

The next discussion-based writing strategy furthers many of the same criteria furthered by Devil's Advocate. It is more suitable to use with content literacy, since it is less like dealing with controversy and more like approaching a problem.

Figure 9.7
Example of Devil's Advocate.

> Mr. Tennyson, a ninth grade social sciences teacher, used the Devil's Advocate strategy to structure a class discussion on banning nuclear testing. His students had read a section of their text that dealt with the horrors of nuclear warfare. As the discussion opens, Tennyson has just finished assigning the students to pairs.
>
> "All right now, you and your partner find a place where you can talk quietly. Each of you should jot down why you believe the United States should stop testing nuclear weapons. Be sure to support your beliefs with evidence from the text. Then take the opposite stance (why the United States should not stop testing nuclear weapons) and again support your beliefs with evidence from the text."
>
> (The students, working individually in pairs, take about ten minutes to complete this task.)
>
> "Okay, now we're ready for the next step. Choose your best arguments and present them to your partner. Be certain that you discuss your beliefs with your partner; for example, seek your partner's ideas and evaluations of the pros and cons that you took on the issue. Is there evidence of any faculty reasoning on either one's part?"
>
> (After approximately fifteen minutes, the noise level in the room drops, an indication that students have finished presenting the arguments they had with themselves.)
>
> "May I have your attention. . . . There are two more things I would like you to do: (1) Think about how your ideas have changed on banning nuclear testing. For example, has your position shifted from your original one? If so, why? (2) Decide whether you have strengthened your original position, abandoned it completely, or only modified it. Then tell your partner your decision and see if he or she agrees."
>
> (After approximately ten minutes, Tennyson drew the students into a whole class discussion by asking them to share some of their ideas on both sides of the issue.)

Note. From Alvermann, Donna E., Dillon, Deborah R., & O'Brien, David G. (1987). *Using Discussion to Promote Reading Comprehension,* IRA. Reprinted with permission of Donna E. Alvermann and the International Reading Association. All rights reserved.

Developmental Discussion

The Developmental Discussion (Maier, 1963) and a slightly modified form called Guided Conversation (Gauthier, 1996) are intended to teach students about the full process of problem solving by involving them in all of its parts: identification and partitioning of the problem, collection of relevant data or information, generation of solutions, and appraisal of solutions. Most importantly, it places heavy emphasis on going beyond existing knowledge. As such, it should be basic to any program to improve creative thinking and problem solving.

Steps in Developmental Discussion/Guided Conversation

1. The teacher instructs students to try to identify certain conflicting points (rather than views) or problems inherent in material presented in text and lecture.

2. The teacher initially provides examples that can serve as models of problem identification (this usually requires comparing textual information to prior knowledge and experiences).

3. The teacher assists students in narrowing and partitioning the problem into manageable segments.

4. Students are divided into cooperative learning groups to solve the smaller parts of the problem. Each group is asked to jot down notes on individual and group members' answers using questions such as the following to guide their analysis:

   a. What do we know about this problem part?

   b. Which parts of the information we have are relevant to the problem?

   c. What more do we need to know to construct a possible solution?

   d. What are some possible solutions given what we now know?

   e. What additional information can we collect—and how—to formulate better solutions?

5. A large-group discussion is held to illustrate the different ways the problem can be viewed and solutions sought. The teacher reminds students to add to their notes during this discussion.

6. The class decides on a solution (usually a synthesis) or—in a significant departure from conventional school practices—may choose to table the matter until the class can collect additional information (see Figure 9.8 for an anecdotal account).

7. Students individually write out the solution as they see it and in the most convincing way possible. Then students exchange papers and give one another feedback on their essays. The teacher invites students and reviewers to read aloud phrases or sections that they feel were particularly well stated.

ON-LINE ENCOURAGEMENT OF CREATIVE/CONSTRUCTIVE THINKING

To provide conceptual readiness, incentives, and further audience for Developmental Discussion/Guided Conversation, the teacher can introduce youngsters to an on-line service that offers examples of innovative questions and solutions and welcomes the contributions of inventive thinkers. The InterNet Web Page called the Registry for Better Ideas allows students

Figure 9.8
Anecdotal account of developmental discussion.

Mr. Freeble, a high school civics teacher, works with a group of average ability students for fifty minutes each morning. In a previous class session the students had read a five page textbook assignment and had completed the accompanying study guide. The assignment covered information about the Supreme Court—what it is, its purpose and charges, and its relationship to the entire governmental system.

Freeble began the developmental discussion by reviewing the previous textbook assignment for five minutes. From the review, students were reminded of the following key concepts: the Supreme Court is the highest court in the land, the individuals sitting on the Supreme Court are charged with interpreting the Constitution, and members of the Supreme Court may change a previous ruling by another branch of the government.

Next, Freeble asked the students to supply current information about events in the news concerning recent Supreme Court rulings. Elicited were facts about prayer in school and nativity scenes set up on public property. Freeble noted that the seasonal influence (it was close to Christmas) play [sic] a large role in students' interest in a local newspaper story about a controversial nativity scene. After ten minutes of discussing that story and its implications for local residents, the class decided on a problem that was text based but of immediate interest to them—should religious groups be allowed to erect nativity scenes on public property?

The teacher guided the students in breaking the larger problem (separation of church and state) into three smaller problems: (1) Does setting up a nativity scene on public property violate the rights of individuals who do not have the same religious beliefs?; (2) What information could the class add that would help solve the problem?; (3) What would be a reasonable way to share what was learned with the people involved in the controversy?

The students broke into smaller groups and began to work on the first part of the problem. Freeble supplied each group with a one page summary of the Pawtucket case involving a Supreme Court ruling on the display of nativity scenes on public property. Freeble circulated among the groups, observing and offering assistance when requested.

During the last fifteen minutes of the period, students participated in a large group discussion in which they reported on their reactions to the Pawtucket case and whether they believed the case had any implications for the local controversy.

Over the next two days, the students worked in small groups to tackle the remaining problem parts. Solutions to the overall problem included working with community leaders to foster improved communication among the dissident groups and writing letters to the editor of the local newspaper on the topic of how the Pawtucket case compared to the local one.

Note. From Alvermann, Donna E., Dillon, Deborah R., & O'Brien, David G. (1987). *Using Discussion to Promote Reading Comprehension,* IRA. Reprinted with permission of Donna E. Alvermann and the International Reading Association. All rights reserved.

to enter a global community that connects people of all ages and stations who have committed dollars to form themselves into microfoundations that award cash incentives to other individuals who simply have submitted better ideas or just more insightfully framed or heuristic questions or problems. There is no charge to peruse the system. To learn more about this system, direct e-mail inquiries to

manzoa@smtpgate.umkc.edu

or simply access it on the InterNet by looking up the Registry for Better Ideas at

HTTP://cctr.umkc.edu/user/rbi/Foundation.HTML

✦ *Looking Back and Looking Ahead* ✦

This chapter detailed some straightforward ways to promote critical-constructive reading, writing, and thinking across the curriculum. It included several references to possible uses of the information superhighway as a supplemental resource and out-of-classroom support system for higher-order literacy. Chapter 10 returns to the more traditional role of school as a place to learn how to study and acquire the information and wisdom stored in books. Chapter 10 will be especially beneficial to those who believe that subject teachers should be part of the effort to teach students how and why to study.

✦ ✦   TRADE SECRET   ✦ ✦

The Big Picture

There essentially are two ingredients to being a good model of constructive thinking. One is to be well-informed on the bases for our current knowledge and perspectives, and the second is to be conversant with the changes that may be looming globally. There are three books that you should consider having in your professional library to achieve the former:

1. *The Great Thoughts,* compiled by George Seldes (New York: Ballantine Books, 1985). This book provides thumbnail sketches of the major ideas that have shaped the history of the world from Abelard (1079–1142), considered the greatest philosopher of his

time, to Zola (1840–1902), the French novelist, who wrote optimistically and, we hope, accurately, "Truth is on the march; nothing now can stop it."

2. *The Encyclopedia of Ignorance: Everything You Wanted to Know about the Unknown,* edited by R. Duncan and M. Weston-Smith (Oxford: Pergamon Press, 1978). These volumes attempt to outline what is not known about the physical world and mathematics. It is not light reading, but it is divided into manageable sections that, unless you are a science or math teacher, you probably will need to reread several times.

3. *The Lessons of History,* a small book (117 pages) by Will and Ariel Durant (New York: Simon & Schuster, 1968). One passage from this book provides a particularly poignant historical perspective on creative thinking, the theme of this chapter. In discussing the many reasons why civilizations rise and fall, they find one common factor:

> . . . the presence or absence of *initiative and of creative individuals* with the clarity of mind and energy of will to mount effective responses to new situations. (p. 91)

That quote logically suggests a second recommendation. It is to join the adventures in thinking that are arising from the electronic discussions that are criss-crossing the globe. If you wish, for example, to join an ongoing electronic dialogue journal for professionals on content area literacy, use the InterNet to access

http://www.ced.appstate.edu/clic/

This home page connects professors and students from several universities who share this interest. Additionally, if the Registry for Better Ideas previously mentioned interests you, you also will wish to look into a similar system in England. It lists solutions to a large array of social problems, from education to basic human relationships. Through the InterNet, you may vote your level of approval for these. Based on worldwide reactions, a yearly award of 1,000 pounds is made to the best social invention. For further information, write The Global Ideas Bank, 20 Heber Road, London NW2 6AA. Telephone 0181208 2853; or e-mail at

rhino@dial.pipex.com

CHAPTER 10

Study Methods and Strategies: For Guided Reading, Learning, and Remembering

Study without reflection is a waste of time; reflection without study is dangerous.

—Confucius

✦ *Organizing Thoughts* ✦

The term *study strategies* refers to the efficient use of time spent in learning. As such, it includes an array of diverse topics such as time management, techniques for active reading and listening, note taking, and test taking. Study strategies may be taught in minicourses or as units in a regular class and/or integrated with the content of various classes. Each approach has merit. The content class approach is gaining in popularity as more teachers learn about these strategies in teacher training and in-service programs.

FROM SKILLS TO STRATEGIES

The techniques and objectives that have been known until quite recently as *study skills* have tended to reflect the educational trends of the times. McMurray wrote the first study skills text for classroom teachers in 1909. It was a no-frills book called simply *How to Study and Teaching How to Study.* Its approach reflected the early-twentieth-century assumption that reading was a bottom-up process of mastering and applying a series of discrete subskills.

This skills-based approach continued through the popularization of self-directed study techniques during World Wars I and II. Armed services inductees needed quick training in how to read and master the contents of the manuals that accompanied increasingly sophisticated weapons and machines. Later, returning veterans willingly enrolled in study skills courses to improve their reading efficiency and grades in technical schools and colleges. By 1930, skills-based books with names like *Outlining as a Study Procedure* (Barton, 1930) were available at the college level.

The open admissions policies initiated in many colleges in the 1960s created a further need to assist underprepared students in meeting college-level reading, writing, and study requirements. By this time, many educators were realizing that effective study, like reading, was not something done to one, but something that one did. The emphasis on imparting study skills gradually evolved into the new emphasis on the learner as an active doer and strategy user.

SQ3R: A STORY UNTO ITSELF

The Survey-Question-Read-Recite-Review (SQ3R) technique is the acknowledged granddaddy of study formulas. It was developed by Francis Robinson (1946), who traced its roots back to 1923. Robinson developed it in response to a need expressed by the U.S. Department of Defense during World War II (N. A. Stahl & Henk, 1986). As noted earlier, U.S. troops had a great deal of technical information to learn and little time in which to learn it. They needed a rigorous, self-guided technique that they could use with minimal instruction in field training situations. SQ3R stresses meticulous, step-by-step analysis of text, followed by repeated reviews to overlearn textual material to the point where key information can be recalled and recited with minimal cuing.

Steps in SQ3R

1. *Survey.*   Survey a chapter before reading it closely.
    a. Read the title, and think about what it says or implies.
    b. Read the headings and subheadings.
    c. Read the summary if there is one.
    d. Read the captions under the pictures, charts, graphs, or other illustrations.
    e. See if there is a bibliography or a list of books related to the content of the chapter.
2. *Question.*   Ask yourself questions about what you are going to read.
    a. What does the title of the chapter mean?
    b. What do I already know about the subject?
    c. What did my instructor say about this chapter when it was assigned?
    d. What questions do the headings and subheadings suggest?
3. *Read.*   Read actively.
    a. Read to answer the questions you raised while doing the survey/question routine.
    b. Read all the added attractions in the chapter (maps, graphs, tables, and other illustrations).
    c. Read all the underlined, italicized, or boldface words or phrases extra carefully.
4. *Recite.*   Go over what you read in step 3 by either orally summarizing what you just read or making notes of some type.

5. *Review.*   Periodically survey what you read and learned.

   a. Use your notes or markings to refresh your memory.

   b. Review immediately after reading.

   c. Review again periodically.

   d. Review again before taking an exam on the subject.

Efficacy of SQ3R for Independent and Content Class Use

The balance of opinion among specialists regarding the efficacy of SQ3R is positive but by no means unanimous. Several studies (Diggs, 1973; Donald, 1967; Gurrola, 1975; McNamara, 1977; Willmore, 1967; Wooster, 1958) found no significant differences between SQ3R and control (i.e., placebo) treatments. Thus, despite the popularity of SQ3R, evidence of its effectiveness as a self-guided reading–study formula still is uncertain.

We continue to endorse SQ3R for content classroom use, especially when each step is practiced under teacher guidance. Used in this way, SQ3R parallels the Directed Reading–Thinking Activity (DR-TA), which has been proven effective. There are several additional obstacles, however, to study strategy instruction in general, which are discussed next.

OBSTACLES TO STUDY STRATEGY INSTRUCTION

Teaching study strategies presents several unique challenges. At a basic managerial level, study strategy instruction is an additional layer of *content* to be taught and learned on top of existing demands.

The second challenge is the quite lofty goal of this type of instruction. The intent is to teach information, processes, and even beyond this, to change habits. And habits are notoriously hard to change. Teaching students to use study strategies like SQ3R is analogous to teaching teachers to use instructional methods like the DR-TA. In each case, what is taught is a set of steps that teachers and students are expected to understand, remember, and then apply *on their own.* This requires preparation, guidance, and lots of practice. Even if students become convinced of the usefulness of a particular study strategy, they are likely to slip back into more accustomed patterns. To be effective, study strategies need to become new habits. Francis Robinson himself observed that SQ3R cannot possibly be effective until it becomes "automatic" and "subordinate to the task of reading" (1946, p. 21).

Another complicating factor is that people tend to resent being given advice, and most study strategies amount to advice. This problem persists even though the strategies and techniques are quite effective.

Finally, teachers tend to believe that what we do when we study is highly individual, and that no one strategy will work for everyone. While it is true that each of us tailors a particular strategy to our own personal style, fundamental principles of learning apply regardless of individual differences. In one of the early textbooks designed for college students with weak academic skills, Walter Pauk (1989) summarized much of what is known about effective learning and study in his "Eight Learning Principles." These research-based principles, shown in Figure 10.1, provide an excellent orientation to the field of developmental studies and a basis for evaluating any study strategies program.

Figure 10.1
Pauk's Eight Learning Principles.

1. **Principle of Motivated Interest.** We remember what interests us. Develop your natural interests, and try to create new interests by reading (e.g., magazine and newspaper articles) in diverse areas. If you find a subject boring, or irrelevant, try to find something in it of personal interest or use, and you will find it easier to learn.

2. **Principle of Selectivity.** Information must be grouped into units of a manageable size for efficient recall. In the nineteenth century, Hermann Ebbinghaus, one of the world's earliest experimental psychologists, found that it took fifteen times as many trials to memorize twelve nonsense syllables as the number of trials needed to memorize six nonsense syllables. One would predict that it would take only twice as many trials.

3. **Principle of Intention to Remember.** Prerequisites to efficient learning include careful attending, getting the facts right the first time, and striving to understand. Recall that this is the basic principle underlying the guided reading procedure, a total reading and study lesson design covered in Chapter 4. Active reading the *first* time saves time in the long run.

4. **Principle of Basic Background.** What we perceive (see, hear, taste, smell, feel, and read) depends in large measure on what we already know. Whenever you are trying to learn something new, connect it to something you know.

5. **Principle of Meaningful Organization.** George Miller, the eminent Harvard psychologist, found that the immediate memory span of the general population seems fixed at approximately seven bits of information, plus or minus two. For effective recall, therefore, information should be categorized into meaningful groups of no more than seven

Figure 10.1, *continued*

bits. The telephone company heeded this research when developing the telephone numbering system. The U.S. Postal Service, on the other hand, has challenged it by implementing a nine-digit zip code system.

6. **Principle of Recitation.** Study reading must be an active process. Recitation is analogous to exercising a muscle: It builds and embeds information in long-term memory. Pauk reminds us of how H. F. Spitzer's classic study compared the amount of information recalled by students seven and sixty-three days after learning. Students who reviewed immediately after learning remembered 83% after seven days and 70% after sixty-three days. Those who did not review immediately after learning remembered 33% after seven days and 14% after sixty-three days. Control groups of students who also did not review immediately after learning remembered approximately 55% after one day, 22% after fourteen days, 18% after twenty-one days, and 1% after twenty-eight days. Obviously, recitation-study works!

7. **Principle of Consolidation.** Information must be harbored in the mind for a certain period before a temporary memory can be consolidated into a more permanent one. Numerous records of accident victims show that a period of unconsciousness can erase the memory of events that occurred from fifteen to five minutes before the person lost consciousness. Spitzer's study, described in principle 6, further illustrates the effectiveness of an immediate review of new information.

8. **Principle of Distributed Practice.** A number of brief reviews are more effective than one long review session. Short sessions prevent physical and emotional fatigue and help sustain interest and motivation.

Note. From *How to Study in College* (4th edition), by Walter Pauk, 1989, Boston: Houghton Mifflin. Copyright 1989 by Houghton Mifflin Company. Adapted with permission.

CONTENT AREA STRATEGIES FOR IMPROVING LECTURE NOTE TAKING AND LISTENING

Palmatier's Unified Note-Taking System

Students need instruction in how to learn from lecture as well as from text. Palmatier's Unified Note-Taking System (PUNS) urges students to review lecture notes immediately after class and supplement them with text information. The note-taking format also provides a built-in study system by separating key words from the body of the notes. PUNS is one of the few note-taking methods that has been validated through empirical research (Palmatier, 1971, 1973; Palmatier & Bennett, 1974).

Steps in PUNS

1. *Record.*   In a loose-leaf binder, use only one side of 8 ½-by-11-inch notebook paper with a 3-inch margin on the left side. (Many college bookstores now stock this type of paper for this purpose.) Record lecture notes to the right of the margin. Use a modified outline form to isolate main topics. Leave space where information seems to be missing. Number each page as you record the notes.

2. *Organize.*   As soon after the lecture as possible, add two sections to the notes. First, place labels inside the left margin. These should briefly describe the information in the recorded notes. Second, insert important text information directly into the recorded notes. If you need more space, you can use the back of the notebook paper.

3. *Study.*   Remove the notes from the loose-leaf binder, and lay them out so that only the left margin of each page is visible. Use the labels as memory cues to recite as much of the information on the right as you can recall. The labels can be turned into questions stems, "What do I need to know about [insert label]?" Verify your recall immediately by lifting the page to read the information recorded to the right of the label. As you master the material on each page of notes, set that page aside in an "I already know" stack. For objective tests, the labels can be approached at random, simulating the format of multiple-choice, true/false, and matching tests. For essay tests, group information into logical units, formulate predicted essay questions, and practice writing answers. Figure 10.2 presents a sample PUNS format.

The notes students take during lectures are influenced as much by listening habits as by note-taking strategy. The next sections suggest ways to improve attention and active listening.

Enabling Questions

The Enabling Questions procedure is a student-initiated strategy that we developed. It is a prepared set of questions that students can use to tune in and reduce distraction during lectures. Using Enabling Questions puts the listener into an active, evaluative thinking mode and invites the teacher or speaker to talk a little less and welcome more interaction. Students should be urged to translate these questions into their own words.

Step 1:   *Record.* Use the right-hand side of a specially divided page, leaving space to add text notes.

Step 2:   *Fill in labels.* Write key word labels in the left margin and text notes in the space provided for lecture notes. Use the back of the previous page if you need more space.

Step 3:   *Study key words.* Lay out pages so that only key words show, and try to recite information from your notes. Remove each page as you master its contents.

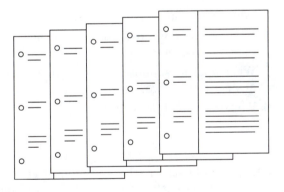

Figure 10.2
PUNS note taking.

Set 1: Questions that Help the Listener Organize and Clarify Information

1. What is/are the main *question(s)* you are answering by your lecture (or lesson) today?

2. Which key terms and concepts are most important for us to remember from what you have said (or will say) today?

3. What is most often misunderstood or confusing about the information or position you are presenting today?

Set 2: Questions that Help the Listener Get a Mental Breather

1. Could you please restate that last point in some other words?

2. Would you please spell ____ and ____ for us?

3. Would you please say which points you especially want us to note at this time?

Set 3: Questions that Invite Give-and-Take with the Speaker

1. How does what you have said compare with positions others have taken, and who might these others be?

2. Is there convincing evidence to support your position that you can share with us?

3. What do you think is the weakest part of the position you have taken?

4. How do you think this position (or new information) affects previously held beliefs?

5. What do you suppose would happen if you extended this point another step or two?

6. Would you mind pausing for a moment to see if there are other views on this in the class/audience? This would help us better understand and follow your points.

Any one of the latter set of questions likely would put the listener back into an active, evaluative thinking mode and reduce the sometimes excessive dominance of the speaker. It is important that the listener who wishes to use these types of questions does so with an eye toward using them for enriching comprehension, learning, and mature interaction, and not as a counteroffensive. One way to help students learn the value and become regular users of Enabling Questions is to write these questions on index cards and distribute a few to each class member. Then urge students to try to use the questions on their card(s) intelligently over a two- to three-day period. Schedule a day to discuss what happened and what students learned and what might need to be modified to make the Enabling Questions even more enabling.

Guided Lecture Procedure

The Guided Lecture Procedure (GLP) (Kelly & Holmes, 1979) is a teacher-directed method for improving listening. It is the listening counterpart of the Guided Reading Procedure (Manzo, 1975).

Steps in the GLP

1. Students are directed to take no notes as they listen carefully to the lecture.
2. The teacher writes the objectives of the lecture on the chalkboard along with key technical terms.
3. The teacher lectures for about half the class period, then stops.
4. Students attempt to write down everything they can recall from the lecture.
5. Students form small cooperative learning groups to review and discuss their notes. This discussion, or language component, helps build related speaking, writing, and thinking strategies.

The GLP has been used effectively with classes from middle school to college levels (Kelly & Holmes, 1979). The small-group activity that forms the latter part of the lesson is an excellent cooperative learning activity.

CONTENT AREA STRATEGIES FOR TEST TAKING

Taking Multiple-Choice Tests

It is difficult to overstate the effects of test taking on the body and the ego. If test taking were a pill, it probably would never pass the Food and Drug Administration guidelines for benefit-to-risk ratio. The growing emphasis on writing and performance-based assessment has begun to decrease the use of multiple-choice tests in the classroom. However, most schools still use standardized multiple-choice tests for evaluation of their overall program. Students' scores on multiple-choice tests can be more a reflection of their test-taking savvy than their knowledge acquisition. See Figure 10.3 for a brief list of helpful hints for taking multiple-choice tests.

PORPE: A Strategy for Taking Essay Tests

Predict-organize-rehearse-practice-evaluate (PORPE) was developed in response to students' anxiety about taking essay examinations (Simpson, 1986). The method evolved from a review of the research literature to

Figure 10.3
Tips for taking multiple-choice tests.

- Block out a rough time plan for timed tests. Note what time it will be when half the time is up, and how many items you should have completed by that time.

- Read slowly and answer quickly. Focus on the question instead of the answer choices. This prevents the frequent and irritating problem of misreading the question.

- Answer the easy questions first, and skip the hard ones. Spending time on difficult questions raises anxiety and may cause you to forget information you knew when the test began. As you go through the test, you may find information that will help you remember answers to earlier difficult items.

- Don't assume that the test is loaded with trick questions. This will cause you to read too much into the questions and spend too much time in needless internal debate. Read each question carefully, but concentrate on the main point rather than the details.

- Avoid anxiety reactions that break concentration: glancing frequently at the clock or the instructor, polishing eyeglasses, examining finger-nails, gazing at the wall or ceiling, excessive yawning or stretching.

- Use all the time allotted. If you finish before the time is up, always check your work. Make sure you answered all the questions, but don't waste time reviewing the answers to easy questions. Change your answers if you have reason to. Research shows that contrary to common belief, three out of four times your changes will be correct. This may be because during a final check, the tension begins to lessen and thought processes are clearer.

find practical ideas about how proficient readers prepare for essay-type tests. PORPE's five steps guide students to behave like "effective readers who have some awareness and control of their own cognitive activities while they read and study" (Simpson, 1986, p. 408).

Steps in PORPE

1. *Predict.* Students are asked to predict essay questions that they might be asked. Teachers should make every effort to help students at this stage to raise synthesizing, analyzing, and application questions as well as more literal *what-* and *when-*type questions. One way to do this is to introduce students to a glossary of the most common words used in essay questions, such as *explain, criticize, compare, contrast, react, support,* and *elaborate.* As follow-up, teachers should model the thought process they go through in preparing

(predicting) and phrasing essay questions on a previously studied body of information. Students then should prepare and share their predicted questions with classmates.

2. *Organize.*   Students are encouraged to organize the information needed to answer predicted questions. Students are encouraged to use semantic maps and outlines for this purpose. Again, teachers should model this strategy.

3. *Rehearse.*   This is the conventional study or recall and recite step. Students should be encouraged to use appropriate memory devices.

4. *Practice.*   In this step students practice composing or answering essay-type questions. They should be reminded of the following in doing so:

    a. Work from an outline.

    b. Make sure your opening sentence rephrases the question and/or takes a clear position.

    c. Make the structure of your answer clear by using transitional words and phrases like *first, on the other hand, furthermore,* and *finally.*

    d. Give examples of major points.

    e. Reread what you wrote, and make appropriate editorial corrections.

5. *Evaluate.*   This step continues logically from the latter portion of the last one but should occur after a brief pause. The idea simply is to consider how a teacher might evaluate your answer. It may be necessary to conduct several sessions where students listen to, read, and discuss the relative merits of various essay answers before they acquire the ability to get outside of themselves and review their own work.

Notes on PORPE

PORPE has been found to be significantly more effective than question–answer recitation in improving comprehension and essay writing (Simpson, Hayes, Stahl, Connor, & Weaver, 1988). PORPE also makes a great deal of sense at an intuitive level. It incorporates attention to metacognitive development, content mastery, effective predicting, organizing, and test writing. Structurally, it progresses in logical movements from teacher instruction, modeling, and guidance to total student independence and control—the purpose of all study strategies instruction.

Study Journals

Keeping a study journal can make students more aware of their present study habits and attitudes. A study journal is simply a written record of thoughts and feelings about studying and about school. Students should be encouraged to make four or five brief journal entries each week, without undue concern for form or style. Guiding questions should be "What am I doing when I study?" and "How do I feel about it?" Some categories for consideration include the following:

✦ Classes: participation or lack of it, difficulty paying attention, confidence level

✦ Homework: difficulty concentrating or getting started, organization of materials, strategies for studying

✦ Tests: thoughts before, during, and after tests; controlling anxiety

✦ Time management: difficulty getting everything done; setting priorities

✦ Symptoms of stress: fatigue, headaches, worry, apathy, guilt, problems in interpersonal relationships, insomnia, excessive snacking, and so on

Following are some sample study journal entries:

9/10   Algebra class always begins in English, but it soon becomes Greek. There must be something I can do to keep from getting lost about midway???

9/14   When I get home from school, I can't stand to face homework. Soon it's dinnertime, then the good programs are on, then I'm too tired. When are you supposed to do homework anyway?

9/25   I hate tests. I never seem to study the right things.

10/2   I've been having trouble falling asleep, and I wake up two hours early thinking about that darn paper due next week. I also find it impossible to stay awake after lunch.

After students have made several entries in their journals, they should be encouraged to look back over what they have written. Are there noticeable patterns? Are there certain kinds of situations that tend to precipitate stress? What coping strategies did students try? How effective were these? We have found that study journals are more likely to be kept when they are combined with the next strategy, which offers a place and time for their use and reinforcement.

Problem-Solving Approach to Study Skills

The Problem-Solving Approach to Study Skills (PASS) (Manzo & Casale, 1980) is an interactive method designed to communicate the attitude that school, learning, and living present a series of typical study problems that generally are quite manageable and often solvable by critical, constructive analysis and personal resolve.

Steps in PASS

1. *Count.* The teacher presents students with a list of common study problems and asks them to check those that apply to them (see Figure 10.4).

2. *Characterize.* The teacher guides students in defining selected problems, and themselves, in specific terms. The teacher urges students to take inventories of learning style, temperament, skills, abili-

Figure 10.4
Checklist of common study problems.

```
_____  1. Taking complete class notes
_____  2. Completing reading assignments
_____  3. Finding the main ideas
_____  4. Remembering details
_____  5. Figuring out what the author/teacher means
_____  6. Staying relaxed when studying
_____  7. Maintaining concentration when reading
_____  8  Maintaining concentration when studying
_____  9. Paying attention in class
_____ 10. Vocabulary meanings
_____ 11. Writing answers to questions
_____ 12. Writing personal opinions about class topics
_____ 13. Writing research papers
_____ 14. Planning and completing class projects
_____ 15. Taking notes while reading/studying
_____ 16. Finding reference materials in the library
_____ 17. Participating in class discussions
Other: _____
       _____
       _____
```

ties, and attitudes in an effort to reach a firmer sense of themselves as learners. (The learning styles inventory called the Impulsivity–Stability Scale, discussed in Chapter 3, Trade Secrets, and found in Appendix A, can be helpful here.)

3. *Consider.* Students consider how they typically have dealt with their particular needs and problems and the possible merit in these intuitive coping strategies.

4. *Collect.* The class discusses and judges standard techniques for dealing with reading/study problems on the basis of their compatibility with each student's style and character. Where these appear incompatible, the procedures are dismissed as inappropriate.

5. *Create.* Students seek inventive alternatives that match their personal styles. This step is best handled initially in small groups and then in larger group discussions.

Notes on PASS

PASS was evaluated in a case study approach and found to be a very sound means of improving study habits and positive attitudes toward learning (Casale & Kelly, 1980). The content teacher's efforts to teach students how to study will be time well spent. Learning is as much attitudinal as it is intellectual. Teaching students how to study tells them that they are as important as the content.

✦ *Looking Back and Looking Ahead* ✦

This chapter suggested some ways in which the content area teacher might help students to build needed study strategies, attitudes, and habits. It focused on the things students do most: listening, note taking, personal problem solving, and test taking. The next chapter addresses some discipline-specific problems that students may encounter and the specific help that each subject teacher might contribute to a schoolwide content area literacy effort.

✦ ✦ TRADE SECRET ✦ ✦

Instant Study Strategies

You may not realize it by the gyrations of day-to-day schooling, but students are influenced by what their teachers genuinely care about. So, care about study, and show it. To show you care, you might post instant study strategies, such as those listed next (based on Friedel,

1976), on a bulletin board for students to read at their leisure (omitting the italicized information). After a week or so, you can begin to call attention to the list, adding the italicized information as warranted by discussions with students. This can be especially impressive to students, parents, and other faculty if it is done by the homeroom and study hall teacher, as well as the content teacher.

Instant Study Strategies

1. *Come early to class and leave late.*   Important guides to the material and tips on exams frequently are given in the first and last minutes of class.

2. *Sit close to the front of the room.*   Studies have shown that students who sit in the front of the class make better grades. Perhaps this is true because those who choose to sit closer to the front are the more motivated students—but why not assume that a positive feedback loop is at work here; that is, proximity to the instructor increases concentration, which enhances motivation.

3. *Take good notes.*   The most effective study time may be the actual hour of the class. Take extensive notes and concentrate during class, and you will have a good record for thought and home study.

4. *Review class notes as soon as possible.*   Immediate review probably is the most powerful learning strategy known. Go over the lecture mentally as you walk to your next class. Make it a habit to briefly review class notes each school night.

5. *Preview a reading assignment before reading it.*   Think about the title and subheadings. Look at the pictures, charts, and other graphic material. Think about what you already know about the topic, and predict what the author's main points are likely to be. This gives focus and purpose to reading.

6. *Underline or highlight after you have read a paragraph.* This focuses attention and concentration and avoids automatic reading or, worse, mindless reading.

7. *Your past and present are your future.*   Your present level of knowledge is the best predictor of how well you will read and learn now and in the future. Build your fund of information by reading an encyclopedia, almanac, or other nonfiction work for fifteen minutes a day. You will be surprised at how quickly the facts and ideas will begin to repeat themselves.

SECTION IV

Reference Information in Content Area Literacy

This final section of the text might be called "Reference Chapters." Even if you have selectively studied the previous chapters, you probably are very close to what in science is called a supersaturated solution—that is, so filled with new information and considerations that to add more could cause most prior learnings to fall to the bottom like excess particles. Nonetheless, there is much more to know.

The next three chapters have been designed to serve some of this ongoing information need, while acknowledging your saturated condition. Therefore, these chapters are presented largely as material for optional assignment by your course professor but also as a reference source, if your initial or subsequent teaching assignment warrants some of this information. To use this information expeditiously, survey each chapter for those things that you think are of immediate value, and mentally note where other topical material is for future possible reference.

By way of overview, Chapter 11 provides you with further specific content area literacy information on your own subject specialization and that of other subjects. Chapter 12 will help you better assist students with special needs as you pursue both discipline-specific and content literacy objectives. Chapter 13 should help you to further see the big picture, or where and how much of the previous information might come together in a schoolwide content area literacy program and toward your personal professional growth.

CHAPTER 11

Discipline-Specific Problems, Contributions, and Applications

Too much new information can drive knowledge out of circulation.
Knowledge is orderly and cumulative, an enduring treasure.

—Dan Boorstin

✦ Organizing Thoughts ✦

In the interest of raising your understanding of some of the special problems, contributions, and methods that are appropriate to your specific discipline, and to the various other disciplines, brief sections follow on each of the subjects found in a typical middle or senior high school. The ensuing information should serve you largely as reference material if you need to function in some interdisciplinary or integrated studies school situation.

ENGLISH

The English curriculum is the focal point for teaching language mastery. The term *English* is a quaint reminder of our colonial and cultural past. In fact, our language is Anglo-American, and the discipline is language arts, or effective listening, speaking, reading, and writing.

Reading and English

Student progress in reading receives its greatest emphasis in the English curriculum. English is the only discipline that traditionally has designated reading improvement as a key objective. It also has traditionally provided direct and systematic instruction in vocabulary, writing, cultural literacy, and literary appreciation. Lately, it has taken to teaching mass media and communications as well. As such, it lays the modern as well as the classical foundations for effective comprehension in all realms and ensures that at least some explicit attention is given to receptive and expressive language in school. There are sound reasons for continuing this focus on language up to and through graduate education. The most obvious is the fact that oral, written, and spoken language, like reading, are developmental processes that can be refined and enhanced throughout one's lifetime.

The English curriculum has special requirements. The most difficult of these is the requirement to read anthologies of prose and poetry that often span hundreds of years in origins, context, and style.

A newer view of the English/language arts curriculum says that a good job is being done with prose and poetry reading but that students need to be taught more about how to read technical writing, something nineteen other industrialized nations already do. Some school reformers maintain that America has moved on from being an industrialized society to one based on technologies and that our curricula are yet to catch up.

Much of the catch-up being called for, we believe, is occurring and will continue at a lively pace. This is largely due to the influence of the content area literacy movement, and the InterNet, which is bringing terse, content-laden, high-tech language into schools and homes via electronic text. For these reasons, we believe there is little reason to panic and revolutionize this aspect of education; rather, educators just need to stay a bit ahead of it and let the process continue to evolve. In this way, new technologies will be folded into the core curriculum without another overswing of the educational pendulum.

While most all of the methods presented thus far would serve the English/language arts curriculum, two are highlighted here: specifications for English textbooks that could be added to the Informal Textbook Inventory (ITI) (see Figure 11.1) and Read-and-Meet-the-Author (Santeusanio, 1967), a method designed to improve creative writing and the art of reading like an author.

Read-and-Meet-the-Author

Ideal for teaching creative writing, Read-and-Meet-the-Author (RAMA) (Santeusanio, 1967) essentially involves taking students' essays, short stories, or poems and treating them as if they were manuscripts being readied for publication.

A few students' works are selected and edited with the teacher's assistance. Questions to accompany each piece are prepared, and the works are duplicated for classroom use. They are then read and discussed by the class. Importantly, authors are present for the discussions and may join in to state their intentions or to clarify ambiguities.

The discussions that ensue are lively and informative. Lessons of this type tend to parallel the objectives of the writing process discussed in Chapter 9 but tend to unfold in a more natural way and with a real audience. Coincidentally, this method is highly motivational, since the material tends to be inherently close to students' interests and experiences.

MATHEMATICS

Repeatedly, reports of the National Assessment of Educational Progress reveal dismal facts about the state of mathematics proficiency in the United States:

+ More than 25% of thirteen-year-olds cannot handle elementary school arithmetic.
+ One-third of eleventh graders agree that they don't even know what their math teacher is talking about.

Figure 11.1
Informal Textbook Inventory questions for English.

I. **Use of Text Aids to Locate Information**

Construct 10 to 15 questions that assess students' ability to use parts of the textbook, such as

A. What is the title of the book?

B. When was it published?

C. Who wrote the book?

D. How many chapters are arranged or grouped?

E. On what page does Chapter 8 begin?

F. In which chapter can you find something about Langston Hughes?

G. In which chapter can you find "Types of Humor in Modern American Literature?"

II. **Rate of Reading and Levels of Comprehension**

Choose a passage from the textbook that students have not read. Have students read the passage and record the time when they finish it. Help them to compute their rate of reading, or words per minute (number of words read divided by number of minutes spent = words per minute). Have students answer questions about the passage that require comprehension at literal, interpretive, and applied levels.

III. **Vocabulary Development**

A. *Contextual Analysis:* Choose sentences from the textbook that contain words that may be difficult for students. List these sentences, with the difficult words underlined. Have students predict the meaning of the underlined words, using clues from the context to make reasonable predictions (evaluate student responses in terms of reasonableness of prediction rather than accuracy of definition).

B. *Structural Analysis:* Select words from the textbook that are made up of affixes and recognizable English root words. Have students identify and explain the meaning or function of the root word, prefix, and/or suffix in each of these words.

Figure 11.1, *continued*

C. *Dictionary Use:* Choose sentences from the textbook that contain a word or words that have multiple meanings. List these sentences, with the multiple-meaning word(s) underlined. Have students check a dictionary to select and write the appropriate meaning of each underlined word according to its use in the sentence.

IV. **Use of Reference Sources to Locate Information**

A. In our classroom dictionary, locate the origin of the word _____ .

B. Using the library card catalog, find the names of two books written by _____ . Who is the author of _____ ?

C. In the *Reader's* Guide to Periodical Literature, locate the journal and the year and month in which you find the short story entitled _____ _____ .

D. In the *Essay and General Literature Index*, find the titles for three stories related to the theme of (family conflict).

E. In the *Current Biography*, locate information about an author's life.

F. In *Bartlett's Familiar Quotations*, locate the person credited with having written: "Go, sir, gallop, and don't forget that the world was made in six days. You can ask me for anything you like, except time."

G. A thesaurus is a book of words grouped by ideas and used to locate precise words to express your idea. In *Roget's International Thesaurus*, locate at least three nouns that could be used instead of *cheerfulness*.

V. **Use of Graphic Aids to Interpret Meaning**

A. Study the cartoon on page _____ of your text. Describe what you believe to be the message of the cartoon.

B. Examine the time line of major English literary periods on page _____ of your text. What years are considered to encompass the neoclassical literary period? List three prominent writers for this period.

C. The diagram on page _____ depicts the plot structure of Jackson's *The Lottery*. After reading the story, briefly discuss the conflict, rising action, climax, and denouement of *The Lottery*.

Note. Section III.C. from an unpublished term paper by Fengfang Lu, 1986, University of Missouri–Kansas City. Sections IV and V from *Content Reading: A Diagnostic/Prescriptive Approach* (pp. 83, 124–125) by B. L. Criscoe and T. C. Gee, 1984, Upper Saddle River, NJ: Prentice Hall. Copyright 1984 by Prentice-Hall. Reprinted by permission of Prentice-Hall, Inc.

✦ Only 6% of seventeen-year-olds can handle algebra or multistep math problems.

✦ Scores for blacks and Hispanics, despite modest gains, lag 7% to 11% behind those of Caucasians.

✦ The average Japanese and Taiwanese high school student does better at math than does the top 5% of American high school students.

The difficulties students experience in dealing effectively with word problems and related mathematical concepts are unparalleled among current educational dilemmas. Clearly, there are more math illiterates than there are people who cannot read. Until recently, however, this problem has been among the lowest-ranked national priorities. Weakness in dealing with math concepts, computation, and word problems is so pervasive that it tends to pass for a fact of life.

Mathematics as a Second Language

Improvement of mathematics and reading instruction has finally begun with the reconstruction of math books to conform more closely to conventional conversational language. See Figure 11.2 for examples of the more conventional language found in modern math texts. Math itself is a system of reality coding that benefits from this more conversational approach. Students can be taught to listen to and speak the language of mathematics in settings and situations that closely parallel the ways in which people successfully learn second languages. Using the principles of second-language instruction, the reason, purpose, and value of mathematical systems can be more easily imparted, reinforced, and internalized. One such principle is to introduce the second language learner to the culture and tools of the new language. A math book is both math culture and a math learning tool.

Informal Textbook Inventory

The math teacher should plan on spending a minimum of three days on the ITI and giving two one-day refresher and extender sessions about two months apart. As students' skills and knowledge base in mathematics grow, so will their perceived need for, and therefore receptivity to, the helping features and value of the text.

The teacher should make an extra effort to conduct all sessions in a relaxed and supportive atmosphere. The ITI experience can be a nonthreatening, teacher-generated means of desensitizing and counterconditioning math anxiety. The examples of Figure 11.2, especially questions 2, 5, 6, and 7, offer useful ways to help students converse in conversational terms about mathematical systems. Note especially question 7 for its possibilities for making math something to be curious about and interested in.

Figure 11.2
Informal Mathematics Textbook Inventory.

1. **Locating Information**

   Directions: Terms used in the book can be found in one of several places; preface, contents, appendix, and glossary/index. You will be able to locate each term on the right in one of the places on the left. Locate the term, and then mark the place where you found it. Do this as quickly as you can.

   Book Section   Term

   A.   Preface   _____ Using your income
                                    _____ Axes
   B.   Contents   _____ Individual differences
                                    _____ 4 pecks = 1 bushel
   C.   Appendix   _____ Cubic units
                                    _____ Objectives
   D.   Glossary/Index   _____ Tables and graphs
                                    _____ 1,760 yards = 1 mile
                                    _____ Dividing fractions
                                    _____ Hourly wage
                                    _____ Measure your progress
                                    _____ Inch
                                    _____ Lesson organization
                                    _____ Overtime
                                    _____ Review

2. **Reading the Mathematics Textbook**

   Directions: Read page 69. When you have finished reading, close your book and answer the following questions. Remember, once you have closed the book, you may not open it for any answers.

   Vocabulary: Mathematical and General

   a.   Define *prime* first in the words of the text, then in your own words.

   What the text said: _____

   Your words: _____

   b.   What did the author mean when he said, "a simple hunting and fishing existence . . . "? _____

   c.   What does the term *signified* mean?_____

   _____

Main Ideas

    d. How did the author explain that early humans needed a method of counting things?

       _____

    e. Why did the author include information about early counting methods in this chapter?

       _____

3. **Interpreting Graphs**

Directions: Turn to page 259, and read the section entitled "Reading Bar Graphs." Study Figure 199, and answer the following questions:

    a. How many students (total number) are represented on the bar graph? _____

    b. Circle the two categories below in which the same number of students is found:

            Poor   Fair   Good   Excellent   Superior

    c. Use the graph to determine an approximate answer to each of the following questions:

       How many students received "poor" grades? _____

       How many students received "good" grades? _____

       How many students received "excellent" grades? _____

       How many students received "superior" grades? _____

    d. Would you say that this test was a good test or a poor test? (Explain your answer.)

4. **Seeing and Using Text Markers**

Directions: Read pages 119–121. When you finish, close your book and fill in the missing parts of the following outline. Do this in pen.

    I. Units of Measurement

        A. Direct: measuring height with ruler

        B. _____

            1. Measuring temperature — thermometer

            2. _____ — _____

            3. _____ — _____

            4. Measuring air pressure — barometer

Figure 11.2, *continued*

    II.   Ancient Measurement Devices
        A.   _____
             1.   Thumb
             2.   Foot
             3.   Hand
             4.   Forearm
             5.   _____
        B.   Difficulties of Ancient Measuring Devices
             1.   _____
             2.   _____

Directions: Now that you have written in your first set of responses in pen, open your book and try to complete the outline in pencil.

5. **Summarizing**
   Directions: You are going to read the section "The Metric System of Weights and Measures," p. 202. When you have finished this section about the consistency of the metric system, close your book. Write a summary of what you have read in four complete sentences.

   _____

   _____

   _____

   _____

6. **Where I Need Help!**
   Directions: Think back to all that you just read and the answers you gave. Indicate in no fewer than two sentences where you think you need help in understanding the information presented.

   _____

   _____

7. **What More?**
   Directions: Think again about what you have read. What are you most curious about? Write at least one sentence telling what you would like to learn more about.

   _____

   _____

The next method for teaching mathematics and reading also imparts something more of the culture that is part of thinking and talking about math. The method addresses the persistent problem of reading and comprehending word problems. There have been many efforts to make math more friendly, such as with the lively and loosely connected quote and colorful names and problems. (See Figure 11.3 from a recent mathematics textbook for examples of both of these.) Nonetheless, word problems remain complex; the one shown from the math book in Figure 11.3 has five major parts and is difficult to translate into computational steps, which most students know how to do.

The Dahmus Method for Word Problems

The Dahmus method for teaching word problems (Dahmus, 1970) emphasizes the translation of English statements into math statements. Recall from previous chapters that translation questions provide a bridge from literal to higher-order thinking skills.

Steps in the Dahmus Method

1. The statements and their parts in the translation must be in the same order as the verbal form.

2. No operations or substitutions should be performed until the translation is completed.

3. Students should read slowly and translate each idea and fact in the verbal form as it appears before reading the entire problem.

4. All other facts suggested by the verbal form and required for the solution should be stated mathematically on students' papers. There should be no verbal forms of translation, only math notation.

5. Students should use deductive reasoning on the translated and implied facts to obtain a solution.

Figure 11.4 provides an example of the Dahmus method.

BIOLOGICAL-PHYSICAL SCIENCES

For over 40 years, science education has called for science to be taught as a narrative of inquiry with emphasis on self-discovery and hands-on learning. In point of fact, science education remains largely textbook dominated. On the plus side, a good deal of the influence of this revisionist view is now being reflected in published science materials and in a revised and more socially sensitive science curriculum in teacher training institutions. Accordingly, the stated goals of science education now

6-2

Area of Rectangles and Squares

WHAT YOU'LL NEED

✓ **Square tiles**

✓ **Graph paper**

Problem Solving Hint

Drawing diagrams may help.

⌐T⌐H⌐I⌐N⌐K⌐ ⌐A⌐N⌐D⌐ ⌐D⌐I⌐S⌐C⌐U⌐S⌐S⌐

Moses is planning a garden. He decides to use 12
square garden plots that measure 1 m on each side.
He wants to arrange them in a rectangle. After he
lays out the plots, he will put a fence around the
outside of the garden.

1. a. How could Moses arrange the plots so that
he would have the least perimeter and use
the least amount of fence? **in a 3 m by 4
m rectangle**

  b. How could Moses arrange the plots so that
he would have the greatest perimeter? **a
12 m by 1 m rectangle**

2. a. What is the area of the arrangement with
the least perimeter? **12 m²**

  b. What is the area of the arrangement with
the greatest perimeter? **12 m²**

  c. Will the area change if Moses arranges the
plots in a nonrectangular shape? Why or
why not? **No; no matter how he arranges
the plots, there are 12 with area 1 m² each.**

In the garden-plot problem you can count the
square plots to find the area of the rectangular
arrangement. When you do not have squares to
count, you can find the area A of a rectangle by
multiplying the length l and the width
w. You can find the perimeter P
by adding $l + w + l + w$ to get
$2l + 2w$, or $2(l + w)$.

In 600 B.C.
Nebuchadnezzar
had the Hanging
Gardens of Babylon built.
They were so beautiful and
complex that they became
one of the seven wonders of
the ancient world.

Source: Encyclopedia Britannica

Area and Perimeter of a Rectangle

$$A = l \times w$$

$$P = 2(l + w)$$

A square is a rectangle in which the
length and the width are equal. You can
find the area A of a square by squaring the
length s of a side. The perimeter P is $4s$.

Figure 11.3 Aids in modern mathematics textbooks.

Note. From *Middle Grades Mathematics: An Interactive Approach* (p. 233), by S. H. Chapin,
M. Illingworth, M. S. Landau, J. O. Masingila, and L. McCracken, 1995. Upper Saddle River,
NJ: Prentice Hall. Copyright 1995 by Prentice-Hall. Reprinted by permission.

Figure 11.4
Example: The Dahmus method.

Mark is twice as old as John. In two years, the sum of their ages M   = 2X   J.   (M + 2)   +   (J + 2) will be five times as much as John's age was four years ago. =   5   X   (J − 4) How old is each now? M = ?   J = ?

Source: Dahmus, 1970.

include understanding the self, appreciating (i.e., reading and following) technology, preparing for college, advancing modern culture, and understanding local issues.

Contribution of Science to Reading

The typical science curriculum, whether textbook or experiment based, already contributes naturally to growth in reading. Simply by teaching science well, the science teacher helps students to better grasp the fundamentals of systematic observation, scientific thinking, problem solving, science vocabulary, science concepts, and the physical world. These elements promote progress in reading by enhancing student schemata, as well as important related linguistic and thinking processes. For these reasons, science and reading have been called a "harmonic convergence" (Johnson, 1995).

The characteristics of an expert reader, such as described in Chapters 4 and 6, strongly resemble and therefore are greatly compatible with the characteristics of a scientifically literate person as defined by the National Science Teachers Association:

> The scientifically literate person has a substantial knowledge base of facts, concepts, conceptual networks, and process skills which enable individuals to continue to learn and think logically.

Problems in Reading Science

The problems students encounter in reading science material stem in large measure from five problem areas:

✦ Inadequate background of information

✦ Misconceptions about the physical world

✦ Inconsiderate or assumptive and inadequately explained text

✦ Difficulty in handling esoteric or technically overwhelming terms

✦ Inadequate preparation and orientation of teachers, particularly at the elementary level, in the basic sciences

Consider now some solutions to these problems as they bear on effective reading and study in science.

Using New-Generation Science Texts

A new generation of science materials offers great promise but has some rough spots that are not easily overcome. These materials are better grounded in compellingly interesting issues, they stress scientific thinking, and they offer opportunities for developing integrated reading, writing, and science skills. The problem they pose is that issues-based materials tend to exceed the mental and social maturity levels of most students and can be quite controversial in some communities. Also, real issues cannot easily be disassembled and reassembled to meet a typical learning sequence. Nonetheless, students do become engaged.

Another new development in science texts is the causal use of and reference to prose and poetry as a common, or known, ground on which to build a sense of familiarity and a basis for new, less familiar knowledge (see Figure 11.5). Admittedly, these connections sometimes appear a bit strained, but in our experience students would rather have them than not.

Use of Science Texts

One ready means of learning how effectively students are using their science text while helping them improve their use is to prepare an ITI on the basic text. See Figure 11.6 for examples of science-oriented items to add to an ITI.

Using Media, Magazines, and Computers

One effective way to build your own as well as students' background knowledge in science is to read lay science magazines, watch public television, and access a multimedia encyclopedia and texts on CD-ROM and the InterNet. A new breed of lay technical writers are turning out articles on such mind-boggling topics as quantum physics and string theory in crystal-clear language—which is not to say that these topics are easily comprehended even then. *Discover* and *Omni* are among the best written of these publications.

5–2 The Excretory System

When the sixteenth-century English poet John Donne wrote that "No man is an island, entire of itself," he was actually talking about the human mind and spirit. However, this phrase can also be used to describe the human body: No human body can function without help from its surroundings. For example, your body must obtain food, water, and oxygen from its surroundings and get rid of wastes that may poison you. In order to do this, three body systems work together to provide a pathway for materials to enter and leave the body.

You have already learned about two of these systems: the digestive system and the respiratory system. The digestive system is the pathway for food and water to enter the body. The respiratory system enables oxygen to enter and carbon dioxide and water vapor to leave the body. The third system is the excretory (EHKS-kruh-tor-ee) system. **The excretory system provides a way for various wastes to be removed from the body.** These wastes include excess water and salts, carbon dioxide, and urea (a nitrogen waste). The process by which these wastes are removed from the body is called **excretion.**

You have just read about one of the organs of the excretory system: the lungs. Because the lungs get rid of the wastes carbon dioxide and water vapor, they are members of the excretory system as well as the respiratory system. The remaining organs of the excretory system are the kidneys, the liver, and the skin.

ACTIVITY
READING

①

Reading Poetry

The first line of John Donne's poem entitled "Meditation XVII" was quoted in this chapter. Find a copy of this poem in the library and read it. Is there another line in this poem that is familiar to you?

The Kidneys

Have you ever made spaghetti? If so, you know that you have to use a strainer to separate the cooked spaghetti from the cooking water or else you will be eating soggy spaghetti! The strainer acts as a filter, separating one material (spaghetti) from the other (water). Like the spaghetti strainer, the **kidneys** act as the body's filter. In doing so, the kidneys filter wastes and poisons from the blood.

The kidneys, which are the main organs of the excretory system, are reddish brown in color and

Figure 11.5 Poetry and the excretory system.

Using Resource Materials

The book *Through the Magnifying Glass* will tell you many ways to use scientific tools:

- How could you find out who wrote the book?
- What is its library call number?
- Where in the library could you locate the titles of filmstrips that deal with ecology?
- In what library index could you locate the title of an article by Asimov?

Applying Theoretical Information

- How can the law of "centrifugal force" be proven?
- Describe an example of inertia that you might see every day.

Formulas and Symbols

- List the meaning of the symbols F and C.

  What do cm and ml stand for in measurement? (Criscoe & Gee, 1984, pp. 124-125)

Using Graphics and Visual Aids

- What does the illustration on page 202 (see below) say about the current flow in electricity?

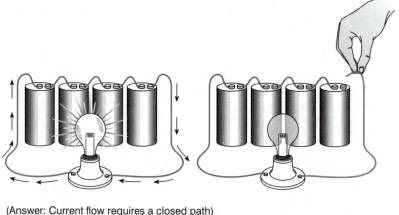

(Answer: Current flow requires a closed path)

Figure 11.6
Sample items for an Informal Textbook Inventory for a science text.

Adaptations of the Guided Reading Procedure for Science

Two adaptations of the Guided Reading Procedure (GRP) (Manzo, 1975) (see Chapter 4) are especially appropriate for pre- and postreading activities using science material (Spiegel, 1980). The GRP-based prereading procedure has students identify clear purposes for study, become aware of specific gaps in their knowledge, and build the scaffolding necessary for forming new concepts. This is achieved by having students bring to mind what they already know about a topic and then organizing this information into an advance outline before reading. Then students read to test their preconceptions.

Steps in the Prereading GRP

1. The teacher identifies a unit or topic of study that is fairly narrow in scope, such as photosynthesis or spiders.

2. The teacher has students tell peer recorder(s) at the chalkboard everything they know about the topic before lecture or reading.

3. The class identifies conflicting information and areas in which no information has been provided. ("Hey, we don't know what spiders eat!" "Are very large spiders insects or animals?")

4. Students construct an outline with conflicting information listed side by side. ("Spiders have six legs/eight legs?") Areas in which no information is known are listed by headings in the outline.

5. The outline is displayed in the classroom throughout the unit of study.

6. The class is told to read to fill in or alter the outline (see Figure 11.7).

Looking Back

Several other methods covered in previous chapters have excellent application to science. Chief among these are the Question-Only strategy (see Chapter 5), which offers an effective means of inquiry training; the Oral

Figure 11.7
GRP prereading outline.

Spiders

I. How they look
    A. Have six legs/eight legs?
    B. Have two body parts
    C. Antennae?

II. How they live
    A. What they eat?
    B. Spin webs
        1. Made of silk
        2. Lots of different kinds of webs
        3. Sticky
            a. What makes them sticky?
            b. Why doesn't the spider get stuck?

Reading strategy (see Chapter 6), for giving direct assistance with science words and phrasing; and Mapping (see Chapters 4 and 7), for imparting a conceptual set for numerous easily confounded details.

SOCIAL STUDIES

Executive Training

The Constitution gives enormous executive power to every citizen. Social studies are the fundamental school-based source of the executive training that every citizen needs in order to read, interpret, and vote on the streams of raw and prepared information emanating from newspapers, magazines, broadcast media, and now the InterNet. The awesome responsibility facing all citizens with such executive power increases the responsibility of those of us who must agonize over what and how to teach them. Accordingly, today's social studies consist not merely of traditional fields like history, government, and geography but fields such as psychology, sociology, and philosophy, and several conceptual approaches that can be applied across these fields, such as social inquiry, moral education, and values clarification (Peters, 1982). Indeed, one of the more welcome changes in the teaching of social studies is the increased focus on people. Look, for example, at the page from a contemporary text (Figure 11.8) to see how immigration has been reduced to human scale in the story of Sacco and Vanzetti; it's not *People* magazine, but it's also not the antiseptic and decontextualized social studies of just a generation ago.

Contribution of Social Studies to Reading

The principles, precepts, and actual content of social studies underlie almost everything written. This may explain why social studies as a discipline is so highly correlated with general reading comprehension (Adams, 1902; Artley, 1944). Also for this reason, the social studies teacher is especially well situated to enhance students' understanding of how best to read and think about nearly all things written. This is done naturally as the teacher and textbook report to students how others think and feel about a variety of issues such as economics, politics, and culture and about the consequences of these beliefs on individual liberties. Most important from the standpoint of reading process, social studies impart a rich fund of general information, a specialized vocabulary, refined critical-relative thinking strategies, and the rudiments of cultural literacy, both about the core culture and the many diverse cultures within the American mainstream. Social studies also are students' main source of information on our growing global awareness.

Sacco and Vanzetti
Millions of Americans mourned when Nicola Sacco and Bartolomeo Vanzetti were executed. They believed the immigrants were victims of prejudice. In this painting by Ben Shahn, the two men are shown handcuffed together as they await their fate. **Citizenship** *How did the Sacco and Vanzetti case fuel anti-immigrant feeling?*

Middle-class Americans worried that communists and anarchists would invade the United States.

Congress responded by passing the Emergency Quota Act in 1921. The act set up a quota system that allowed only a certain number of people from each country to enter the United States. "America must be kept American," said Calvin Coolidge.

The quota system favored immigrants from Northern Europe, especially Britain. In 1924, Congress passed new laws that further cut immigration, especially from Eastern Europe. In addition, Japanese were added to the list of Asians denied entry to the United States.

Immigrants From Latin America

Latin Americans and Canadians were not included in the quota system. In 1917, the Jones Act made Puerto Ricans American citizens. Poverty on the island led to a great migration to the United States. In 1910, only 1,500 Puerto Ricans lived in the mainland United States. By 1930, there were 53,000.

Farms and factories in the Southwest depended on workers from Mexico. By 1930, a million or more Mexicans had crossed the border. Most came to work in the vegetable fields, orchards, and factories of the Southwest. The pay was

low and the housing was poor. Still, the chance to earn more money was a very powerful lure. During the 1920s, more and more Mexicans began to settle in the large cities of the Midwest, too.

Solo in Chicago

Just before World War I, exciting news began filtering across the border into Mexico:

❝ In the early days . . . one heard only of the states of Texas and California. The few Mexicans that left Mexico went there and wrote back from there. After a while we heard of New Mexico and Arizona, but beyond that there was no more United States to us. I remember distinctly with what great surprise we received a letter in our pueblo from a Mexican who had gone to Pennsylvania. 'Oh, where can that be! That must be very, very far away.' ❞

As news about jobs in the United States spread, young Mexican men made their way to El Paso or Laredo, Texas. There, they

---

Figure 11.8

Putting the *story* back in history.

Note. From *The American Nation* (p. 700), by J. W. Davidson and M. B. Stoff, 1995. Upper Saddle River, NJ: Prentice Hall. Copyright 1995 by Prentice-Hall. Reprinted by permission.

Obstacles to Reading and Studying in Social Studies

The major problems students encounter in reading in social studies stem in large measure from the very elements to which social studies ultimately contribute in general reading. Reading in social studies often requires conceptual and informational preparation. It also requires considerable assistance with objective reasoning and in connecting loose factual elements into a structure that subsequently can be used to read, grasp, and interpret still more.

Reasoning Guides

Reasoning Guides were developed and popularized in direct response to the preceding concerns. A Reasoning Guide is a specialized form of reading guide that strongly emphasizes interpretive and applied levels of reading and thinking (Herber, 1978). See Figure 11.9 for an example of the format and question types in a Reasoning Guide.

Steps in Using a Reasoning Guide

1. The teacher constructs a guide that draws focused attention to the key portions of a longer section (see Figure 11.10).
2. Students read the longer selection first before using the guide.
3. Students complete the Reasoning Guide, rereading the key portions of the text as necessary.
4. A class discussion in which students compare their answers and their reasons follows.
5. Students further discuss what they learned about their own thinking and about thinking in general, for example:
   a. In what way(s) can we discover what attitudes we and others hold other than by what we or they say? (By our or their actions?)
   b. Is there really any value in trying to form generalizations without all the facts? (Life requires that we do, but any new piece of information may change all previous thoughts and conclusions.)

Building Good Judgment

No one is born with good judgment. It is painstakingly acquired. An interesting format for promoting good judgment, or critical-evaluative thinking, in social studies was borrowed from experimental tests (Manzo & Manzo, 1990a) and further developed by ninth-grade teachers Susan Tarwater and the late Phyllis McConnel. McConnel and Tarwater used these formats in a team-taught core curriculum program combining

Figure 11.9
Sample Reasoning Guide for social studies.

Directions: Reread the sentences below taken from John F. Kennedy's inaugural address, which you just read in its entirety in your textbook. Then complete the exercises called for below.

  A. The world is very different now.

  B. For man holds in his mortal hands the power to abolish all forms of human poverty and all forms of human life.

  C. [T]he rights of man come not from the generosity of the state but from the hand of God.

  D. United there is little we cannot do in a host of cooperative ventures.

  E. To those people in huts . . . we pledge our best efforts . . . not because the communists are doing it, . . . but because it is right.

  F. We dare not tempt them with weakness.

  G. So let us begin anew, remembering on both sides that civility is not a sign of weakness.

  H. Let both sides explore what problems unite us instead of belaboring those problems which divide us.

  I. And so, my fellow Americans, ask not what your country can do for you, ask what you can do for your country.

---

social studies and English. The team approach permitted team members to relieve one another from classroom teaching duties to enable them to develop the necessary materials.

In the Critical Judgments Exercise, students first decide and then discuss their judgments of the relative values of certain pieces of information. The format can be used with general or background information or with items selected from a section of text that students read in class. Figure 11.10 presents examples of both general information and text-based items.

Physical Education

"Reading is sport," wrote Gentile (1980). "It requires mastering the fundamental skills, sufficient practice, a well-balanced diet of literary experiences, and a lifetime of development" (p. 4). The artificial separation of physical and academic education that exists in most schools is unfortunate, unnecessary, and uncaring. Plato placed gymnastics at the highest level for training his philosophers.

Figure 11.9, *continued*

Directions: Now consider each of the statements below, and decide based on the statements above whether J.F.K. would have approved or disapproved of each. In column A, answer yes or no. In column B, write the letter indicating the quotation from J.F.K. that influenced your decision. For number 10, write an original statement that you think J.F.K. might have made. Quote some part of the address (in your text) other than the quotations listed above as evidence.

A   B

____ ____ 1. The problems we are facing today are not much different from those that faced our forefathers.

____ ____ 2. The oriental world is immensely different from our own.

____ ____ 3. Our rights are given to us out of the goodness of humans' love for humankind.

____ ____ 4. If we are to win over the threat of world communism, we must give money, supplies, and help to underdeveloped nations of the world.

____ ____ 5. Let us demonstrate our goodwill to the world by disarming.

____ ____ 6. Only the federal government can solve the complex problems of our society.

____ ____ 7. We will never resort to violence.

____ ____ 8. The events of the past have helped us to realize the truth of Washington's policy of isolationism. We should continue to heed the advice of our president.

____ ____ 9. The greatest threat to humankind is not famine and sickness but the threat of world communism.

____ ____ 10. _____

_____

_____

Figure 11.10
Critical judgments exercise.

Part 1: General Information Items
Directions: Using your best judgment, decide what you think would be the value to society in knowing each of the statements listed below. Consider each statement to be true. We shall discuss these momentarily.

$$1 = \text{of no use}$$
$$2 = \text{of little use}$$
$$3 = \text{of moderate use}$$
$$4 = \text{very useful}$$
$$5 = \text{extremely useful}$$

____ 1. Mary Queen of Scots inherited the throne at the age of six days.

____ 2. Simplicity and elegance in writing are more desirable than length or vocabulary.

____ 3. The first European to sail into New York Harbor was Henry Hudson.

____ 4. The tomato is not a vegetable but a fruit.

____ 5. Left-handedness is a recessive genetic trait.

____ 6. Mary Goddard was the only woman to have her name on the Declaration of Independence.

____ 7. Diamond dust is black.

____ 8. Red meats are high in fat content.

Part 2: Text-Based Items
Directions: Indicate your judgment of the relative values of the statements below taken from your text. Use the five-point scale—
1 = lowest, 5 = highest value— that we have used previously.

A. ____ 1. The Nobel Prize is given at least once every five years.

____ 2. The Nobel Prize is awarded for important discoveries or inventions in the five categories of knowledge.

____ 3. No Nobel Prizes were given in 1940 to 1942.

____ 4. The Nobel Prize was founded by Alfred Nobel, a Swedish chemist and philanthropist.

____ 5. Women as well as men have been awarded the Nobel Prize.

B. ____ 1. Oliver Cromwell was called "The Protector."

____ 2. Cromwell was born in 1599.

____ 3. Cromwell was a violent and persuasive speaker.

____ 4. Cromwell expanded England's territories and increased its commerce.

____ 5. Cromwell's court was frugal but dignified.

The Physical Domain
Linking Physical and Academic Development.   The relationship between physical and academic development is more than coincidental. As we noted in earlier chapters, all learning enters through and takes place in the body as well as in the mind. The linking of motor involvement with language and academic learning can be a natural for the physical education class, as illustrated in a recent news report that went something like this:

> In the gymnasium at the Jackson Avenue Elementary School of Mineola, New York, eight-year-olds ran through the pathways of a human circulatory system drawn on the parquet floor.
> Pretending they were blood cells, they grabbed oxygen molecules (bean bags) from a bucket, raced through the heart chambers (red and blue Hula-Hoops), and completed the circuit by exchanging the oxygen for carbon dioxide (crumpled waste paper). Their warm-up finished, the panting pupils checked their pulse rates.
> Watching them, Kathleen Kern, the school's physical education teacher, said, "You can't teach kids about aerobic fitness until they understand the circulatory system."

In the same vein, Gentile (1980) suggests an interesting metacognitive activity involving reading, appreciation of the physical domain, and provocative discussion: In gym class, have students read and discuss statements, such as one from Michener's *Sports in America*, which says, in effect: "If I had a child determined to be a writer, I'd expect that child to take two courses: one in ceramics so that he or she could feel form emerging from inchoate clay and a second in eurythmic dancing so that child could feel within his or her own body the capacity for movement, form, and dramatic shifts in perspective."

The highest goal of the reading curriculum, as noted several times previously, is not merely to teach youngsters to read but to promote language, thinking, and socioemotional maturity. Following, in slightly paraphrased form, are a few methods recommended by Maring and Ritson (1980), professors of reading and physical education, respectively, for fostering content area literacy in gym classes.

Method 1: Reading to Reinforce Instruction.   Make up one-page handouts that summarize and reinforce the physical education content and skills that have just been taught via lecture explanation, demonstration, or charts and diagrams. Type key terms in all-capital letters, and underline portions of the text that explain their meanings. On the bottom or back of each handout, include a set of questions that relate to the main ideas in the lesson. After students have read the handout, have them form small groups to answer the questions (see Figure 11.11).

Figure 11.11
Reading to reinforce instruction: The basic rules of basketball.

Directions: Review the underlined information about the capitalized key terms below. Then answer the questions that follow.

Key Terms

1.   Each team is composed of five MEMBERS who play the entire court area.

2.   A team scores 2 points when the ball passes through the hoop during regular play (FIELD GOAL).

3.   A team may score additional points by means of free throws when a member of the opposing team commits a PERSONAL FOUL (hacking, pushing, holding, etc.).

Questions

1.   Where on the court do team members play?

2.   Explain in your own words what a field goal is.

3.   Name two kinds of personal fouls.

Method 2: Read and Do.   Prepare "read and do" instruction sheets so that students will learn required content and at the same time improve their ability to follow written directions (see Figure 11.12).

Method 3: Book Checkout.   In the locker room or near your office, place a revolving book rack displaying high-interest paperbacks with checkout cards pasted inside the back covers that relate to aspects of your physical education curriculum. Consult the school librarian and reading specialist for assistance in book selection. Have the class or team elect a librarian to be responsible for the lending and returning of the books.

Figure 11.12
Read and do: Motor development exercise.

Single-Heel Click
Jump into the air, click heels together once, and land with feet apart (any distance). This can be turned into an amusing exercise in which students try to write out totally unambiguous expository directions for their peers to follow. You might invite an English teacher to cooperate with you on this project.

Method 4: "Testlets." Evaluate students' performance skills and knowledge by giving short tests that require students to read and follow directions (see Figure 11.13). Each test can be presented on an individual card. Students should be familiar with this format before being tested.

Method 5: Student Reports. Have students read and write a brief (half-page) report on any person making news in sports. Invite different students to give these reports in the opening five minutes of class. Tack up the best reports on a cork display board (Gentile, 1980).

CONTENT AREA READING IN THE SUPPORT SUBJECT AREAS

Business, Vocational Technology, Art, Music, and Speech

The contemporary forces that have led to the information explosion in the core areas of the curriculum have profoundly influenced the support subjects as well. The evidence for this is readily apparent in even a casual inspection of any support area syllabus. In music, students now study jazz and rock as well as choral, orchestral, and symphonic works. In industrial arts, particularly automotive technology, there now is a strong emphasis on electronics. Home economics now addresses complex issues in nutrition, parenting, and diverse family relationships. Business education, which formerly meant typing and shorthand, now means word processing, inventory control, networking, and purchasing. In short, the traditional separation between academic subjects and what once were known as minor-area subjects has all but vanished. These support areas involve complex technologies and require considerable and ongoing reading, research, and critical analysis. In some very real sense, the so-called support area subjects are our best hope for a curriculum that is both authentic, in the sense of real, and interdisciplinary.

Today's teachers of these subjects rarely need to be convinced that their subjects contain a heavy academic component. Thus, the support area teacher now has a heavy investment in, and commitment to, nourishing reading, writing, studying, language, and thinking strategies.

Vocational Technology

Problems and Goals

Federal Public Law 98-524, also known as the Carl D. Perkins Vocational Act of 1984, has as one of its main purposes the goal of improving the academic foundations of vocational technology students. Simply put, the

Figure 11.13
Testlets.

Grapevine Test
Stand with heels together. Bend trunk forward, extend both arms down
between legs and behind ankles, and hold fingers of hands together
in front of ankles. Hold this position for five seconds. Failure: (a) loss of
balance, b) not holding fingers of both hands together, (c) not holding
the position for five seconds.

Three-Dip Test
Take a front leaning-rest position. Bend arms, touching chest to the floor,
and push body up again until forearms are in a straight line with upper
arms. Execute three performances in succession. Do not touch the floor
with legs or with abdomen. Failure: (a) not pushing body up three times,
(b) not touching chest to floor, (c) touching the floor with any part of the
body other than hands, feet, and chest.

Full-Left-Turn Test
Stand with feet together. Jump upward, making a full turn to the left.
Land at approximately the same place from where the test was started.
(Feet may be separated when landing.) Do not lose your balance or
move your feet after they have touched the floor. Failure: (a) not making
a full turn to the left, (b) moving feet after they have returned to the floor,
(c) loss of balance.

---

objective is to create a workforce able to adjust to the changing content
of jobs. This act contains provisions to support schools willing to develop
quality programming in reading, computing, and vocational areas.

The justification for such programming is well supported by several
studies that have shown that the average workday for nonprofessional
workers requires between 24 minutes and 4 hours of reading per day
(Rush, Moe, & Storlie, 1986). Related research indicates that workers
themselves underestimated by an average of 45% the amount of time
they spent reading (Mikulecky, 1982). Furthermore, job-related reading
is by no means easy. The materials essential to job competency in eleven
fields, ranging from account clerk to welder, have readability levels that
rarely dip as low as ninth grade and typically reach as high as the sixteenth grade level. Secretarial reading is the most difficult, ranging from
sixteenth to college graduate levels (Diehl & Mikulecky, 1980).

Not surprisingly, one of the nagging problems of vocational technology has been the difficulty level of school texts and the information and
schematics that come up on computer screens. Although this situation is
changing, examples of inconsiderate text still are plentiful. Derby (1987)
offers examples from one vocational technology textbook:

✦ "This chapter is devoted to a study of the various ways in which the basic engine theory and parts are utilized to produce multicylinder engines of several types." This, Derby explains, is an awkward way of saying that this chapter is about the different kinds of engines used in today's cars.

✦ In a second example, the same textbook states, "Although a number of three-rotor and four-rotor experimental engines have been built, common usage at this time employs either a one-rotor or a two-rotor engine." A more considerate-text version would read, "Although a number of experimental engines have been built with three or even four rotors, most engines being built today have just one or two rotors" (pp. 309–312).

Following are some services and functions that vocational technology teachers can offer to help promote literacy in this domain.

Seven Services Vocational Technology Teachers Can Provide

1. Work with students to use, and where necessary create, text aids such as advance organizers, pivotal questions, glossaries of terms, and concept maps.

2. Follow the simple steps of the Listen-Read-Discuss (see Chapter 2) method so that students will be better empowered for reading dense and often inconsiderate text.

3. Using the ITI, give students practice and instruction in using basic texts and reference books. For students of electricity, teach the use of the National Electrical Code; for health assistants, demonstrate the *Physicians' Desk Reference* on diseases; and for automotive students, develop familiarity with Chilton's repair manuals and other motor company services manuals.

4. Use the Question-Only procedure (see Chapter 5) as a prereading and prelecture method: Instead of merely announcing a topic, show the class a vital engine part, and have them conduct a systematic inquiry into its nature, functions, and most frequent failure points.

5. Vocational technology subjects offer abundant opportunities to use the Typical to Technical Meaning Approach (see Chapter 8) (Walker, 1985). This strategy also can be used to concurrently improve abstract thinking. Here are some examples of automotive terms, suggested by Piercy (1976), for which students might have culled meanings from everyday life:

   ✦ *Differential*—a set of gears that permit rear wheels to revolve at different speeds

   ✦ *Differential*—a peculiarity, distinction, feature, or earmark

✦ *Governor*—a device for automatically controlling the speed of an engine by regulating the intake of fuel

✦ *Governor*—the elected head of any state in the United States

✦ *Distributor*—a mechanical device for distributing electric current to the spark plugs of a gas engine

✦ *Distributor*—a business firm that distributes goods to customers

6. Guiding a pre- and postreading analysis of diagrams and illustrations is a powerful way to promote strategic reading. This can be done in a survey fashion before reading and in a very careful way following silent reading. When this procedure is followed routinely, students will be keyed into the supportive graphic material as they begin to read and anticipate further analysis following reading. This combination should increase the probability that they will use the illustrations, like the one in Figure 11.14, to grasp and clarify meanings when they

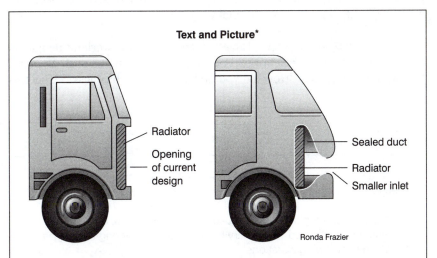

Text and Picture*

Radiator

Opening of current design

Sealed duct

Radiator

Smaller inlet

Ronda Frazier

Current truck radiator installation design (left) requires flat front. Air resistance can be reduced by a streamlined design (right) where ducts bring sufficient cooling air to the radiator.

*Through design improvement, over-the-road trucks can function with radiator openings one-third as large as those used currently. Sealing of ducts is necessary so that all cooling air is directed to the radiator. Applications of such truck designs have existed in the aircraft industry for many decades. Automotive engineers should examine aeronautical engineering practices in their quest for aerodynamic efficiency.

Figure 11.14
Using illustrations to grasp and clarify meaning.
Note. From Rush, R. Timothy, Moe, Alden J., & Storlie, Rebecca L. (1986). *Occupational literacy education.* Newark, DE: IRA. Reprinted with permission of R. Timothy Rush and the International Reading Association. All rights reserved.

read silently. It also should help them become better strategic readers when they must read independently in school and on the job.

Career-Oriented Literature

Quite apart from textbooks and manuals, the vocational technology teacher needs a ready and readable supply of career-oriented literature (COL). COL refers to articles and stories about jobs and career areas. It tends to reflect how real people feel about their jobs and vocations.

COL materials tend to touch on matters that textbooks and manuals rarely address, such as apprenticeship programs and various employee benefit options. For publishers who offer other special, hard-to-find, human elements, see Figure 11.15.

Language Experiences

Most activities undertaken in career and vocational education can be performed better with student input. Language Experience Activities (LEAs) provide such opportunities. Here are a few LEA-type activities that are especially suitable for the vocational technology class:

1. *Celebrity interview.* Have students interview working people as though the latter were celebrities. Ask concerned questions such as might be asked of celebrities: "How did you first get into this business?" "Has this

Figure 11.15
Career-oriented literature sources.

The Globe Book Company has two books containing true, brief anecdotal accounts of work situations that are unusual and sometimes humorous: *All in a Day's Work* and *It Happened on the Job.*

Pitman Learning offers Pacemaker Vocation Readers, a set of ten high-interest, controlled vocabulary books describing young trade-type people in challenging situations.

Scholastic Magazine has an Action Series that has a number of job-related storybooks like the *Plumber's Line, Rosina Torres, L.P.N., Demolition Man*, and *Paramedic Emergency*.

Vocational Biographies, Inc., offers *Project Earth* and *Project Explore,* describing jobs and careers in the context of scientific principles and actual vocational biographies highlighting real individuals.

Career World (formerly *Real World*) is a color newspaper, written in the vein of *USA Today*. It addresses the work-a-day world and contains actual reading skill exercises.

Note. Adapted from "Reading Instruction and Course Related Materials for Vocational High School Students" by T. Derby, 1987, *Journal of Reading, 39,* pp. 308–316.

work been fulfilling for you?" "Have you ever wished that you could have done something else?" "Can you tell me an interesting or amusing experience that you have had in this line of work?" Students could be instructed to watch television interview shows to get some ideas for "people questions." Discuss the questions they might ask before they ask them.

2. *Dialogue journal.* As previously noted, have students keep a journal in which they write a sentence or two every other day regarding their career interests and experiences. Periodically, read and write a brief reaction to these: "Charlie, I didn't realize that your father is an electrician!" "Mary, if you will see me after class, I can tell you where to get more information on summer jobs with the city."

3. *Vocabulary from the workplace.* To help build respect and support for the vocational program throughout the school, have students interview friends and family about words and expressions that they use on the job but laypeople would be unlikely to know. Ask English teachers, for example, to use the Vocabulary Self-Collection Strategy (Haggard, 1982) to include some of these words on English vocabulary lists (see Chapter 8). Vocabulary collections of this type can contribute to students' sense of accomplishment and make English teachers realize that many students who might not know what *onomatopoeia* means probably do know what a rocker panel is (the name for the narrow shelf beneath all car doors). Terms such as these, which the English teacher probably doesn't know and which rarely can be found in most standard dictionaries, constitute a wider and richer language system than most academically oriented teachers have considered.

4. *Magazines.* Have students subscribe to a few quality news and trade magazines. These can be read in class or for homework. Assign groups to give well-organized reports on different articles.

5. *Computer networks.* Browse the InterNet for home-page sites that correspond to specific vocational technical interests.

Art, Music, and Speech

Pleasure and Elevated Expression

Art, music, and speech teachers are important advocates and shapers of cultural literacy in the schools. Studies in art, music, and speech contribute to progress toward higher literacy in a variety of ways. Art and music raise students' level of cultural literacy; speech raises phonemic awareness (discussed later); and together they contribute to effective decoding and comprehension. Further, art, music, and speech offer a sheltering and enriching alternative to the sometimes harsh sounds and the challenges of life. As such, they enhance emotional well-being and simple joy in living. Art, music, and speech also tend to reflect diverse perspectives, dialects, and historical periods, and therefore contribute to a broader and more multicultural outlook. They also provide pleasure and offer an outlet for more elevated expression. For these reasons, it is important to consider ways to gently weave together content area literacy and the art, music, and speech curricula, since each benefits the other.

The Challenge

Writing in art and music almost by nature tends to be esoteric and difficult to read. Sentences often contain complex syntax, unusual phrasings, assumptive references, sophisticated ideas, and names and words of foreign origin. It has been said that "One does not really read a music theory book . . . one grapples with it" (Duke, 1987). A typical passage from even a popular library book on music reads like this:

> In all of art's best periods, creative people were brought together, and thus we had Pericles' Athens, the Medici's Florence, Elizabeth's London, Goethe's (and later Liszt's) Weimar, Beethoven's (and later Brahms') Vienna, Emerson's Concord, Lowell's Boston and Monet's Paris. These were by no means smooth waters, but they were lively. (Bacon, 1963, p. 130)

The reader needs to be quite well informed in the areas of art, music, literature, and history and in the characteristics of several different cultures to take in the full significance of this almost casual observation by pianist and teacher Earnest Bacon.

Meeting the Challenge

The art, music, and speech teacher can help students meet and profit from the challenge of inconsiderate text in several ways. Some of these are specified in the following list. Consider a suggestion to be applicable to all three subjects unless otherwise specified.

1. Use the Oral Reading Strategy (see Chapter 6) to familiarize students with syntax, phrasing, proper breathing, enunciation, and pronunciations.

2. Ask frequent translation questions: "Can you say this in your own words?"

3. Add information as needed to enhance schema, or background knowledge: "Have you read or heard about the Medici family in world history class yet? They were a wealthy and influential Italian family in medieval Florence—a thriving seaport city in Italy. They were great patrons of the arts."

4. Use the Listen-Read-Discuss method (see Chapter 2) and Note Cue (see Chapter 12) to guide reading and discussion in art, music, and effective speaking.

5. Have students use the Subjective Approach to Vocabulary with illustrations: Divide a page into quarters, have students write the new word in quadrant 1, write its dictionary meaning in 2, draw a pictorial representation in 3, and write the subjective association in 4. Then the class discusses these and stores them in their notebooks.

6. The ambitious speech/theater teacher or speech pathologist can incidentally help youngsters to become better decoders of words by raising their phonemic awareness, or sense of the speech sounds represented in print. In fact, an approach to reading by the Lindamoods (1975) is based on such training. The program, used largely across a wide range of ages and intellects, from preschool to professional adult levels, teaches students to feel and label various speech sounds, which are the basis for phonics in reading. Due to genetics, about one-third of the population cannot accurately identify sounds within spoken words. They cannot benefit from traditional phonics instruction because it primarily *exercises* rather than *develops* phonemic awareness. The terms used for the speech sounds are descriptive, rather than the technical terms used in linguistics (e.g., *fricatives, continuents*, etc.). See Figure 11.16 for sample descriptive labels that conceptualize the distinctive place and manner of the articulatory-motor features of speech sounds and develop phonemic awareness. For more precise information on this technique, see Manzo and Manzo (1993).

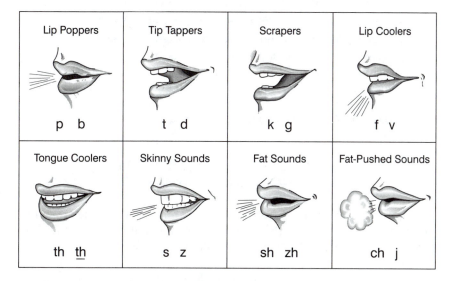

Figure 11.16
The Lindamood approach to reading.
Note. From *The A.D.D. Program, Auditory Discrimination in Depth* (Books 1 & 2) by C. H. Lindamood and P. C. Lindamood, 1975. Austin, TX: Pro-ed. Reprinted by permission.

7. Work with science, literature, and social studies teachers to have students produce various forms of artistic representations of significant ideas.

8. Work with the school principal to use music in appropriate settings. Music has been shown to facilitate creative writing, mathematics, spelling, and art (Greenhoe, 1972; Taylor, 1980). While music sometimes can be distracting during reading, classical music has been found to be conducive to comprehension gains (Mullikin & Henk, 1985). The classical music played in the study was Pietro Mascagni's "Intermeggio" from *Cavalleria Rusticana.* A no-music condition produced better performance than did rock music, which is to say that rock is disruptive. The researchers decided that it seemed to be the complexity of the music that stimulated reading and thinking. U. C. Manzo found this to be true while using taped music during sustained silent reading time with urban junior high school reading classes. Music was played during the first ten minutes of class, when students who were caught up with class work had the privilege of reading anything of their choosing. Manzo began the year with a few classical and easy-listening instrumental selections for free reading time. Not knowing about Mullikin and Henk's (1985) findings, Manzo succumbed several times to students' pleas to use rock music instead. It never worked: With a rock music background, students were more distracted than they would have been otherwise. When Manzo eliminated rock music, however, they appreciated the more traditional melodic pieces enough to hush one another rather than lose the privilege.

9. Outstanding television shows are dramatized with music. Work with the English teacher to have students think through and try to score selections of literature with appropriate musical pieces and/or poignant oral readings. This takes a good deal of thinking and analysis. If you feel daring, ask students to select or compose theme tunes for the school and/or individual teachers.

IN CONCLUSION: BE CREATIVE AND ENCOURAGE CREATIVITY

We urge you to encourage creative thinking and problem solving and to be encouraged to be creative in your own thinking and teaching. The three main ingredients for encouraging creativity follow:

✦ Connect your students and yourself to creative thinkers whenever and wherever you can. You might look up the web page of the Foundation for Better Ideas on the InterNet. It is one way to provide exposure to creative questions, creative answers, and even monetary and social incentives for creative production in a variety of disciplines and across disciplines.

✦ Teach students to formulate appropriate guiding questions, or purposes, for which to read and listen.

✦ Request and expect expression and creative production from your students, and they will not disappoint you.

✦ *Looking Back and Looking Ahead* ✦

This reference chapter was intended to provide you with further possible in-depth knowledge of content literacy in your own area of specialization and with an overview of the specific values and problems of the other disciplines. Logically, now, you may wish to know a bit more about how to attend to students with specific or special needs in these same situations. The next chapter will equip you to better understand and provide for such needs.

✦ ✦ TRADE SECRET ✦ ✦

Daily Diet and Teaching/Learning

Teaching and learning can be very taxing. However, a proper daily diet can help. You probably know your own dietary needs better than anyone, but here are some tips that might help you meet the challenges of effective teaching and that you can share with students as aids for effective learning.

1. Avoid full meals; they tend to induce lethargy.
2. Remember to eat a bit of something with complex carbohydrates (such as a bagel) and a little oil or fat (add some light cream cheese) to get the three or more hours of energy needed for continuous classes.
3. Soft drinks and mild coffee with caffeine are good stimulants, especially if taken in moderate quantities. (Paradoxically, the drug Ritalin, taken by many children with hyperactivity and learning disabilities, isn't much different from caffeine.)
4. Most importantly, drink as much water as you reasonably can.

The last suggestion bears some reinforcement, since there is a tendency to avoid drink when toilet facilities are not readily accessible.

By the end of each day, the average person is relatively dehydrated. It has been determined, for example, that a 120-pound woman living in a temperate climate uses about two and a half quarts of water a day simply breathing. Even mild dehydration will cause many of the same symptoms of fatigue, headaches, and irritability caused by low blood sugar. So, drink lots of water, and feel better and more energetic.

CHAPTER 12

Special Needs Students and Issues in Remediation and Diversity

A helping word to one in trouble is often like a switch on a railroad track—an inch between wreck and smooth-rolling prosperity.

—Henry Ward Beecher

✦ *Organizing Thoughts* ✦

This reference chapter opens with a discussion of some guiding ideas that touch each area of special needs. The intent is to reclaim some partial solutions that should not have, but in fact, *have* lost favor in recent times. Ideally, this admittedly provocative discussion will encourage you to think through what your professional positions eventually will be on these critical issues.

SPECIAL NEEDS STUDENTS: GUIDING IDEAS

The term *special needs* is used here to refer to youngsters who are at risk of underachieving for a variety of reasons that are not typically provided for in a regular classroom setting. The chief approach is *compensatory*. This refers to methods, materials, and means of helping students with such needs to make up, or compensate, for some deficit or difference that may be putting them at increased risk to underachieve. Reasons might include limited English proficiency (LEP), different cultural orientation, learning disability, or simply a lack of motivation to learn.

What even fleas can tell us. Try this: Put some fleas in a glass jar with a lid, and observe. At first the fleas will try eagerly to get out, jumping all around and up and down in the jar. After just a few minutes, however, they will no longer hit the lid. Now take the lid off. The fleas will still jump now and then, but they never will jump out of the jar.

The lesson in this is obvious, but bears stating. The content area teacher must be especially careful about inadvertently creating a glass ceiling of literal level expectations for students, particularly those whom one might presume to be too slow to learn. It is just as important to "teach up" (Estes, 1991) for remedial-level learners as for those who are average and above. Several studies have definitively shown that teaching weaker students to read between and beyond the lines actually boosts their ability to read the lines, or at the literal level (Collins, 1991; Cooter & Flynt, 1986; Haggard, 1976). However, this is not the same thing as saying that those labeled slow are not slow, or that they can do anything if teachers would only challenge or teach them properly. Everyone does better when they are treated as if they are whole and unique, rather than totally defined by a given deficiency, or, for that matter, even by a superior proficiency, as in the cases of those who are academically gifted but may nonetheless have areas of specific need. Consider now two other

239

related and intermingled messages that have come to be overstated and may need a modification of perspective.

Two overstated perspectives: Diversity is to be encouraged and perpetuated, and remedial reading doesn't work and is oppressive. Two important aspects of schooling have taken an unfortunate turn where at-risk students are concerned. One is that cultural diversity and language differences necessarily need to be perpetuated by being formally structured into the school curriculum, and the other is that remedial reading programs don't work and may even be oppressive. Our conclusions on both accounts are somewhat different.

Should cultural and language differences be encouraged?   Efforts to bring about greater tolerance of differences are always proper and reasonable. However, efforts to underscore cultural and language differences may be countereffective to the natural evolution of both and may be a serious disservice to individuals who may wish to be equipped to conduct most of life and business in a dominant culture and language different from their own. Importantly, too, the dominant culture is ever evolving: It regularly shifts to be more like those who accumulate power to influence it; whereas excessive efforts to represent different cultures can perpetuate stereotypes that often have no life outside the representations presented in staged multicultural situations.

It is further notable that parents from America's diverse backgrounds overwhelmingly expect schools to prepare their children to speak, write, and acclimate to the mainstream as a means of becoming an influential part of it. The methods suggested throughout this text, and in this chapter, tend to have this as a goal. Of equal importance, the methods selected have the goal of empowering youngsters to influence culture and language by being highly competent and effective in telling their individual and collective stories and forming the literary, intellectual, and economic base from which to conduct business and win empathy for their particular ways of thinking, speaking, and behaving. In this way diverse cultural and linguistic orientations traditionally have come to be legitimate entries into the competition for the conduct and character of the ever evolving mainstream, or dominant culture.

Should remedial reading continue in a state of neglect?   The evidence is overwhelming that most remedial reading programs work quite well, although you might never know this by the criticisms and faint praise leveled at them even by traditional reading people (Johnston & Allington, 1991; Ruddell, 1993). Remedial reading programs are proven to help many youngsters achieve at approximately twice the average rate in reading per semester and four times the prior pace of these same students (Manzo & Manzo, 1993; Spache, 1976). The fundamental reason that this goes unnoticed is because an almost irreducible number of students do not make progress even with remedial assistance. Ironically, this number would be even smaller if remedial and early prevention programs and efforts were more fully supported, rather than reduced and maligned, which has been the case now for over twenty years.

The disrepute into which remedial reading has fallen is part of a complex set of dynamics that have little bearing on the real efficacy of such programs. Three confluences are especially worth noting. Understandably, middle-class parents wanted a way to get help for their underachieving children without social stigma. In response, they created *learning disabilities (LDs)*, a condition that clearly has some reality base but still no educationally sound definition and in any case is 80% reading related. These facts aside, legislative bodies have designated LD as a physically handicapping condition that otherwise is not the result of a socioeconomic deficit, a cultural difference, or an emotional problem. This entitled students with LDs to receive special and personalized help in a least restrictive environment (i.e., in a socially acceptable fashion), with services to continue through college. Accordingly, students so designated receive a great deal more than remedial readers ever did, including the right to have tests read to them and other such personalized accommodations. This gain for students with LDs has been with great cost to taxpayers and has overburdened teachers. These considerations are not unjustified, but in a world of limited resources, they have resulted in the loss of support for remedial reading programs that previously served the total population.

A second trend that has weakened belief and support for remedial reading, ironically, has been the overgeneralization of an argument in favor of content area literacy. The argument was that content teachers should provide a certain measure of helpful scaffolding to all youngsters, especially those with special needs, and in a regular classroom setting. By a twist of fate, this regular class accommodation of readers came to replace remedial reading because the reading specialists who taught these sections felt overburdened by the responsibility both to guide the school's content area literacy program and to teach the separate remedial groups. Of course, the logical thing to have done was to hire more reading specialists, but the funds went to create and hire more LD specialists.

Finally, important social activists, such as Paulo Freire (1985, 1987) and Ira Shor (Shor & Freire, 1987), have had their messages of *liberation education* convoluted to mean that remedial reading is oppressive. They have argued, as we just have, that school should empower individuals to compete in society where the playing field often is not level. However, these social activists noticed that schooling, largely in the third world, seemed to be designed to educate individuals only sufficiently to make them cogs in someone else's machine, but not to aspire to be, or to run, their own economic engines. This message became erroneously attached to remedial and corrective reading programs in the United States, which because of the high percentage of enrollment of African

American students became viewed as another symbol of oppression. This connection was intensified by the concern of some very well-meaning American educators and humanists who were largely whole-language enthusiasts. They felt that underachievement was almost exclusively the result of social policies, lowered expectations, and poor self-esteem. Further, since whole language is largely based on an incidental learning model and an abhorrence of all testing, it was quick to condemn remedial reading, which is based on a direct and intensive teaching with lots of (diagnostic) testing. In fact, of course, the two positions are not oppositional to one another, but complementary.

The bottom-line issue is that the facts, as previously mentioned, suggest that even the most old-fashioned remedial/corrective reading programs work quite well, with most youngsters achieving at two to four times their prior average rate per unit of time. Furthermore, remedial/corrective reading programs are sensible and necessary because content area teachers cannot reasonably provide explicit and intensive instruction to youngsters who are several grade levels below expected norms and hence unable to reasonably learn from most print sources. Ironically and sadly, efforts to make classroom teachers responsible for such dramatic differences in instructional need, without remedial/corrective reading support, may well have been the impetus for causing some of them to lower their expectations for many students and to quietly pass and graduate youngsters who hardly read at all.

Consider now just a few of the methods that can be used to help youngsters with special needs. Frankly, most of these require somewhat, to considerably, more energy and effort than the methods in previous chapters. But, then, with few remedial/corrective programs still operating, it necessarily falls on content teachers to do whatever they reasonably can to accommodate special needs youngsters in the regular classroom.

TEACHING METHODS FOR SPECIAL NEEDS STUDENTS

The methods presented next focus on the needs of students who are said to have reading/learning disabilities, those with limited English proficiency, personal-social adjustment problems, and/or those who are culturally different.

Fortunately, most of the methodology and ideas developed for special needs students are of benefit to most typical students as well. This is because people are more alike than they are different from one another. And, almost all students, at one time or another, are likely to need some of the same kind of extraordinary thought, concern, and assistance that tend to be reserved for the different, the reluctant, and the chronic underachieving.

Throughout we have tried to select methods that are conducive to both teacher and student discovery and learning. Many of the ideas and practices advocated also are valuable in promoting tolerance, a multicultural outlook, and diversity in education.

We have not directly addressed the gifted as a category of special needs student in this chapter, because many further issues confounding the definition of *giftedness* are well beyond the scope of this text. Also, you probably already have noticed that many of the methods presented in previous chapters, especially those on writing and higher-order literacy, serve the gifted quite nicely.

Motivating the Unmotivated

An earlier chapter defined and developed the role of engagement theory in motivation. This section adds a few more thoughts and devices for reaching the reluctant, and occasionally resentful, reader. It begins with ideas for encouraging reading, discusses means and methods for dealing with disruptive behavior in the classroom, and concludes with techniques for improving basic word attack, comprehension, personal-social adjustment problems, and content-based mainstreaming efforts.

Encouraging Reading

Here are several methods designed to encourage reading. If you were to turn this section into a checklist and commit yourself to doing half of what is suggested for one full year, you would help weak readers and contribute to creating a school environment conducive to higher-literacy and content learning.

1. *Establish a Sustained Silent Reading (SSR) program.* Once or twice a week, have students read anything they choose that is content related. Increase the time from seven to twenty minutes over a few months. This lengthening period of SSR can become an effective management tool as well as a means of teaching students how to read in an increasingly sustained manner. To be sure that everyone has something to read and to allay students' sense that this is an idle-time activity, it is best to store SSR materials in class and to periodically invite individual students to discuss what they are reading. This classroom-based activity can be broadened to include the entire school. It is most conducive if teachers, administrators, and all other personnel read for the sustained period as well.

2. *Keep interesting newspaper and magazine articles, and make them available in the classroom for students to read before or after class or during downtime.*

3. *Have students fill out a reading interest inventory, indicating the types of books they enjoy reading.* Invite the school librarian to help you select an appropriate inventory and to develop a list of suggested book titles related to areas of interest.

4. *Encourage students to join a book club and/or subscribe to magazines in areas of special interest.* Concerned members of the business community often will pay for these.

5. *Become a reading motivator.* Most everyone likes to be read to. Set aside a few minutes of classroom time to read a poem, newspaper, or magazine article, or portion of a cherished book to the class.

6. *Let two or more students read the same book for a book report to the class.* Encourage them to discuss the book with one another.

7. *Use technology to encourage reading.* The school can buy multimedia CD-ROM disks or borrow them from libraries and hook up to the InterNet to encourage reading for pleasure and expanded knowledge.

8. *Cut out and display the weekly book review section of the newspaper.*

9. *Ask students to see a movie or television program either before or after reading a book on which one or the other is based.*

10. *Have student groups create a book or article of the week poster.* Display books and articles with the caption "Read All About It." Invite students to share their books or articles with the class, noting the titles, authors, and sources of critiques.

11. *Invite local authors or poets to class to discuss and read their works.*

12. *Give students incentives to read.* Students who read three or more books during a quarter or a semester can be rewarded with a donated gift certificate from a bookstore, record store, clothing store, or food store.

13. *Conduct reading conferences with students.* Personalized discussion and interest in a student's reading can be deeply motivating.

14. *Teach students to use the closed caption option on television to incidentally work on their own reading effectiveness* (Koskinen, Wilson, Gambrell, & Jensema, 1987). Similarly encourage weak readers to listen to books on tape while they follow along; however, this may have a slightly negative effect with above-average readers (Cloer & Denton, 1995).

The next section offers insights into dealing with behavioral as well as literacy problems. The thrust of each of these methods is to help teachers and students deal with the sometimes corrosive effects of daily teaching and learning situations more than the explosive ones—a need poignantly expressed by the playwright Chekhov's observation that "Any idiot can face a crisis. It is this day-to-day living that wears you down."

Personal-Social Adjustment through Bibliosupport and Dialogue Journals

Bibliosupport

For students who are inclined to read, bibliosupport (Manzo & Manzo, 1995) can be an effective means of aiding with personal-social adjustment. Bibliosupport is based on bibliotherapy, which essentially means healing through reading (Edwards & Simpson, 1986). Generally, it entails redirecting students' perceptions and attitudes in a healthy direction by getting the right reading material to the right student at the right time.

The sources of problems students encounter as they grow and mature are varied: cultural differences, family relationships, moving, divorce, peer pressure, physical handicaps, racial prejudice, death of loved ones, gender identification, and many others. Bibliosupport is merely a means of becoming more broadly informed on and dealing with these personal-social dilemmas so that schooling does not suffer irreversibly.

Whenever possible, the teacher or counselor who recommends a book to a student should invite the student to retell the story, highlighting incidents and feelings that are relevant to the central situation. Changes in behavior, feelings, and relationships should be looked at closely to permit reasonable identification and empathy with the textual characters (Heaton & Lewis, 1955). Most important, the reader should have an opportunity to form a conclusion about the consequences of certain behaviors or feelings to determine whether or not these behaviors or feelings improve the human condition, as well as one's self-centered concerns or personal situation.

Reading and discussion are most fruitful when they are built around two questions, one which most everyone can answer easily, "What have you read that reminds you of someone you know?" and another that few of us can answer easily, "What reminds you of yourself?"

Dialogue Journals

Bibliosupport can be greatly enhanced by the addition of a writing component. The easiest way to do this is to have students keep personal journals in which they write brief reactions—at least one sentence—to whatever they read. These can be stored in a box in the classroom or in a word processor, where, with students' prior approval, the teacher may read through them and write back personal notes and thoughts. Of course, notes and dialogue need not be limited to textual material; they can be extended to anything a student wishes to write or to anything a teacher may be interested in communicating. The idea of dialogue journals (Staton, 1980) is as old as conversation between caring friends. Teachers who use this approach regularly report touching insights revealed and warm relationships formed with students who at first appeared apathetic, hostile, or otherwise reluctant to learn (Kirby & Liner, 1981). In time, a teacher who uses this interactive means of teaching will learn a great deal about how to respond to many common complaints and potentially seething concerns of pre- and early adolescents. One teacher we know, for example, reminds teens, who frequently complain about the material things that they do not have, that even the poor today live better then the rich did 100 years ago, and infinitely better than did many kings and emperors 1,000 years ago. To dramatize the point, he has them list ten things that most of them have that the Czar of Russia did not have in 1900.

As classroom disruptions begin to diminish and participation starts to rise, it is necessary to simultaneously begin closing gaps in the literacy levels of underachieving students. Failure to do so can inhibit progress and even foster a more embittered and hopeless attitude. The methods described next are particularly useful for helping to make quick-paced progress.

Improving Decoding

The most essential facets of effective reading are decoding, or phonics, and comprehension. Poor readers, by definition, have difficulty with either or both. Here now is a way for a nonexpert to help with phonics.

Glass Analysis Approach: No-Rules Phonics

Glass Analysis (Glass, 1973) is a simple procedure that enables virtually anyone who knows how to read to teach others how to do so. It can be used at opportune times as a whole-class method when introducing or reinforcing difficult content terms. Moreover, it takes some of the mystery out of dealing with the lowest readers. Teachers need not know about diphthongs, digraphs, and other phonic elements and rules. Teachers simply provide occasional assistance, based on their own ability to decode, as time and circumstances permit.

Glass Analysis is based on two verbal protocols, or scripts. The scripts are designed to teach students to focus attention on the word and increase their familiarity with the sounds of the most common letter clusters in the English language. The sound for *ing*, for example, has a high frequency of occurrence and is more easily learned as a cluster than as three separate letter sounds that then must be synthesized. Following are some general guidelines and steps for teaching with Glass Analysis.

General Guidelines for Teaching Glass Analysis.   Students should continuously look at the word. Never cover part of the word or point to letters when presenting the word. Do not include definitions of words in the instruction unless a student asks. Reinforce students for correct responses. If a student cannot answer a word attack question, state the answer and return to the same question before finishing with the word.

Steps in Glass Analysis

1. Write the word to be taught on the chalkboard or a large card.
2. Pronounce the word. Then teach it using as many combinations of letter clusters as are sensible.
3. Use the following questions or verbal scripts:

   ✦ "What letters make the <ch> sound?"
   ✦ After you have used this question with the possible combinations, ask
   ✦ "What sound do the letters <c/h> make?"

Figure 12.1 illustrates how Glass would use this approach with a new word before silent reading. See Figure 12.2 for a listing of common letter clusters, grouped according to difficulty level.

Figure 12.1
Example of Glass Analysis.

The teacher writes the word *forgetfulness* in large letters on the chalkboard. Then the teacher uses the Glass analysis script as follows:
   In the word *forgetfulness*, what letters make the *for* sound?
   The *or* sound?
   What letters make the *et* sound?
   The *get* sound?
   What letters make the *forget* sound?
   In the word *forgetfulness*, what letters make the *ful* sound?
   The *forgetful* sound?
   What letters make the *fulness* sound?
   What letters make the *getfulness* sound?
(Notice how many structures can be learned in just one word—all transferable to other words.)

In the word *forgetfulness*, what sound do the letters f/o/r make?
What sound do the letters e/t make?
The g/e/t?
The f/o/r/g/e/t?
What sound do the letters f/u/l/ make?
What sound does g/e/t/f/u/l make?
What sound does e/s/s make?
n/e/s/s?
In the word *forgetfulness*, what sound do the letters f/u/l/n/e/s/s make?
If I took off the letters f/o/r, what sound would be left?
If I took off the *ness* sound, what sound would be left?
What is the whole word?

Figure 12.2
Letter clusters (by difficulty level).

STARTERS	MEDIUM 1	MEDIUM 2	HARDER 1	HARDER 2
1. at	1. ed	1. all	1. fowl	1. er
2. ing	2. ig	2. aw	2. us	2. air
3. et	3. ip	3. el(l)	3. il(l)	3. al
4. it	4. ud	4. eck	4. ite	4. ied
5. ot	5. id	5. ice	5. es(s)	5. ew
6. im	6. en	6. ick	6. om	6. ire
7. op	7. ug	7. if(f)	7. oke	7. ear
8. an	8. ut	8. ink	8. ore	8. eal
9. ay	9. ar	9. ob	9. tow	9. tea
10. ed	10. em	10. od	10. ast	10. ee
11. am	11. up	11. og	11. ane	11. care
12. un	12. ate	12. ub	12. eat	12. deaf
13. in	13. ent	13. uf(f)	13. as(s)	13. oat
14. ap	14. est	14. ush	14. ev	14. ue
15. and	15. ake	15. able	15. ind	15. oo
16. act	16. ide	16. ight	16. oss	16. ou
17. um	17. ock	17. is(s)	17. oem	17. ound
18. ab	18. ade	18. on	18. ost	18. ure
19. ag	19. ame	19. or	19. rol(l)	19. ture
20. old	20. ape	20. l(l)	20. one	20. ur
21. ash	21. ace	21. ac	21. ate	21. ir
22. ish	22. any	22. af(f)	22. ave	22. ai
	23. enk	23. ook	23. ove	23. au
	24. ong	24. tion	24. folly	24. oi
			25. age	

Uses of Glass Analysis. Glass Analysis can be used in three ways to create an effective schoolwide remedial/corrective decoding program:

1. Content teachers can incidentally use this simple letter-clustering approach each time a new technical or content word is introduced: "The word is *photosynthesis*. What letters make the *photo* sound? What letters make the *syn* sound? The *thesis* sound? What is the whole word again?"

2. Content teachers also can occasionally preview textual material assigned for reading and use Glass Analysis to teach other challenging words, especially foreign-language terms, that occur in text. "This is the Italian word *ciao*. Which letters make the *ch* sound in Italian? Which make the *ow* sound? How is the whole word pronounced again?"

3. All students with serious decoding deficiencies can be scheduled for one to five fifteen-minute sessions per week in which Glass Analysis tutoring is provided. Decoding stations can be set up in convenient, unobtrusive places throughout the school. These can be staffed by teachers serving a duty period and/or by volunteer paraprofessionals. (Glass Analysis letter cluster kits for such intensive training are available from Easier-to-Learn, Inc., P.O. Box 329, Garden City, NY 11530, 516-475-3803.)

MAINSTREAMING METHODS

Federal Public Law 94-142 mandates that youngsters with learning disabilities and handicaps attend school in a least restrictive environment. This has been taken to mean that wherever possible such students will be mainstreamed or expected to attend and be accommodated in regular classes.

Most of the methodology of the content area reading movement is suitable for meeting this requirement. Maring and Furman (1985) have made an especially strong case for seven whole-class strategies for helping mainstreamed youngsters read and listen better in content area classes:

1. Use the Oral Reading Method (described in Chapter 6) at least once a week to increase familiarity and comfortableness with the language of the text.
2. Use the whole-class graphic organizer called *pyramiding* (Clewell & Haidemos, 1983). This activity offers group assistance to students with learning disabilities in identifying, classifying, and properly subordinating terms and ideas found in text.
   a. Each student reads silently to identify and write down key facts and ideas.
   b. The teacher leads a discussion, using the chalkboard to pyramid, or group, facts and phrases into logical categories.
   c. The class decides on a sentence that answers the question, "What is the author saying about these ideas?" This sentence forms the base of the triangle (see Figure 12.3).
3. Enhance and review the informal textbook inventory described in Chapter 3 and add some easier questions to help make the course textbook more instructive and user friendly, for example:
   a. How many pages are in the glossary?
   b. Where could you find more information about a term defined in the glossary? (Answer: the index.)
   c. What are the first and last page numbers of the index?

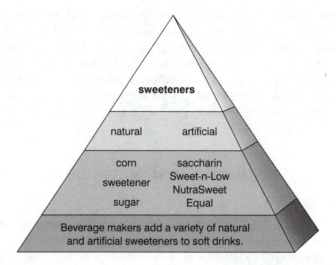

Figure 12.3
Whole-class graphic organizer called *pyramiding,* a strategy for special needs students.

Note. From "Seven 'Whole Class' Strategies to Help Mainstreamed Young People Reading and Listen Better in Content Area Classes," by G. Maring and G. Furman, 1985, *Journal of Reading 28,* p. 696. Reprinted with permission of G. Maring and the International Reading Association. All rights reserved.

4. Use the Contextual Redefinition method described in Chapter 8 to improve vocabulary while reading (Moore, Readence, & Rickelman, 1982).

5. Use Words on the Wall (J. W. Cunningham, Cunningham, & Arthur, 1981) as an uncomplicated means of providing students with learning disabilities and other students with an easily available set of key words from the text to which they can refer for meaning, significance, spelling, and increased familiarity. Simply write key words with a felt-tip marker on half-sheets of paper, and tape them on the walls during a given unit of study.

6. Conduct the Guided Reading Procedure (see Chapter 4 for details) with the following specifications:

   a. Use the procedure every two weeks, and administer a delayed retention test in the intervening week.

   b. Try to get mainstreamed readers to contribute free recalls early in the lesson before the more able students contribute all of the easiest information.

   c. Reread the information on the board as students try to decide which items are main ideas, which are related details, and how to sequence the information.

7. Build further crutches, or scaffolding, into reading guides:

    a. Mark with asterisks those questions you feel are most necessary and appropriate for mainstreamed youngsters to answer. Tell them to answer these questions first.

    b. Put page, column, and paragraph numbers after certain questions to better guide those students who might have difficulty finding these (Wilkins & Miller, 1983); for example, "92, 2, 2" means page 92, second column, second paragraph.

LIMITED ENGLISH PROFICIENCY, CULTURAL DIFFERENCES, AND PROMOTING DIVERSITY

Methods for Second-Language Students

The increasing numbers of youngsters pouring into our schools from foreign and diverse cultural backgrounds are once again hastening the need for all educators to be conversant with the precepts of teaching to those with limited English proficiency. Past efforts to accommodate non-English–speaking American youngsters have consistently resulted in a richer, more diverse, and stronger nation.

Many of the methods devised and developed for content area literacy have proved especially appropriate for use with linguistically and culturally different students. In many instances, these methods need not even be modified but merely used as described. This certainly applies to methods that create a rich instructional conversation such as ReQuest, reported to be profoundly effective in English as a second language classes (McKenzie, Ericson, & Hunter, 1988), as well as other interactive methods such as Question-Only, the Cultural-Academic Trivia game, the Subjective Approach to Vocabulary, Vocabulary Development through Cooperative Learning, most variations on the cloze procedure, and the various discussion methods presented in Chapters 8 through 10, on promoting higher-order literacy.

The most appealing feature of the methods presented next is that, in addressing second-language and limited English needs, they simultaneously account for certain universal needs shared by all students. Among the most prominent of these are the need for a multicultural outlook; the need to reconnect ourselves to certain traditional human values and wisdom; the need to think abstractly as a requisite to thinking adaptively; and the need to actively participate in class, that is, conduct ourselves in harmony with others while pursuing individual goals. The final method presented in this chapter can help teachers achieve these and other valued educational goals. This method is appropriate for the unmotivated and occasionally disruptive student as well.

Note Cue: For Improving Oral Language, Comprehension, and Class Participation

Typically, students are not taught how to participate in class discussion, that is, how to ask, answer, and make relevant and appropriate comments. Students with LEP, students learning English as a second language, and culturally different and other at-risk students typically have found these social-academic strategies especially difficult to acquire. These students often are unfamiliar with the more subtle aspects of the English language, such as tempo, volume, and social protocols such as waiting one's turn to speak, and speaking cogently.

Note Cue (Manzo & Manzo, 1987) is a form of parroting designed to show students how a well-orchestrated lesson might occur. In some ways it resembles spotting, a technique used in physical education to guide initial attempts at tumbling (see Figure 12.4). It is a form of sensorimotor involvement in which the mind and the body learn complex new language, thinking, and social routines.

Steps in Preparing for and Conducting the Note Cue Method

Teacher Preparation. Prepare two sets of cards, one for prereading and one for postreading. On the prereading cards, write prereading questions (one per card), answers (one per card), and comments (one per card). Write the label "Question," "Answer," or "Comment" at the top of each card. Leave a few blank cards, initially just one, then about one more blank each time you use the method until only 20% of the cards contain statements. Questions, answers, and comments should focus on predicting main topics, important events, and outcomes. Write in pencil, and remember to reread and edit your cards. Prepare the postreading cards the same

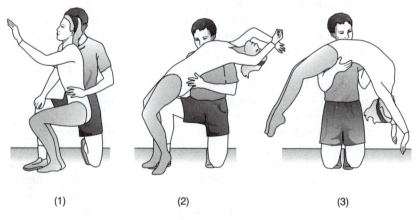

(1)   (2)   (3)

Figure 12.4
Note cue is like acrobatic spotting.

way, but shift the focus from prediction to verification—what the passage actually states—and related evaluative questions and comments.

In preparing both sets of cards, be sure the answer card is phrased clearly enough to be easily matched to the question card (e.g., Q: Who followed Abraham Lincoln into the presidency? A: Andrew Johnson followed Abraham Lincoln into the presidency [not simply A: Andrew Johnson]).

Prereading Activity

1. Instruct students to survey the reading material to try to predict what it will be about. Inform them that a brief written test will follow reading and discussion of the selection.
2. While students are surveying, place one or more random or selected prereading cards on each student's desk.
3. Instruct students to read their card(s) silently and think about when they should read it (them) and about whether they wish to add anything else.
4. Instruct students with blank cards to think of a question, answer, or comment and, if time permits, write it on their cards.
5. Begin the prereading, or prediction, stage of the discussion by asking who has a question or comment that seems to provide a good idea of what the selection will be about. If a question is read, ask who has an answer that seems to fit it. This process continues until students have a sense of what the passage will be about. This should take no more than ten minutes; a brisk pace and aura of evolving a purpose for reading will convey to students that not all cards need to be read to establish a reasonable purpose for reading.
6. Instruct students to read the selection silently to test their predictions. Remind them to read their postreading cards, which will be placed on their desks while they are reading. Announce that you will come to the desk of any student who raises a hand for assistance.

Postreading Discussion

7. Ask, "Who has a good question to check comprehension of this selection?" then, "Who has a good answer to that question?" then, "Who has a comment that seems right to state?" and finally, "Who has reaction(s) or personal comment(s)?" The last question is intended to encourage extemporaneous statements as well as statements read from cards.

Follow-up

8. Within the same class period, or later if preferred, give a test of five to ten questions that require brief written responses. Most questions should be taken directly from the cards to build an appreciation of the cooperative value in reading a cue card for all to hear and profit from.

Notes on Note Cue

If initial participation is slow to develop, try these options:

1. Get things going by reading a question or comment card yourself.
2. Simply call on students by name to read their card.
3. Stimulate interest by inverting the process slightly: Request that an answer card be read, then ask, "What is the question?"
4. Call on at least two students with question cards to read their cards aloud. Then, rather than immediately requesting an answer, ask, "Which question do you think should come first?"
5. Have students write their names in pencil on the back of each card. Junior high teacher Betty Bennett says this heightens students' sense of ownership and accountability for the cards' contents and offers a good way to check afterward which students did not volunteer to read their cards.

To foster greater independence and transfer of learning, try these options:

1. Reinforce high-quality extemporaneous responses by handing the student a blank card and saying, "That was very good. Would you please write it on this card for further use?"
2. Divide the class into groups, and have them prepare the Note Cue cards for the next selections to be read.
3. Once students are familiar with the activity, prepare some cards with prompts ("Try to ask a question to show that one should doubt what is being said") or an incomplete statement to be completed by students ("Make a comment by completing this statement: 'I enjoyed reading this story because . . . ' or 'The reaction would have been different in my family or culture. We would have . . . '"). Other types of prompter cards can be personalized ("Come on, Fred, don't you have something you can say about this selection?").

To foster higher-level thinking, develop evocative comment cards, preferably ones related to students' experiences. One vivid example of this kind of bridging comes to mind from a lesson observed in an English class. The selection read had been excerpted from a popular book. It described how a fifteen-year-old boy set out on a solitary voyage across the Pacific in a small craft. The questions and answers the teacher had put on the cue cards were primarily from the teacher's manual for the text. One of the comments that she added, however, raised the class's interest and even indignation: "How in the world did this young man raise the money and supplies to do this, and why did his parents permit him to risk his life in such a silly venture?" A student might not have worded the comment quite like that, but such real reactions tend to invite equally real responses and lively discussion.

Finally, Note Cue, unlike many conventional lesson designs, is cumulative. The cards a teacher composes for today's lesson can be stored for future use. Through cooperative work and sharing, teachers can develop starter sets of Note Cues for most key selections of a text. More important, with each use, previously written cards can be modified following use, and new cards generated by students can be added. In this way, lessons can be kept fresh and current.

✦ *Looking Back and Looking Ahead* ✦

This chapter discussed some misunderstandings that have arisen regarding how to help remedial-level readers and youngsters from diverse cultural and language backgrounds. It strongly supported the need for remedial reading programs and offered methods to improve reading, language, thinking, and personal-social adjustment among special needs students in content classrooms. Methods included means of motivating the unmotivated, mainstreaming strategies, bibliosupport and dialogue journals, Glass Analysis to manage decoding problems, and Note Cue to heighten classroom participation. Most of these methods are applicable to broader student groups. The next chapter sets out ways to bring students, faculty, and community together in activities that are beneficial to all.

✦ ✦ TRADE SECRET ✦ ✦

Catch Them Being Good

Occasionally, a teacher and a student, or even an entire class, gets locked into a deadly cycle of misbehavior, criticism, defensive reactions, threats, and punishment—and more misbehavior. One way to break this cycle is to "catch them being good" and then reward them. This simple strategy, though sometimes difficult to mount in a negative atmosphere, is the basis of all behavior modification. As such, it is a great mechanism for preventing the deadly cycle from occurring as well as for teachers to find their way back to civility if and when it begins.

If this strategy comes easily to you, we're sorry to say that you still have something else to beware of: turning kids into praise junkies. But don't worry too much about this, since most of us have trouble finding the opportunity and the will to praise.

Praise, by the way, is most effective when it highlights a specific behavior: "That was a good idea to write your homework assignment in your notebook, George." By matching praise to a specific behavior, you often can buy enough grace to later be able to engage in some constructive criticism in the same direction without unsettling consequences: "You know, George, if you write your assignments from the rear to the front of your notebook, they'll take up only a few pages over the entire semester. They also will be easier to find, and you'll have a record of everything assigned when you need to review for a test."

Within this teaching tip is an example of another: Address students by name whenever possible. It helps to form a more personal bond. Good salespersons practice this routinely. And, in case you didn't realize it, teachers are in sales.

CHAPTER 13

Schoolwide Content Area Literacy Programming and Professional Development

And that's . . . the big picture!

—A. Whitney Brown

✦ *Organizing Thoughts* ✦

This chapter is structured to answer two organizing questions that a classroom teacher and/or reading specialist in training would need to understand to be an effective participant in a school's content area literacy program:

1. What do schoolwide content area literacy programs typically look like? This question contains two other implicit questions:

    a. What help can I expect in the way of assistance and from whom?

    b. What is expected of me as a teacher?

2. What more can be done?

The term *program* here means any plan targeted at a stated goal or objective.

COMPONENTS OF CONTENT AREA LITERACY PROGRAMS

Day-to-day events may appear random and even fragmented while they are being experienced. For this reason alone, it can be satisfying to get a glimpse of the big picture. But there is another reason to try to gain a top-down perspective: It offers a solid opportunity to exercise a more assertive role as a professional educator as well as classroom teacher.

Successful content area literacy programs, typically, are built around eight key elements that together equal the big picture:

- ✦ An ideology
- ✦ Objectives and goals
- ✦ Clear roles and responsibilities
- ✦ Special services for various segments of the student body
- ✦ Ongoing needs assessment and program evaluation
- ✦ A curriculum implementation plan
- ✦ A staff development program that provides consultation, in-service training, and sharing opportunities
- ✦ Activities that promote collaboration and cooperation

The following sections show how some of these elements might be or are being implemented in actual school programs. The examples and discussions include some optional as well as essential elements.

Ideology

The term *ideology* is used loosely here to mean a guiding philosophy or perspective. It usually is expressed in the form of a unifying theme or focus that serves as the conceptual basis for guiding programming.

Several philosophies have held sway in recent years. Most notable among these has been the mastery learning perspective that emphasizes heavy doses of direct instruction, a strong concern for transmission of knowledge, and a skills-based orientation. In counterpoint is the whole language orientation, which emphasizes indirect teaching; transactional, or constructionist, subjectivity in reading; and the integration of content learning, reading, writing, and speaking largely through interdisciplinary and theme units of study.

The most popular philosophy, however, is an eclectic one. *Eclecticism* is a philosophy that permits one to pragmatically pick and choose parts, principles, and practices from all others. Our own choice is a form of eclecticism that we have labeled the *New, or Informed, Eclecticism* (Manzo & Manzo, in press). This philosophy differs from conventional eclecticism in several important ways. There are two primary differences. One is that every effort should be made to reconcile seemingly competing ideas and political crosscurrents, since there is a good chance that these will enhance rather than displace each other. The second is that instructional decisions should be guided not merely by subjective judgments but rather by an assessment of student needs and reference to research findings that support or fail to support various practices. The chief value of these simple guidelines is that they encourage attention to innovations but help schools to resist fads and hollow buzzwords.

Objectives and Goals

Goals and objectives represent the first fleshing out of an ideology or philosophical bent. School districts are very good at cranking out hair-splittingly specific objectives. However, the sheer weight of these tends to sink their usefulness.

We recommend that those goals and objectives that largely already exist be taken and used to focus teacher, student, and community efforts into a cogent sentence or two. Here are some examples that suit content area literacy:

1. Promoting progress toward reading-language-thinking-content-social/emotional maturity as opposed to mere reading competence

2. Promoting higher-order literacy, or working to diagnose and remedy shortfalls in critical-constructive thinking, among the academically proficient as well as remedial readers

3. The improvement of reading, writing, speaking, listening, and thinking

4. Cooperative and competitive reading and learning, or the school as an authentic community

Realistically speaking, these themes may not always play well in a particular school or community, even though they should be an integral part of the school's philosophical or ideological goals. In such situations, it is more practical to express the focus for the school program in more conventional terms, such as the following:

+ Effective comprehension and vocabulary
+ Efficient reading and study
+ Reading and writing to learn

In most cases, the ideology of the school program will be expressed in a combination of the preceding terms with some locally recognized need. Examples of specific local needs might include functional literacy for job flexibility, college preparation, or effective reading and use of technology.

Organization, Roles, and Responsibilities

The chief element in translating program ideals into practice is the assignment of role responsibilities. Following are the most commonly acknowledged responsibilities of the school administrator, reading specialist, and classroom teacher.

The School Administrator

The school principal has the primary responsibility for initiating and supporting the development and implementation of the goals, objectives, curriculum, and design of the literacy program. In this capacity, the principal is the one to initiate school-wide survey testing, program evaluation, and ongoing literacy-related faculty development programs. Equal to all else, it is the principal's responsibility to cultivate a positive school climate. It is important to note, however, that "a poor climate can inhibit learning, but a positive climate does not guarantee success" (Hoffman, 1991, p. 926).

The Reading Specialist

As a rule of thumb, an intermediate and secondary school should have one full-time reading specialist for every 250 students. Reading specialists are expected to serve as resource persons in the development of the goals, objectives, curriculum, and design of the literacy program. They typically are responsible for coordinating and interpreting schoolwide survey testing to assist in the ongoing evaluation of the literacy program and for administering additional diagnostic tests as needed based on survey test results and/or referrals. Reading specialists provide ongoing assistance to teachers in a variety of forms: planning in-service activities, evaluating and/or preparing instructional materials, and demonstrating new methods. In addition, they should be responsible for eliciting and coordinating the contributions of other support services such as librarians, counselors, outside consultants, and parents.

The Content Area Teacher

The ultimate power and responsibility for the overall literacy program rests with classroom teachers. A vital content area literacy program enlists teachers' participation in the development of the goals, objectives, curriculum, design, and evaluation procedures for the schoolwide literacy program. This participation helps to ensure whole-hearted implementation of the program.

Special Services Component

In the context of this discussion, *special services* mean assistance available for students with special needs. This typically involves pull-out programs, elective or minicourses, and centers.

Pull-Out Services

In pull-out programs, a reading specialist offers diagnostic and/or remedial/corrective tutoring for youngsters who cannot be adequately provided for in regular classes. This component is intended to ensure that

1. No remedial-level reader falls between the cracks and leaves school only quasi-literate after twelve years
2. Foreign-born and other language-handicapped students receive special attention where this appears necessary
3. Diagnosis and treatment are provided for other difficult, different, or sometimes overlooked problems (e.g., higher-order literacy needs, cultural differences, study skills deficiencies, and reading-related writing, grammar, and spelling)
4. Consultation is provided for all teachers in selecting and using appropriate methods and materials

Elective Courses

Content area and reading specialists in upper elementary, middle, and high schools frequently offer exploratory minicourses or full elective courses on topics such as study strategies, speed reading, critical reading, and vocabulary enrichment. This type of short-term, focused instruction reinforces and builds on the ongoing content reading instruction provided daily in content classrooms.

Learning Centers

The learning center usually is the hub out of which a reading or literacy department may operate. Bernice Bragstad (1985), an International Reading Association award-winning content area literacy specialist, says that her former high school's learning center provided these three services:

1. Individualized or small-group tutoring in any subject or skill, provided by a select cadre of proficient student-tutors or the reading specialist
2. Individualized help with writing, provided by several English teachers who served their duty periods in this way
3. A preventative biweekly summer tutoring program conducted by high school students for middle and junior high students

In addition to these services, learning centers can offer walk-in assistance with almost any pressing homework or academic problem. The Kansas City Public School District has extended this concept to a homework hotline. The hotline is available after school hours and staffed by volunteer teachers.

Needs Assessment

Information about students' academic status and about the effects of the school program on them is essential to determining what needs to be done and how to best do it. This type of information should be collected regularly by school leaders and cross-verified by an independent audit from an outside team of consultants about every three to five years. Surveys guided by outside consultants help identify problems that have a way of cropping up in virtually every operation in which day-to-day pressures erode educators' sensitivity to flaws in policy and procedure. Most effective businesses routinely budget for such periodic surveys and reviews. It is a fundamental form of quality control.

Curriculum Implementation Plan

Apart from the obvious effort to infuse each content subject with the necessary reading-related strategies, each discipline can be designated, by common agreement, to give special attention to specific features of the content area literacy curriculum. Distribution and assignment of reading and literacy-related objectives to each subject area proceeds best when school units volunteer to play a role. This horizontal distribution also can be detailed vertically by age/grade level (see Figure 13.1).

Figure 13.1
Possible distribution of literacy objectives by major disciplines.

English

1. Story comprehension
2. Poetry comprehension
3. Language patterns
4. Creative writing
5. Summary writing
6. Systematic vocabulary
7. Literary reference books

Social Studies

1. Analytical discussion
2. Critical reading
3. Metaphorical thinking
4. Critique and reaction writing
5. Note taking
6. Social studies vocabulary
7. Almanac, encyclopedia, and related reference skills
8. Reading maps, charts, graphs, and cartoons

Science

1. Inquiry training
2. Thesis and detail writing from expository material and observation
3. Cooperative reading–learning
4. Accurate recall
5. Science vocabulary
6. Hypothesis formulation and testing
7. Abstract thinking

Mathematics

1. Recitation
2. Translation
3. Test taking
4. Mathematics vocabulary
5. Expository writing: What did this problem ask, and why did I solve it as I did?
6. Cooperative problem solving

Staff Development

A well-planned staff development program is an important means of ensuring that programs endure and evolve over time in an institutional setting that undergoes frequent changes in administration and staff. An effective plan for staff development should include four basic components:

1. A means of enlisting teacher support in program development and an ongoing sense of program ownership
2. A way to provoke program review and renewal
3. A means of fine-tuning a program and accommodating individual teacher's needs
4. Attention to innovation and resistance of fads and hollow words

Three means are discussed next for addressing some of the these components: action research as a way to enlist teacher support and ownership, in-service training as a means of providing ongoing training, and the growing force of media and computer technology in contemporary life and education.

Action Research

Classroom experimentation is a proven way to change instructional routines. It has been pointed out that by involving teachers in planning, conducting, and reporting classroom research, teachers greatly increased their sense of ownership of ideas while providing hands-on evidence of the value of several basic content area literacy methods (Santa, Isaacson, & Manning, 1987).

The process of involving teachers in action research projects is more manageable today than ever before. Assistance with research design and statistics usually can be had for a small fee or even free from a school district's own office of research, from advanced degree-seeking teachers, and/or from nearby university campuses. The idea of teacher-scholars has a rich history in education (Chall, 1986). No doubt you have noticed that several of the methods and ideas presented in this text were suggested by classroom teachers and other school practitioners.

In-Service Education

In-service education, or staff informing and transforming, is a key feature of successful school programming. This can take several forms. The action research model just discussed is one means of broadening horizons. The most practical methods, however, involve direct in-service training.

There are no clear formulas for conducting in-service teacher training. Nonetheless, there has been a good deal of research on the efficacy of various generic approaches. A metaanalysis (broad-summary analysis) of many studies (Wade, 1984–1985) and our own more recent research (Manzo & Manzo, 1995) support the following conclusions:

1. Regardless of who conducts in-service sessions (trainers come under many different job classifications), teachers are more likely to benefit when they use methods that permit learning by doing.

2. There is no magical combination of methods for successful in-service education. Nevertheless, in-service programs that use observation, microteaching, auditory and visual feedback, and practice, either individually or in some combination, are more effective than programs that do not use these methods.

3. Contrary to recent populist trends, in-service education is most successful when led by an expert but organized to encourage participant involvement and contributions.

Two features of contemporary life are serving as valuable catalysts to literacy and content objectives. They are the media—a sleeping giant— and computing—a rapidly growing one.

MEDIA: A SLEEPING GIANT

As used here, the term *media* refers primarily to television but includes radio, magazines, and newspapers. Media bashing has become a popular sport, even within media circles. This heavy assault, especially on nonprint media, clearly needs reevaluation. A school's entire curriculum can be enhanced by the judicious use of film, broadcast television, and access to videotape libraries and CD-ROMs. These, after all, are powerful sources of information and, as such, a potentially painless means of building a fund of knowledge, cultural literacy, schema, and a worldview.

A recent cable news network story reported that adults are watching three and one-half to four and one-half hours of television per day, and children much more. It is difficult to see why this is considered inherently bad. In a typical day's offerings, one easily can be exposed to quick news and thorough news; entertainment and educational programs; documentaries and docudramas; financial and medical programs; foreign language programming; multicultural and multiracial stories, news, and outlooks; courses for college credit; discussions and perspectives on many of life's pleasures and woes; and a good deal of sports and entertainment. Obviously, not all of these offerings are of the highest quality or always very high-minded. But the same can be said of books.

MICROCOMPUTING AND TELECOMPUTING:
RAPIDLY GROWING GIANTS

Microcomputing and telecomputing can add cohesiveness to a reading program and relieve a staff of some otherwise tedious chores. In several places throughout this text, we have made passing reference to microcomputer usage and teleconnection to the InterNet. In view of the decisions many educators face as to whether and how many computers to purchase for home or school use, it seems appropriate to comment briefly on their potential value. Courses on computer literacy, now being offered by most institutions, will answer more technical questions.

Consider the question of whether computers are a justifiable expense from the standpoint of the content and literacy programs. Clearly they are, but there are some nagging problems. The biggest problem is the lack of compatibility of equipment and software programs. The computer industry could help us all if it would strive harder to agree on a standard language and compatible components. The industry argues that this is difficult because so much computer technology is in a state of growth and flux. However, it is now more than thirty-five years since the first computer-assisted instructional programs were piloted, and from a user's point of view, the situation is exasperating. It's as though each maker of audiotape and record players required a different size and speed of recording and playback equipment. The problem is magnified by rigorous training requirements for most word processing programs and huge manuals of documentation that can make a pencil look very attractive.

Having said all this, it is worth considering what can be done with microcomputers, which, while still expensive, now rival the power and flexibility of the million-dollar machines of two generations past. Microcomputers are wonderful electronic instructional packages. There are software programs and CD-ROM systems that present and even generate vocabulary reinforcement and mathematics practice exercises. Best of all, the machine doesn't get tired, bored, or ill; it provides immediate feedback; and some programs actually keep score and provide printouts of patterns of individual student responses. There also are more inventive programs that teach active reading, allow the student to write or choose different endings to stories, and provide simulation activities in science, social studies, and economics. The most ambitious effort by far is a growing interest in developing electronic textbooks that contain hypertext—that is, imbedded aids and other material to supplement and support the basic text.

Notable, too, is the fact that we are about to see another significant breakthrough in computing that is due to telecommunications. Companies are developing computers that will be less expensive than television sets, since they will receive all needed software and computing power via electronic hookups to large companies such as CompuServe, America

On-Line, and future educational services that probably will partner with existing textbook publishers.

Computers for Teachers

For the most part, the greatest potential benefit of computers in education has yet to be realized. It is not in computer-assisted instruction for students, or even telecommunication distance learning, but computer-managed instruction for teachers. As a rule, teachers have not yet been given desktop micro- or telecommunications computer capacity. When these are made readily available, teachers can use them to

- ✦ Quickly and easily spot-check readability of text and supplementary materials.
- ✦ Manage grades.
- ✦ Store and generate tests.
- ✦ Store and suggest teaching methods.
- ✦ Score and even interpret tests.
- ✦ Globally connect teachers and students in their responses to and discussion of books.
- ✦ Access expert systems and consultants to help them assess needs and select appropriate means and methods.
- ✦ Store scanned-in student works and portfolios, and assemble personal or teacher portfolios.

A teacher portfolio is a place where teachers keep a record of their evolving ideas and experiences. It is a form of résumé collection that can be used to periodically reflect on where one has been and where one is, or wishes to go. See Appendix B for an organizational format for a teacher portfolio.

A word of caution is in order regarding computers. As useful as computers can be, there is little vital to the school content and literacy program that can be done with them that cannot be done without them. Further, any aspect of program development begun in earnest without computers will further help justify their future purchase.

✦ *Looking Back and Looking Ahead* ✦

This chapter provided an overview of the parts and roles of successful content area literacy programs. It was intended to provide you with the schema base, or framework, you will need to continue to learn and think more about these categories and ideally to begin to map a place for yourself and your potential contribution to these efforts.

✦ ✦ **TRADE SECRET** ✦ ✦

Your Ability to Pay

As part of the complex tapestry of modern life, teachers need to plan for how to meet their rudimentary financial needs. This is complicated by several factors: the huge financial demand of continuing education; the increase in job insecurity; our modest salaries; and the absence of opportunities for bonuses, stock options, and ownership that are common in the private sector. Further, home purchases no longer can be expected to accrue greatly in value, and the aging of the population will add to the burden on Social Security and other retirement systems.

However, there is a way to keep pace and perhaps even establish some financial security. It is through supplementary retirement savings plans, called 403Bs and 401Ks. Basically, these are deferred income plans that permit teachers and some government workers to save up to about 9% of an annual salary in a program managed by designated insurance and mutual fund companies.

Talk to your business or personnel office about this option. It is one that shouldn't be overlooked. Basically, it will permit you to save, say, $50 per month, in a plan that invests all of it before tax is taken out. In other words, each such investment automatically gains 15% to 50% in value for the period it is invested, depending on your tax bracket at the time it is invested. Some companies even will permit you to borrow against this retirement money at a reduced interest rate for further schooling for you or your children and for a first home purchase.

Don't overlook this opportunity to build a personally secure future. In so doing, you also will be building respect for the teaching profession.

APPENDIX A

Impulsivity–Stability Scales and Scoring Guide

The Impulsivity–Stability Scales (D. E. P. Smith, 1967) presented here originally were abstracted from two scales of the widely used Minnesota Multiphasic Personality Inventory. Impulsivity and stability are considered to be fundamental affective characteristics that influence basic motivation, learning and teaching style, and career interests. These scales offer a hands-on way to better know oneself and improve understanding of students.

Impulsivity–Stability Scales

Directions: There are no right or wrong answers to the following questions. Indicate your responses by marking Y (yes), N (no), or ? (not sure) in the space before each question. A few questions require an "a" or "b" answer. Do not spend time pondering questions. You should mark an item ? (not sure) only when it is impossible to say yes or no. Be sure to answer every question.

___ 1. Are you given to quick retorts and snap judgments?

___ 2. When you meet someone new, do you usually start the conversation?

___ 3. Are you inclined to express your thoughts without much hesitation?

___ 4. Are you apt to say things you may regret later rather than keep still?

___ 5. Do you think much and speak little?

___ 6. Do you get very excited by new ideas and new people?

___ 7. Would you say that you have (a) many friends or (b) just a few friends?

___ 8. Do you often find yourself making comments to a friend while listening to a lecture or watching a movie?

___ 9. In discussion, do you think better when you are challenged to defend your position?

___ 10. Would you rather take (a) an oral test or (b) a written test?

___ 11. Does it irritate you to listen to someone who speaks slowly?

___ 12. Do you recover your emotions rapidly after a sudden upset?

___ 13. Are you inclined to be quick and a little careless in your actions?

___ 14. Would you rather talk than listen in a social situation?

___ 15. Can you turn out a large amount of work in a short time if you are under pressure?

___ 16. Do you usually start to work on a new academic subject with a great amount of enthusiasm?

___ 17. Do you hesitate to volunteer remarks in class?

___ 18. Do you quickly form larger concepts from a few disconnected ideas?

___ 19. Do you find that your recall of past conversations is more accurate than that of most of your friends?

___ 20. Do you usually find that you understand a complex situation with a minimum of explanation?

___ 21. Do you tend to be submissive and apologetic (a) often or (b) seldom?

___ 22. Are you likely to complain about your suffering and hardships?

___ 23. Do you sometimes have a feeling of fear as though you had done something wrong?

___ 24. Do you often have trouble falling asleep at night?

___ 25. Do people tell you that you worry too much?

___ 26. Do you become discouraged when things go wrong?

___ 27. Are you usually tired when you get up in the morning?

___ 28. Do you have nightmares (a) seldom or (b) often?

___ 29. Do you usually have a feeling of being able to handle minor crises?

___ 30. Do you sometimes feel that life would be happier if people only treated you better?

___ 31. Do you sometimes perspire or feel tense without any reason?

___ 32. Do you think of yourself sometimes as neglected and unloved?

___ 33. Would you say that one is wise to be very careful about whom one trusts?

___ 34. Are your ideas generally well organized and systematic?

___ 35. Are you frequently troubled by pangs of conscience?

___ 36. Are you often concerned that you may not have done right in social situations?

___ 37. Do you feel sometimes that people disapprove of you?

___ 38. Is the control of your emotions (a) easy or (b) difficult?

___ 39. Are you easily discouraged when people make fun of you?

___ 40. Are there times when you can't help feeling sorry for yourself?

Impulsivity–Stability Scoring Guide

Key: There are no right answers, but just put a check beside the numbers where this answer is the same as yours. A total score of 0 to 8 is considered a low score; 9 to 11 is moderate; 12 to 20 is high.

1. Yes	11. Yes	21. b	31. No
2. Yes	12. Yes	22. No	32. No
3. Yes	13. Yes	23. No	33. No
4. Yes	14. Yes	24. No	34. Yes
5. No	15. Yes	25. No	35. No
6. Yes	16. Yes	26. No	36. No
7. a	17. No	27. No	37. No
8. Yes	18. Yes	28. a	38. a
9. Yes	19. No	29. Yes	39. No
10. a	20. Yes	30. No	40. No

Total, Items 1–20 ____   Total, Items 21–40 ____
(Impulsivity Score)   (Stability Score)

Use this chart to convert your impulsivity and stability scores into a quadrant score.

I	II
High stability High impulsivity	High stability Low impulsivity
Low stability High impulsivity	Low stability Low impulsivity
III	IV

Interpretation of Quadrant Scores on the Impulsivity–Stability Scale

With no other factors taken into account, here is what placement in each quadrant tends to mean:

✦ Quadrant I: High stability/high impulsivity. Quick thinking; secure; gregarious; appetitively or intrinsically motivated; executive type; tends to like social studies, generally not as good in arithmetic calculations and precise work.

✦ Quadrant II: High stability/low impulsivity. Secure; reserved and methodical; accountant type; tends to like math, grammar, and lengthy books.

✦ Quadrant III: Low stability/high impulsivity. Worries a great deal; given to exaggeration; driven but seldom able to satisfy needs; salesperson type; preference for subject is greatly influenced by who is teaching it.

✦ Quadrant IV: Low stability/low impulsivity. Worries a great deal; tends to be fear motivated (motivated by what you don't want to happen); also may appear either apathetic or standoffish; librarian type; tends to like literature, art history, crafts, and repetitive tasks.

In general, scores between 9 and 11 constitute an indefinite range. In all probability, the two factors this scale measures simply are not critical factors in your life. But that's the way it is with most learning-style factors: important when they are definitive and largely inconsequential otherwise.

APPENDIX B

Model Professional Portfolio Recorder and Planner

A professional portfolio, begun early in your career, can be an invaluable lifelong resource. To construct a model portfolio, you will need the following materials.

+ A three-ring binder (you may want to begin with a 1-inch binder and transfer materials to a larger size binder as your collection grows)
+ Nine three-hole notebook pockets for storing materials in various sections of the portfolio (see below)
+ Attachable index tabs to mark each section (attach these to the pockets, since these extend farther than regular-sized sheets)
+ Section titles (described next), copied onto separate sheets for insertion into the notebook, between pockets

With these simple materials, and a bit of reflection on your past, present, and future, you are ready to assemble a model portfolio that will grow with you through your professional career.

Section I: Guiding Thoughts
In this section, record relevant quotations you run across that strike you as worth remembering and that can serve to keep your thinking and instructional decision making on track.

A. Thoughts and perspectives on careers in general

Examples
+ Successful careers don't just happen; they are the result of vision, planning, and effort.
+ Most successful careers are beset by occasional setbacks. Expect these, and be ready to push on.
+ When truth stands in your way, you are headed in the wrong direction.

B. Thoughts and perspectives on teachers and teaching

Examples

- ✦ The art of teaching is the art of assisting discovery.
- ✦ The enthusiastic teacher is a lifelong student.
- ✦ The finer the instruction, the more it invites; the poorer it is, the more it compels.

C. Thoughts and perspectives on schools and schooling

Examples

- ✦ Nowadays, school heads are chosen to run a school rather than lead it.
- ✦ The school's task is to take a lot of live wires and see that they get well grounded.

Section II: Employment Record
In this section, keep a running record of both teaching and nonteaching experiences, and store an updated résumé.

A. Nonteaching job experiences
B. Educational job experiences
C. Other

(Pocket: current résumé)

Section III: Personal History (Birth to High School)
In this section, make relevant notes about your family and early school background, and store related documents.

A. Family background
B. Medical/health factors
C. Social, athletic affiliations
D. Academic record, K–12
E. Hobbies and interests
F. Significant memories

(Pocket: birth certificate, passport, school records, early photos, letters, memorabilia)

Section IV: Personal History (Postsecondary)

In this section, make notes about your college life and education, and store related documents.

A. Academic record (degrees, majors, minors)
B. Activities (extracurricular; organizations, religious, athletic)
C. Social life (personal and family)
D. Intellectual development (books, magazines, ideas)

(Pocket: transcripts, letters of reference, other records)

Section V: Material Accounting

In this section, keep notes about your financial standing and store related documents.

A. Gifts, trusts, support
B. Income history
C. Loan history
D. Assets (stocks, car, furniture, property)
E. Approximate net worth
F. Prospects (likely legacies and/or opportunities)

(Pocket: financial records, photos, memorabilia)

Section VI: Professional History

In this section, make notes about your teaching career, and store related documents.

A. Certificates
B. Evaluations/recommendations
C. Memorable teachers and colleagues
D. Teaching experiences: subjects, grade levels, situations
E. Related nonteaching roles and experiences
F. Memorable in-service sessions, conferences, sabbaticals
G. Memorable articles, books, papers
H. Membership and roles in committees and professional organizations
I. Grants, travel, awards
J. Summer activities and employment

(Pocket: teaching certificates, letters, articles or summaries)

Section VII: Self-Appraisals
In this section, keep notes on an ongoing self-assessment, and store related records.

A. Attitudes
B. Interests and abilities
C. Temperament/personality
D. Teaching/learning style
E. Personal assessment of strengths and weaknesses as a person and as a teacher

(Pocket: records)

Section VIII: Occasional Notes
In this section, make additional notes of memorable events and experiences, and store related records.

A. Notes on memorable personal events (marriage, deaths, births, friendships)
B. Notes on memorable professional experiences (significant mentor relationships, special students)

(Pocket: records)

Section IX: Blueprints
In this section, keep notes about long-term career plans, and store related documents.

A. Personal career goals
B. Objectives that might contribute to your professional education

(Pocket: related articles, notes, and documents)

Section X: Teaching Competence
In this section, keep notes about your experiences in using various teaching approaches and methods, and store related materials.

A. Teaching methods you have mastered
B. Teaching methods you intend to try

(Pocket: related articles and notes on each method)

REFERENCES

Aaronson, E., Blaney, N., Sikes, J., Stevan, C., & Snapp, N. (1975, February). The jigsaw route to learning and liking. *Psychology Today, 43–50.*

Aaronson, E., Stephan, C., Sikes, J., Blaney, N., & Snapp, M. (1978). *The jigsaw classroom.* Beverly Hills, CA: Sage.

Adams, M. J. (1990). *Beginning to read: Thinking and learning about print.* Cambridge, MA: MIT Press.

Alder, J. (1974). *Individualized language arts.* Weehawken, NJ: Weehawken School District.

Alley, G., & Deshler, D. (1980). *Teaching the learning disabled adolescent: Strategies and methods.* Denver, CO: Love.

Alvermann, D. E., & Boothby, P. R. (1983). A preliminary investigation of the differences in children's retention of "inconsiderate" text. *Reading Psychology, 4,* 237–246.

Alvermann, D. E., Dillon, D. R., & O'Brien, D. G. (1987). *Using discussion to promote reading comprehension.* Newark, DE: International Reading Association.

Anders, P. L., Bos, C. S., & Filip, D. (1984). The effect of semantic feature analysis on the reading comprehension of learning-disabled students. In J. A. Niles & L. A. Harris (Eds.), *Changing perspectives on research in reading/language processing and instruction. Thirty-third yearbook of the National Reading Conference* (pp. 162–166). Rochester, NY: National Reading Conference.

Anderson, R. C., & Nagy, W. E. (1989). *Word meanings.* (Tech. Rep. No. 485). Cambridge, MA: Bolt, Beranek and Newman.

Ankney, P., & McClurg, E. (1981). Testing Manzo's Guided Reading Procedure. *The Reading Teacher, 34,* 681-685.

Applebee, A. N. (1981). *Writing in the secondary school.* Urbana, IL: National Council of Teachers of English.

Artley, A. S. (1944). A study of certain relationships existing between general reading comprehension and reading comprehension in a specific subject-matter area. *Journal of Educational Research, 37,* 464–473.

Aschner, M. J., Gallagher, J. J., Perry, J. M., Afsar, S. S., Jenne, W., & Farr, H. (1962). *A system for classifying thought processes in the context of classroom verbal interaction.* Champaign: University of Illinois, Institute for Research on Exceptional Children.

Ausubel, D. P. (1960). The use of advance organizers in the learning and retention of meaningful verbal material. *Journal of Educational Psychology, 51,* 267–272.

Bacon, E. (1963). *Notes on the piano.* Syracuse, NY: Syracuse University Press.

279

Baker, L., & Brown, A. L. (1984). Metacognitive skills and reading. In P. D. Pearson (Ed.), *Handbook of reading research* (pp. 333–394). New York: Longman.

Baldwin, R. S., & Kaufman, R. K. (1979). A concurrent validity study of the Raygor readability estimate. *Journal of Reading, 23,* 148–153.

Bandura, A., & Walters, R. (1963). *Social learning and personality development.* New York: Holt, Rinehart & Winston.

Barrett, T. C. (1967). *The evaluation of children's reading achievement.* Newark, DE: International Reading Association.

Barton, W. A. (1930). *Outlining as a study procedure.* New York: Columbia University, Teacher's College.

Baumann, J. F., & Kameenui, E. J. (1991). Research on vocabulary instruction. In J. Flood, J. M. Jensen, D. Lapp, & J. Squire (Eds.), *Handbook of research on teaching the English language arts* (pp. 604–631). Upper Saddle River, NJ: Prentice Hall.

Bean, T. W., & Pardi, R. (1979). A field test of a guided reading strategy. *Journal of Reading, 23,* 144–147.

Behle, P. (Ed) (1982). *The double helix: Teaching the writing process.* Florissant, MO: Ferguson-Florissant Writers Project.

Benge-Kletzien, S., & Balocke, L. (1994). The shifting muffled sound of the pick: Facilitating student-to-student discussion. *Journal of Reading, 37,* 540–545.

Blanc, R. A. (1977). Cloze-plus as an alternative to "guides" for understanding and appreciating poetry. *Journal of Reading, 21,* 215–218.

Bloom, B. S. (Ed.). (1956). *Taxonomy of educational objectives: The classification of educational goals. Handbook 1. Cognitive domain.* New York: Longman, Green.

Bormuth, J. R. (1965). Validities of grammatical and semantic classifications of cloze test scores. In J. A. Figurel (Ed.), *Reading and inquiry. International Reading Association Conference Proceedings* (Vol. 10, pp. 283–286). Newark, DE: International Reading Association.

Boyer, P. S., et al. (1993). The Progressive Era. In *The enduring vision: A history of the American people. Vol. 2: From 1856* (2nd ed., pp. 724–761). Lexington, MA: D. C. Heath.

Bragstad, B. (1985, March). *Mapping: Using both sides of the brain.* Lecture handout, International Reading Association State Council Meeting. Orlando, FL.

Bromley, K. D. (1985). Précis writing and outlining enhance content learning. *The Reading Teacher, 38,* 406–411.

Bruer, J. T. (1993). *Schools for Thought: A Science of Learning in the Classroom.* Cambridge, MA: A Bradford Book of MIT Press.

Bruner, J. C. (1971). *Toward a theory of instruction.* New York: W. W. Norton.

Calfee, R. C., Dunlap, K. L., & Wat, A. Y. (1994). Authentic discussion of texts in middle school. *Journal of Reading, 37*(7), 546–556.

Camperell, K. (1982). Vygotsky's theory of intellectual development: The effect of subject-matter instruction on self-regulated cognitive processes. In G. H. McNich (Ed.), *Reading in the disciplines. Second yearbook of the American Reading Forum* (pp. 33–35). Athens: University of Georgia.

Carr, E. M., & Ogle, D. M. (1987). K-W-L Plus: A strategy for comprehension and summarization. *Journal of Reading, 30,* 626–631.

Carver, R. P. (1985). Is the Degrees of Reading Power test valid or invalid? *Journal of Reading, 29,* 34–41.

Casale, U. P. (1985). Motor imaging: A reading-vocabulary strategy. *Journal of Reading, 28,* 619–621.

Casale, U. (P.), & Kelly, B. W. (1980). Problem-solving approach to study skills (PASS) for students in professional schools. *Journal of Reading, 24,* 232–238.

Casale, U. P., & Manzo, A. V. (1983). Differential effects of cognitive, affective, and proprioceptive approaches on vocabulary acquisition. In G. H. McNinch (Ed.), *Reading research to reading practice. Third yearbook of the American Reading Forum* (pp. 71–73). Athens, GA: American Reading Forum.

Caverly, D. C., Burrell, K., & McFarland, J. (1992, November). *Evaluation results of a whole language TASP reading program.* Paper presented at the annual conference of the Conference on Academic Support Programs, Fort Worth, TX.

Caverly, D. C., Mandeville, T. F., & Nicholson, S. A. (1995). PLAN: A study-reading strategy for informational text. *Journal of Adolescent and Adult Literacy, 39*(3), 190–199.

Chall, J. S. (1986). The teacher as scholar. *The Reading Teacher, 39,* 792–797.

Clewell, S. E., & Haidemos, J. (1983). Organizational strategies to increase comprehension. *Reading World, 22,* 314–321.

Cloer, T., Jr., & Denton, G. R. (1995). The effects of read-along tapes on the comprehension of middle school students. In K. Camparell, B. L. Hayes, & R. Telfer (Eds.), Linking literacy: past, present, and future. *American Reading Forum Yearbook* (Vol. 15, pp. 85–92). Logan, Utah: American Reading Forum Yearbook.

Collins, C. (1987). Content mastery strategies aid classroom discussion. *The Reading Teacher, 40,* 816–818.

Collins, C. (1991). Reading instruction that increases thinking abilities. *Journal of Reading, 34,* 510–516.

Commeyras, M. (1993). Promoting critical thinking through dialogical-thinking reading lessons. *The Reading Teacher, 6,* 486–493.

Condus, M. M., Marshall, K. J., & Miller, S. R. (1986). Effect of the key-word mnemonic strategy on vocabulary acquisition and maintenance by learning disabled children. *Journal of Learning Disabilities, 19,* 609–613.

Cooter, R. B., & Flynt, E. S. (1986). *Reading comprehension: Out of the ivory tower and into the classroom.* Unpublished paper, Northwestern State University, Natchitoches, LA.

Crafton, L. K. (1983). Learning from reading: What happens when students generate their own background information? *Journal of Reading, 26,* 586–592.

Criscoe, B. L., & Gee, T. C. (1984). *Content reading: A diagnostic/prescriptive approach.* Upper Saddle River, NJ: Prentice Hall.

Culver, V. I., Godfrey, H. C., & Manzo, A. V. (1972). A partial reanalysis of the validity of the cloze procedure as an appropriate measure of reading comprehension [Research report summary]. *Journal of Reading, 16,* 256–257.

Cunningham, D., & Shablak, S. L. (1975). Selective Reading Guide-O-Rama: The content teacher's best friend. *Journal of Reading, 18,* 380–382.

Cunningham, J. W., Cunningham, P. M., & Arthur, S. V. (1981). *Middle and secondary school reading.* New York: Longman.

Cunningham, P. M., & Cunningham, J. W. (1976). SSSW, better content-writing. *The Clearing House, 49,* 237–238.

Cunningham, P. M., Moore, S. A., Cunningham, J. W., & Moore, D. W. (1983). *Reading in elementary classrooms: Strategies and observations.* New York: Longman.

Dahmus, M. E. (1970). How to teach verbal problems. *School Science and Mathematics, 70,* 121–138.

Davey, B. (1983). Think aloud—Modeling the cognitive processes of reading comprehension. *Journal of Reading, 27,* 44–47.

Davidson, J. L. (1970). The relationship between teachers' questions and pupils' responses during a directed reading activity and a directed reading-thinking activity (Doctoral dissertation, The University of Michigan, Ann Arbor). *Dissertation Abstracts International, 31,* 6273A.

Derby, T. (1987). Reading instruction and course related materials for vocational high school students. *Journal of Reading, 30,* 308–316.

Deutsch, M. (1962). Cooperation and trust: Some theoretical notes. In M. R. Jones (Ed.), *Nebraska Symposium on Motivation: Vol. 10. Current theory and research in motivation* (pp. 275–319). Lincoln: University of Nebraska Press.

Diehl, W. A., & Mikulecky, L. (1980). The nature of reading as work. *Journal of Reading, 24,* 221–227.

Diggs, V. M. (1973). The relative effectiveness of the SQ3R method, a mechanized approach, and a combination method for training remedial reading to college freshmen (Doctoral dissertation, West Virginia University, Morgantown, 1972). *Dissertation Abstracts International, 33,* 5964A. (University Microfilms No. 74-4, 786)

Doctorow, M., Wittrock, M. C., & Marks, C. (1978). Generative processes in reading comprehension. *Journal of Educational Psychology, 70,* 109–118.

Donald, M., Sr. (1967). The SQ3R method in grade seven. *Journal of Reading, 11,* 33–35, 43.

Duckworth, S., & Taylor, R. (1995). Creating and assessing literacy in at-risk students through hypermedia portfolios. *Reading Improvement, 32*(1), 26–31.

Duke, C. R. (1987). Integrating reading, writing, and thinking skills into the music class. *Journal of Reading, 31,* 152–157.

Durkin, D. (1978–1979). What classroom observations reveal about comprehension instruction. *Reading Research Quarterly, 14,* 481–533.

Eanet, M. G., & Manzo, A. V. (1976). REAP—A strategy for improving reading/writing/study skills. *Journal of Reading, 19,* 647–652.

Ediger, M. (1992). The middle school student and interest in reading. *Journal of Affective Reading Education, 10*(2), 9–13.

Edwards, P. A., & Simpson, L. (1986). Bibliotherapy: A strategy for communication between parents and their children. *Journal of Reading, 30,* 110–118.

Estes, T. H. (1991). Ten best. In E. Fry (Ed.), *Ten best ideas for reading teachers* (p. 59). New York: Addison Wesley.

Farr, R. (1992). Putting it all together: Solving the reading assessment puzzle. *The Reading Teacher, 46*(1), 26–37.

Feathers, K. M., & Smith, F. R. (1987). Meeting the reading demands of the real world: Literacy based content instruction. *Journal of Reading, 30,* 506–511.

Fowler, G. L. (1982). Developing comprehension skills in primary students through the use of story frames. *The Reading Teacher, 36*, 176–179.

Freire, P. (1985). *The politics of education: Culture, power, and liberation.* South Hadley, MA: Bergin & Garvey.

Freire, P. (1987). Literacy: Reading the word and the world. South Hadley, MA: Bergin & Garvey.

Friedel, G. (1976, September). *Instant study skills.* Workshop handout, University of Missouri-Kansas City.

Fry, E. (1968). A readability formula that saves time. *Journal of Reading, 11*, 513–516, 575–578.

Fry, E. (1977). Fry's readability graph: Clarification, validity, and extension to level 17. *Journal of Reading, 21*, 242–252.

Garber, K. S. (1995). *The effects of transmissional, transactional, and transformational reader-response strategies on middle school students' thinking complexity and social development.* Unpublished doctoral dissertation, University of Missouri, Kansas City.

Gauthier, L. R. (1996). Using guided conversation to increase students' content area comprehension. *Journal of Adolescent & Adult Literacy, 39*, 310–312.

Gee, T. C., & Rakow, S. J. (1987). Content reading specialists evaluate teaching practices. *Journal of Reading, 31*, 234–237.

Gentile, L. M. (1980). *Using sports and physical education to strengthen content area reading skills.* Newark, DC: International Reading Association.

Geyer, J. J. (1972). Comprehensive and partial models related to the reading process. *Reading Research Quarterly, 7*, 541–587.

Gipe, J. P. (1978–1979). Investigating techniques for teaching word meanings. *Reading Research Quarterly, 14*, 624–644.

Glass, G. G. (1973). *Teaching decoding as separate from reading.* Garden City, NY: Adelphi University Press.

Gomez, M. L., Graue, M. E., & Bloch, M. N. (1991). Reassessing portfolio assessment: Rhetoric and reality. *Language Arts, 68*(8), 620–628.

Goodman, K. S. (1984). Unity in reading. In A. Purves & O. Niles (Eds.), *Becoming readers in a complex society. Eighty-third yearbook of the National Society for the Study of Education. Part I* (pp. 79–114). Chicago: University of Chicago Press.

Goodman, K. S., Bird, L. B., & Goodman, Y. M. (1991). *The whole language catalog.* Santa Rosa, CA: American School Publishers.

Gough, E. B., & Cosky, M. J. (1977). One second of reading again. In N. J. Castellan, Jr., D. Pisoni, & G. Potts (Eds.), *Cognitive theory* (Vol. 2, pp. 271–288). Hillsdale, NJ: Erlbaum.

Greenewald, M. J., & Wolf, A. E. (1980). Professional journals in secondary education: Which ones do teachers recommend most? *The Clearing House, 53*, 349–350.

Greenhoe, M. L. (1972). Parameters of creativity in music education: An exploratory study (Doctoral dissertation, The University of Tennessee, Knoxville). *Dissertation Abstracts International, 33*, 1766A.

Grobler, C. Van E. (1971). Methodology in reading instruction as a controlling variable in the constructive or destructive channeling of aggression (Doctoral dissertation, University of Delaware, Newark, 1970). *Dissertation Abstracts International, 32*, 6197A.

Gurrola, S. (1975). Determination of the relative effectiveness and efficiency of selected combinations of SQ3R study method components (Doctoral dissertation, New Mexico State University, 1974). *Dissertation Abstracts International, 35,* 6938A. (University Microfilms No. 75-10, 822)

Guszak, E. J. (1967). Teacher questioning and reading. *The Reading Teacher, 21,* 227–234.

Guthrie, J. T. (1984). Lexical learning. *The Reading Teacher, 37,* 660–662.

Haggard, M. [Ruddell]. (1976). *Creative Thinking-Reading Activities (CT-RA) as a means for improving comprehension.* Unpublished doctoral dissertation, University of Missouri-Kansas City, Kansas City, MO.

Haggard, M. R. (1982). The vocabulary self-collection strategy: An active approach to word learning. *Journal of Reading, 27,* 203–207.

Harker, W. J. (1972–1973). An evaluative summary of models of reading comprehension. *Journal of Reading Behavior, 5,* 26–34.

Harker, W. J. (Ed.). (1977). Classroom strategies for secondary reading. Newark, DE: International Reading Association.

Harste, J. (1978). Instructional implications of Rumelhart's model. In W. A. Diehi (Ed.), *Secondary reading: Theory and application. The 1978 Lilly conference on secondary reading* (Monographs in Teaching and Learning No. 1, pp. 21–23). Bloomington: Indiana University, School of Education.

Harste, J. C. (1994). Whole-language assessment. In A. Purves (Ed.), *Encyclopedia of English studies and language arts* (Vol. 2, pp. 1262–1263). New York: Scholastic.

Heaton, M. M., & Lewis, H. B. (1955). *Reading ladders for human relations* (3rd ed.). Washington, DC: American Council on Education.

Henderson, E. H. (1963). A study of individually formulated purposes for reading in relation to reading achievement, comprehension and purpose attainment (Doctoral dissertation, University of Delaware, Newark). *Dissertation Abstracts, 24,* 5529.

Henry, G. H. (1974). *Teaching reading as concept development: Emphasis on affective thinking.* Newark, DE: International Reading Association.

Herber, H. L. (1978). *Teaching reading in content areas* (2nd ed.). Upper Saddle River, NJ: Prentice Hall.

Hirsch, E. D. (1987). *Cultural literacy: What every American needs to know.* Boston: Houghton Mifflin.

Hittleman, C. (1984, Spring/Summer). Peer response groups: The writing process in action. *Language Connections: Hofstra University Newsletter, 4.*

Hittleman, D. K. (1978). Readability, readability formulas, and cloze: Selecting instructional materials. *Journal of Reading, 22,* 117–122.

Hoffman, J. (1991). Teacher and school effects in learning to read. In R. Barr, M. Kamil, P. Mosenthal, & D. P. Pearson (Eds.), *Handbook of reading research* (Vol. 11, pp. 911–950). White Plains, NY.

Hori, A. K. O. (1977). *An investigation of the efficacy of a questioning training procedure on increasing the reading comprehension performance of junior high school learning disabled students.* Unpublished master's thesis, University of Kansas, Lawrence.

Johnson, A. P. (1995). Science in reading: A harmonic convergence. *Iowa Reading Journal, 8*(1), 12–13.

Johnson, D. D., Toms-Bronowski, S., & Pittelman, S. D. (1982). *An investigation of the effectiveness of semantic mapping and semantic feature analysis with intermediate grade students* (Program Report 83-3). Madison: University of Wisconsin, Wisconsin Center for Education Research.

Johnson, D. D., & Pearson, P. D. (1984). *Teaching reading vocabulary* (2nd ed.). New York: Holt, Rinehart & Winston.

Johnson, D. W., Johnson, R. T., & Holebec, E. J. (1993). *Cooperation in the classroom.* Edina, MN: Interaction Books.

Johnson, D. W., Maruyama, R. T., Johnson, R. T., Nelson, D., & Skon, L. (1981). Effects of cooperative, competitive and individualistic goal structures on achievement: A meta-analysis. *Psychological Bulletin, 89,* 47–62.

Johnson, R. T., & Johnson, D. W. (1985). Student–student interaction: Ignored but powerful. *Journal of Teacher Education, 46,* 22–26.

Johnston, P. H., & Allington, R. (1991). Remediation. In R. Barr, M. L. Kamil, P. B. Mosenthal, & P. D. Pearson (Eds.), *Handbook of reading research* (Vol. 2, pp. 984–1012). New York: Longman.

Jonassen, D. H. (Ed.). (1982). *The technology of text: Principles for structuring, designing, and displaying text* (Vol. 1). Englewood Cliffs, NJ: Educational Technology Publications.

Jonassen, D. H. (1985a). Generative learning vs. mathemagenic control of text processing. In D. H. Jonassen (Ed.), *The technology of text: Principles for structuring, designing, and displaying text* (Vol. 2, pp. 9–45). Englewood Cliffs, NJ: Educational Technology Publications.

Jonassen, D. H. (Ed.). (1985b). *The technology of text: Principles for structuring, designing, and displaying text* (Vol. 2). Englewood Cliffs, NJ: Educational Technology Publications.

Kay, L., Young, J. L., & Mottley, R. R. (1986). Using Manzo's ReQuest model with delinquent adolescents. *Journal of Reading, 29,* 506–510.

Kelly, B. W., & Holmes, J. (1979). The Guided Lecture Procedure. *Journal of Reading, 22,* 602–604.

Kibby, M. W. (1995). The organization and teaching of things and the words that signify them. *Journal of Adolescent and Adult Literacy, 39,* 208–223.

Kirby, D., & Liner, T. (1981). *Inside out: Developmental strategies for teaching.* Montclair, NJ: Boynton/Cook.

Konopak, B. C., & Williams, N. L. (1988). Using the key word method to help young readers learn content material. *The Reading Teacher, 41,* 682–687.

Koskinen, P. S., Wilson, R. M., Gambrell, L. B., & Jensema, C. J. (1987). *Using the technology of closed-captioned television to teach reading to handicapped students.* (Performance Report, U.S. Department of Education Grant No. G-00-84-30067). Falls Church, VA: National Captioning Institute.

Krathwohl, D. R., Bloom, B. S., & Masia, B. B. (Eds.). (1956). *Taxonomy of educational objectives: The classification of educational goals. Handbook 2. Affective domain.* New York: Longman, Green.

Legenza, A. (1978). Inquiry training for reading and learning improvement. *Reading Improvement, 15,* 309–316.

Lehr, E. (1984). Cooperative learning. *Journal of Reading, 27,* 458–460.

Levin, J. R., Morrison, C. R., McGivern, J. E., Mastropieri, M. A., & Scruggs, T. E. (1986). Mnemonic facilitation of text-embedded science facts. *American Educational Research Journal, 23,* 489–506.

Lindamood, C. H., & Lindamood, P. C. (1975). *The A.D.D. program, auditory discrimination in depth* (Books 1 & 2). Hingham, MA: Teaching Resources.

Lordon, J. (1981) Small group instruction: To make it work. *The Clearing House, 54,* 265–266.

Lovett, M. B. (1981). Reading skill and its development: Theoretical and empirical considerations. In G. MacKinnon & T. Waller (Eds.), *Reading research: Advances in theory and practice* (Vol. 3, pp. 1–37). New York: Academic Press.

Maier, N. R. E. (1963). *Problem solving discussions and conferences: Leadership methods and skills.* New York: McGraw-Hill.

Mandeville, T. F., & Caverly, D. C. (1993, February). *Helping middle school poor readers keep up with their classmates.* Paper presented at the annual conference of the Texas Middle School Association, Corpus Christi, TX.

Mandeville, T. F., & Van Allen, L. (1993). Middle school poor readers need more than good literature and skill drills. *Texas Middle School Journal, 2*(2), 24–28.

Manzo, A. V. (1969a). Improving reading comprehension through reciprocal questioning (Doctoral dissertation, Syracuse University, Syracuse, NY, 1968). *Dissertation Abstracts International, 30,* 5344A.

Manzo, A. V. (1969b). The ReQuest procedure. *Journal of Reading, 13,* 123–126.

Manzo, A. V. (1970). CAT—A game for extending vocabulary and knowledge of allusions. *Journal of Reading, 13,* 367–369.

Manzo, A. V. (1973). CONPASS English: A demonstration project. *Journal of Reading, 16,* 539–545.

Manzo, A. V. (1974). The group reading activity. *Forum for Reading, 3,* 26–33.

Manzo, A. V. (1975). Guided reading procedure. *Journal of Reading, 18,* 287–291.

Manzo, A. V. (1977). *Recent developments in content area reading.* Keynote address, Missouri Council of Teachers of English, Springfield, MO.

Manzo, A. V. (1980). Three "universal" strategies in content area reading and languaging. *Journal of Reading, 24,* 146–149.

Manzo, A. V. (1983). "Subjective approach to vocabulary" acquisition (Or " . . . I think my brother is arboreal!"). *Reading Psychology, 3,* 155–160.

Manzo, A. V. (1985). Expansion modules for the ReQuest, CAT, GRP, and REAP reading/study procedures. *Journal of Reading, 28,* 498–502.

Manzo, A. V., & Casale, U. P. (1980). The five C's: A problem-solving approach to study skills. *Reading Horizons, 20,* 281–284.

Manzo, A. V., & Casale, U. P. (1985). Listen-read-discuss: A content reading heuristic. *Journal of Reading, 28,* 732–734.

Manzo, A. V., & Garber, K. (1995). Study guides. In A. Purves (Ed.), *Encyclopedia of English studies and language arts* (pp. 1124–1125). New York: Scholastic.

Manzo, A. V., Garber, K., Manzo, U. C., & Kahn, R. (1994). *Transmission, transaction, and transformation: Response to text perspectives.* Paper presented at the National Developmental Educators Conference, Kansas City, MO.

Manzo, A. V., Garber, K., & Warm, J. (1992). *Dialectical thinking: A generative approach to critical/creative reading.* Paper presented at the National Reading Conference, San Antonio, TX, 1992.

Manzo, A. V., & Legenza, A. (1975). Inquiry training for kindergarten children. *Journal of Educational Leadership, 32*, 479–483.

Manzo, A. V., & Manzo, U. C. (1987). *Asking, answering, commenting: A participation training strategy.* Paper presented at the annual meeting of the International Reading Association, Anaheim, CA.

Manzo, A. V., & Manzo U. C. (1990a). *Content area reading: A heuristic approach.* Upper Saddle River, NJ: Merrill/Prentice Hall.

Manzo, A. V., & Manzo, U. C. (1990b). Note cue: A comprehension and participation training strategy. *Journal of Reading, 33*, 608–611.

Manzo, A. V., & Manzo, U. C. (1993). *Literacy disorders: Holistic diagnosis and remediation.* Fort Worth, TX: Harcourt Brace Jovanovich.

Manzo, A. V., & Manzo, U. C. (1995). *Teaching children to be literate: A reflective approach.* Fort Worth, TX: Harcourt Brace College Publishers.

Manzo, A. V., & Manzo, U. C. (in press). The new eclecticism: An inclusive philosophy for literacy education. *Journal of Reading Research and Instruction.*

Manzo, A. V., & Sherk, J. K. (1971–1972). Some generalizations and strategies for guiding vocabulary acquisition. *Journal of Reading Behavior, 4*, 78–89.

Maring, G. H., & Furman, G. (1985). Seven "whole class" strategies to help mainstreamed young people read and listen better in content area classes. *Journal of Reading, 28*, 694–700.

Maring, G. H., & Ritson, R. (1980). Reading improvement in the gymnasium. *Journal of Reading, 24*, 27–31.

Martin, D. C., Lorton, M., Blanc, R. A., & Evans, C. (1977). *The learning center: A comprehensive model for colleges and universities.* Grand Rapids, MI: Central Trade Plant.

Marzano, R. J., & Marzano, J. S. (1988). *A cluster approach to elementary vocabulary instruction.* Newark, DE: International Reading Association.

McFadden, C., & Yaeger, R. E. (1993). *Science plus.* Austin, TX: Holt, Rinehart & Winston.

McKenzie, J. V., Ericson, B., & Hunter, L. (1988). *Questions may be an answer.* Unpublished manuscript, California State University at Northridge.

McNamara, L. P. (1977). A study of the cloze procedure as an alternate group instructional strategy in secondary school American government classes (Doctoral dissertation, Northern Illinois University, DeKalb). *Dissertation Abstracts International, 39*, 216A.

Meichenbaum, D., & Asarnow, J. (1979). Cognitive-behavioral modifications and metacognitive development. In P. C. Kendall & S. D. Hollan (Eds.), *Cognitive-behavioral interventions: Theory, research and procedures* (pp. 11–35). New York: Academic Press.

Meyer, B. J. E. (1975). *The organization of prose and its effect on memory.* Amsterdam: North-Holland.

Michael Jackson: Junk culture triumph. (1984, May). *Working Woman*, p. 192.

Mikulecky, L. (1982). Job literacy: The relationship between school preparation and workplace actuality. *Reading Research Quarterly, 17*, 400–419.

Miller, W. E., & Dollard, J. (1941). *Social learning and imitation.* New Haven, CT: Yale University Press.

Missouri Department of Elementary and Secondary Education. (1986). *Core competencies and key skills for Missouri schools: For grades 2 through 10.* Jefferson City, MO: Author.

Mitchell, D. C. (1982). *The process of reading: A cognitive analysis of fluent reading and learning to read.* Somerset, NJ: John Wiley & Sons.

Moje, E. B. (1996). "I teach students, not subjects": Teacher–student relationships as contexts for secondary literacy. *Reading Research Quarterly, 31*(2), 172–195.

Moore, D. W., Readence, J. E., & Rickelman, R. J. (1982). *Prereading activities for content area reading and learning.* Newark, DE: International Reading Association.

Mulliken, C. N., & Henk, W. A. (1985). Using music as a background for reading: An exploratory study. *Journal of Reading, 28,* 353–358.

Nagy, W. E. (1988). *Teaching vocabulary to improve reading comprehension.* Newark, DE: International Reading Association.

Niles, O. (1965). Organization perceived. In H. L. Herber (Ed.), *Developing study skills in secondary schools* (pp. 57–76). Newark, DE: International Reading Association.

Ogle, D. (1989). Study techniques that ensure content area reading success. In D. Lapp, J. Flood, & N. Farnam (Eds.), *Content area reading and learning* (2nd ed.). Boston: Allyn & Bacon.

Ogle, D. M. (1996). Study techniques that ensure content area reading success. In D. Lapp, J. Flood, & N. Farnan (Eds.), *Content area reading and learning* (2nd ed.). Boston: Allyn & Bacon.

Otto, W., & Hayes, B. (1982). Glossing for improved comprehension: Progress and prospect. In G. H. McNinch (Ed.), *Reading in the disciplines. Second yearbook of the American Reading Forum* (pp. 16–18). Athens, GA: American Reading Forum.

Padak, N. D. (1986). Teachers' verbal behaviors: A window to the teaching process. In J. A. Niles & R. V. Lalik (Eds.), *Solving problems in literacy: Learners, teachers, and researchers. Thirty-fifth yearbook of the National Reading Conference* (pp. 185–191). Rochester, NY: National Reading Conference.

Palincsar, A. S., & Brown, A. L. (1984). Reciprocal teaching of comprehension monitoring activities. *Cognition and Instruction, 1,* 117–175.

Palincsar, A. S., & Brown, A. L. (1986). Interactive teaching to promote independent learning from text. *The Reading Teacher, 39,* 771–777.

Palmatier, R. A. (1971). Comparison of four note-taking procedures. *Journal of Reading, 14,* 235–258.

Palmatier, R. A. (1973). A notetaking system for learning. *Journal of Reading, 17,* 36–39.

Palmatier, R. A., & Bennett, J. M. (1974). Notetaking habits of college students. *Journal of Reading, 18,* 215–218.

Pauk, W. (1989). *How to study in college* (4th ed.). Boston: Houghton Mifflin.

Pearce, D. L. (1983). Guidelines for the use and evaluation of writing in content classrooms. *Journal of Reading, 27,* 215.

Perry, M. (1971). *Man's unfinished journey.* Boston: Houghton Mifflin.

Pepitone, E. A. (1980). *Children in cooperation and competition.* Lexington, MA: D. C. Heath.

Peters, C. W. (1982). The content processing model: A new approach to conceptualizing content reading. In J. P. Palberg (Ed.), *Reading in the content areas: Application of a concept* (pp. 100–109). Toledo, OH: University of Toledo, College of Education.

Petre, R. M. (1970). Quantity, quality and variety of pupil responses during an open-communication structured group directed reading-thinking activity and a closed-communication structured group directed reading activity (Doctoral dissertation, University of Delaware, Newark). *Dissertation Abstracts International, 31,* 4630A.

Piercy, D. (1976). *Reading activities in content areas.* Boston: Allyn & Bacon.

Pinnell, G. S. (1984). Communication in small group settings. *Theory into Practice, 23,* 246–254.

Pressley, M., Johnson, C. J., & Symons, S. (1987). Elaborating to learn and learning to elaborate. *Journal of Learning Disabilities, 20,* 76–91.

Pressley, M., Levin, J. R., & MacDaniel, M. A. (1987). Remembering versus inferring what a word means: Mnemonic and contextual approaches. In M. C. McKeown & M. E. Curtis (Eds.), *The nature of vocabulary acquisition* (pp. 107–129). Hillsdale, NJ: Erlbaum.

Pressley, M., Levin, J. R., & Miller, G. E. (1981). How does the keyword method affect vocabulary comprehension and usage? *Reading Research Quarterly, 16,* 213–225.

Putnam, L., Bader, L., Bean, R. (1988). Clinic directors share insights into effective strategies. *Journal of Clinical Reading, 3,* 16–20.

Rakes, S. K., & Smith, L. J. (1987). Strengthening comprehension and recall through the principle of recitation. *Journal of Reading, 31,* 260–263.

Ratekin, N., Simpson, M. L., Alvermann, D. E., & Dishner, E. K. (1985). Why teachers resist content area reading instruction. *Journal of Reading, 28,* 432–437.

Raygor, A. L. (1977). The Raygor readability estimate: A quick and easy way to determine difficulty. In P. D. Pearson (Ed.), *Reading: Theory, research, and practice.* Clemson, SC: National Reading Conference.

Reeve, R. A., Palincsar, A. S., & Brown A. L. (1985). *Everyday and academic thinking: Implications for learning and problem solving* (Journal of Curriculum Studies Technical Report No. 349). Champaign: University of Illinois, Center for the Study of Reading.

Reutzel, D. R., Larson, C. M., & Sabey, B. L. (1995). Dialogical books: Connecting content, conversation, and composition. *The Reading Teacher, 49*(2), 98–109.

Robinson, E. (1946). *Effective study.* New York: Harper Brothers.

Roby, T. (1983, April). *The other side of the question: Controversial turns, the devil's advocate, and reflective responses.* Paper presented at the annual meeting of the American Educational Research Association, Montreal.

Rosenblatt, L. (1938). *Literature as exploration.* New York: Appleton-Century.

Rosenblatt, L. (1968). *Literature as exploration* (2nd ed.). New York: Appleton-Century.

Rosenblatt, L. (1970). *Literature as exploration* (3rd ed.). New York: Noble & Noble.

Rosenblatt, L. (1976). *Literature as exploration* (4th ed.). London: Heineman.

Rosenblatt, L. (1983). *Literature as exploration* (5th ed.). New York: Noble & Noble.

Rosenshine, B. V. (1984). Content, time, and direct instruction. In P. L. Peterson & H. J. Walberg (Eds.), *Research on teaching: Concepts, findings, and implications* (pp. 102–106). Berkeley, CA: McCutchan.

Ruddell, M. R. (1993). *Teaching content reading and writing.* Boston: Allyn & Bacon.

Ruddell, R. B., & Ruddell, M. H. (1995). *Theoretical processes and models of reading* (3rd ed.). Newark, DE: International Reading Association.

Rumelhart, D. E. (1977). Toward an interactive model dreading. In S. Dornic (Ed.), *Attention and performance VI: Proceedings of the Sixth International Symposium on Attention and Performance, Stockholm, Sweden, July 28 to August 1, 1975* (pp. 573–603). Hillsdale, NJ: Erlbaum.

Rush, T., Moe, A., & Storlie, R. (1986). *Occupational literacy education.* Newark, DE: International Reading Association.

Samuels, S. J. (1977). Introduction to theoretical models of reading. In W. Otto, N. A. Peters, & C. W. Peters (Eds.), *Reading problems: A multidisciplinary perspective* (pp. 7–41). Reading, MA: Addison-Wesley.

Sanders, P. L. (1969). Teaching map reading skills in grade 9. *Journal of Reading, 12*, 283–286, 337.

Santa, C. M., Dailey, S. C., & Nelson, M. (1985). Free-response and opinion proof: A reading and writing strategy for middle grade and secondary teachers. *Journal of Reading, 28*, 346–352.

Santa, C. M., Isaacson, L., & Manning, G. (1987). Changing content instruction through action research. *The Reading Teacher, 40*, 434–438.

Santeusanio, R. (1967). RAMA: A supplement to the traditional college reading program. *Journal of Reading, 11*, 133–136.

Schell, L. M. (1988). Dilemmas in assessing reading comprehension. *The Reading Teacher, 42*, 12–16.

Schumm, J. S., & Mangrum, C. T., II (1991). FLIP: A framework for content area reading. *Journal of Reading, 35*, 120–123.

Shannon, P. (1990). *The struggle to continue: Progressive reading instruction in the United States.* Portsmouth, NH: Heinemann.

Shepherd, D. (1978). *Comprehensive high school reading methods* (3rd ed.). Upper Saddle River, NJ: Merrill/Prentice Hall.

Shor, I., & Freire, P. (1987). *A pedagogy for liberation: Dialogues on transforming education.* South Hadley, MA: Bergin & Garvey.

Simpson, M. (1986). PORPE: A writing strategy for studying and learning in the content areas. *Journal of Reading, 29*, 407–414.

Simpson, M. L., Hayes, C. G., Stahl, N. A., Connor R. T., & Weaver, D. (1988). An initial validation of a study strategy system. *Journal of Reading Behavior, 20*, 149–180.

Singer, H. (1976). Theoretical models of reading. In H. Singer & R. B. Ruddell (Eds.), *Theoretical models and processes of reading* (2nd ed., pp. 634–654). Newark, DE: International Reading Association.

Singer, H., & Dolan, D. (1980). *Reading and learning from text.* Boston: Little, Brown.

Singer, H., & Ruddell, R. B. (1976). *Theoretical models and processes of reading* (2nd ed.). Newark, DE: International Reading Association.

Slavin, R. E. (1980). Cooperative learning. *Review of Educational Research, 50*, 315–342.

Smith, D. E. P. (1967). *Learning to learn.* New York: Harcourt Brace Jovanovich.

Smith, E. (1978). *Understanding reading: A psycholinguistic analysis of reading and learning to read* (2nd ed.). New York: Holt, Rinehart & Winston.

Smith, E. (1979). *Reading without nonsense.* New York: Teachers College Press.

Smith, R. J., & Dauer, V. L. (1984). A comprehension-monitoring strategy for reading content area materials. *Journal of Reading, 28,* 144–147.

Spache, G. D. (1976). *Diagnosing and correcting reading disabilities.* Boston: Allyn & Bacon.

Spiegel, D. L. (1980). Adaptations of Manzo's guided reading procedure. *Reading Horizons, 20,* 188–192.

Stahl, N. A., & Henk, W. A. (1986). Tracing the roots of textbook study systems: An extended historical perspective. In J. A. Niles & R. V. Lalik (Eds.), *Solving problems in literacy: Learners, teachers, and researchers. Thirty-fifth yearbook of the National Reading Conference* (pp. 366–374). Rochester, NY: National Reading Conference.

Stahl, S. A., & Fairbanks, M. M. (1986). The effects of vocabulary instruction: A model-based meta-analysis. *Review of Educational Research, 56,* 72–110.

Staton, J. (1980). Writing and counseling: Using a dialogue journal. *Language Arts, 57,* 514–518.

Stauffer, R. (1969). *Directing reading maturity as a cognitive process.* New York: Harper & Row.

Stevens, K. C. (1982). Can we improve reading by teaching background information? *Journal of Reading, 25,* 326–329.

Stieglitz, E. L., & Stieglitz, V. S. (1981). SAVOR the word to reinforce vocabulary in the content areas. *Journal of Reading, 25,* 48.

Taylor, G. C. (1980). Music in language arts instruction. *Language Arts, 58,* 363–367.

Tharp, R. G., & Gallimore, R. (1989). *Rousing minds to life: Teaching, learning, and schooling in social context.* New York: Cambridge University Press.

Tharp, R. G., & Gallimore, R. (1990). *Rousing minds to life: Teaching, learning, and schooling social context.* New York: Cambridge University Press.

Thorndike, E. L. (1917). Reading as reasoning: A study of mistakes in paragraph reading. *Journal of Educational Psychology, 8,* 323–332.

Tierney, R. J., Readence, J. E., & Dishner, E. K. (1990). *Reading strategies and practices* (3rd ed.). Needham Heights, MA: Allyn & Bacon.

Tierney, R. J., Soter, A., O'Flahavan, J. F., & McGinley, W. (1989). The effects of reading and writing upon thinking critically. *Reading Research Quarterly, 24,* 134–137.

Tishman, S., Perkins, D., & Jay, E. (1995). *The thinking classroom.* Boston: Allyn & Bacon.

UMKC Insider. (1996). *2*(2), Kansas City, MO: University of Missouri-KC Press.

Uttero, D. A. (1988). Activating comprehension through cooperative learning. *The Reading Teacher, 41,* 390–395.

Vacca, R. T., & Vacca, J. L. (1986). *Content area reading* (2nd ed.). Boston: Little, Brown.

Vygotsky, L. S. (1978). *Mind in society: The development of higher psychological process.* Cambridge, MA: Harvard University Press.

Wade, R. K. (1984–1985). What makes a difference in inservice teacher education? A meta-analysis of research. *Educational Leadership, 42*(4), 48–54.

Walker, B. J. (1985). Right brain strategies for teaching comprehension. *Academic Therapy, 21*, 133–141.

Walker, A., & Parkman, M. (1924). *The study readers: Fifth year.* New York: Merrill.

Watkins, J., McKenna, M., Manzo, A., & Manzo, U. (1995). *The effects of the listen-read-discuss procedure on the content learning of high school students.* Unpublished manuscript.

Weaver, W. W., & Kingston, A. J. (1963). A factor analysis of cloze procedure and other measures of reading and language ability. *Journal of Communication, 13*, 252–261.

Welker, W. A. (1987). Going from typical to technical meaning. *Journal of Reading, 31*, 275–276.

Wilkins, G., & Miller S. (1983). *Strategies for success: An effective guide for teachers of secondary-level slow learners.* New York: Teachers College Press.

Williams, J. P. (1973). Learning to read: A review of theories and models. *Reading Research Quarterly, 8*, 121–146.

Willmore, D. J. (1967). A comparison of four methods of studying a college textbook (Doctoral dissertation, University of Minnesota, 1966). *Dissertation Abstracts, 27*, 2413A.

Wooster, G. E. (1958). Teaching the SQ3R method of study: An investigation of the instructional approach (Doctoral dissertation, The Ohio State University, 1953). *Dissertation Abstracts International, 18*, 2067–2068.

Name Index

Aaronson, E., 129
Adams, M. J., 218
Adler, J., 177
Afsar, S. S., 81
Alley, G., 73, 88
Allington, R., 240
Alvermann, D. E., 27, 29, 63, 122, 178, 179, 181
Anders, P. L., 155
Andersen, O., 177
Anderson, R. C., 157
Ankney, P., 73
Applebee, A. N., 170
Arthur, S. V., 153, 250
Artley, A. S., 218
Asarnow, J., 104
Aschner, M. J., 81
Ausubel, D., 93

Bacon, E., 232
Bader, L., 152
Baker, L., 103, 104
Baldwin, R. S., 49
Balocke, L., 126
Bandura, A., 84
Barrett, T. C., 81
Barton, W. A., 185
Baumann, J. F., 142
Bean, R., 152
Bean, T. W., 73
Behle, P., 43
Benge-Kletzien, S., 126
Bennett, J. M., 188
Bird, L. B., 21
Blanc, R. A., 106
Blaney, N., 129
Bloch, M. N., 47
Bloom, B. S., 81
Boothby, P. R., 63
Bormuth, J. R., 40
Bos, C. S., 155
Bragstad, B., 263
Bromley, K. D., 170

Brown, A. L., 88, 90, 91, 92, 93, 103, 104
Bruer, J. T., 93
Bruner, J. C., 26
Burrell, K., 65

Calfee, R. C., 127
Camperell, K., 84
Carr, E., 73, 75
Carver, R. P., 21
Casale, U. P., 26, 150, 151, 198
Caverly, D. C., 63, 65, 67, 68, 69
Chall, J. S., 265
Chapin, S. H., 212
Clewell, S. E., 249
Cloer, T., Jr., 244
Collins, C., 125, 239
Commeyras, M., 167, 176
Condus, M. M., 160
Connor, R. T., 195
Cooter, R. B., 239
Cosky, M. J., 20
Crafton, L. K., 28, 95
Criscoe, B. L., 206, 216
Culver, V. I., 40
Cunningham, D., 112
Cunningham, J. W., 73, 153, 170, 250
Cunningham, P. M., 73, 153, 170, 250

Dahmus, M. E., 211
Dailey, S. C., 165, 176
Dauer, V., 107
Davey, B., 104
Davidson, J. L., 59
Davidson, J. W., 219
Denton, G. R., 244
Derby, T., 227, 228, 230
Deshler, D., 73, 88
Deutsch, M., 129
Dewey, J., 165
Diehl, W. A., 227
Diggs, V. M., 187
Dillon, D. R., 27, 122, 178, 179, 181
Dishner, E. K., 29, 153

293

Subject Index